Narrative Of Captivity In Abyssinia

With Some Account Of The Late Emperor Theodore, His Country And People

by

Henry Blanc

Double 9
BOOKS

Narrative Of Captivity In Abyssinia

With Some Account Of The Late Emperor Theodore, His Country And People

by Henry Blanc

ISBN: 978-93-63052-63-5

Published by

DOUBLE 9 BOOKS

2/13-B, Ansari Road
Daryaganj, New Delhi – 110002
info@double9books.com
www.double9books.com
Tel. 011-40042856

ABOUT THE AUTHOR

Henry Blanc, a distinguished chronicler of historical events, penned the masterpiece "Narrative of Captivity in Abyssinia: With Some Account Of The Late Emperor Theodore, His Country And People," an insightful and gripping account of his harrowing experiences as a captive in Abyssinia (modern-day Ethiopia). In this captivating narrative, Blanc provides readers with a detailed firsthand perspective of the tumultuous events surrounding his captivity under Emperor Theodore II. Through vivid descriptions and compelling storytelling, Blanc offers readers a glimpse into the culture, customs, and politics of Abyssinia during the mid-19th century. His narrative not only sheds light on the complexities of Ethiopian society but also delves into the character and motivations of Emperor Theodore himself. With its blend of adventure, history, and personal reflection, Blanc's "Narrative of Captivity in Abyssinia" stands as a testament to the resilience of the human spirit in the face of adversity and offers invaluable insights into a little-known chapter of African history.

CONTENTS

PREFACE

With a view of gratifying the natural curiosity evinced by a large circle of friends and acquaintance to obtain accurate information as to the cause of our captivity, the manner in which we were treated, the details of our daily life, and the character and habits of Theodore, I undertook the task of writing this account of our captivity in Abyssinia.

I have endeavoured to give a correct sketch of the career of Theodore, and a description of his country and people, more especially of his friends and enemies.

In order to make the reader familiar with the subject, it was also necessary to say a few words about the Europeans who played a part in that strange imbroglio—the Abyssinian difficulty. My knowledge of them, and of the events that occurred during our captivity, was acquired through personal experience, and also by intercourse with well-informed natives, during long months of enforced idleness.

In preparing this work for the press, I found it necessary to the completeness of the narrative, to incorporate some portions of my Report to the Government of Bombay on Mr. Rassam's mission, which appeared in an Indian newspaper, and was subsequently republished in a small volume.

For the same reason I have also included a few articles contributed by me to a London newspaper.

The sufferings of the Abyssinian captives will be ever associated, in the annals of British valour, with the triumphant success of the expedition, so skilfully organized by its commander, whose title, Lord Napier of Magdala, commemorates the crowning achievement of a glorious career.

London, July 23, 1868.

CHAPTER I

Lij Kassa, better known as the Emperor Theodore, was born in Kouara about the year 1818. His father was a noble of Abyssinia, and his uncle, the celebrated Dejatch Comfou, had for many years governed the provinces of Dembea, Kouara, Tschelga, &c. On the death of his uncle he was appointed by Ras Ali's mother, Waizero Menen, governor of Kouara; but, dissatisfied with that post, which left but little scope for his ambition, he threw off his allegiance, and occupied Dembea as a rebel. Several generals were sent to chastise the young soldier; but he either eluded their pursuit or defeated their forces. However, on the solemn promise that he would, be well received, he repaired to the camp of Ras Ali. This kind-hearted but weak ruler thought to attach to his cause the brave chieftain, and to accomplish that object gave him his daughter Tawavitch (she is beautiful). Lij Kassa returned to Kouara, and for a time remained faithful to his sovereign. He made several plundering expeditions in the low lands, carried fire and sword into the Arab huts, and always returned from these excursions bringing with him hordes of cattle, prisoners, and slaves.

The successes of Kassa, the courage he manifested on all occasions, the abstemious life he led, and the favour he showed to all who served his cause, soon collected around him a band of hardy and reckless followers. Being ambitious, he now formed the project of carving out an empire for himself in the fertile plains he had so often devastated. Educated in a convent, he had not only studied theological subjects, but made himself conversant with the mystic Abyssinian history. His early education always exercised great influence on his after-life, giving to his intercourse with others a religious character, and impressed vividly upon his mind the idea that the Mussulman race having for centuries encroached on the Christian land, it should be the aim of his life to re-establish the old Ethiopian empire. Urged on, therefore, both by ambition and fanaticism, he advanced in the direction of Kedaref at the head of 16,000 warriors; but he had soon to learn the immense superiority of a small number of well-armed and well-trained troops over large but undisciplined bodies of men. Near Kedaref he came in sight of his mortal foes the Turks, a mere handful of irregulars; yet they were too much for him: for the first time, defeated and disheartened, he had, for a while, to abandon his long-cherished scheme.

Instead of returning to the seat of his government, he was obliged, on account of a severe wound received during the fight, to halt on the frontier of Dembea. From his camp he informed his mother-in-law of his condition, and requested that she would send him a cow—the fee required by the Abyssinian doctor. Waizero Menen, who had always hated Kassa, now took advantage of his fallen condition to humble his pride still more; she sent him, instead of the cow, a small piece of meat with an insulting message. Near the couch of the wounded chieftain sat the brave companion who had shared his fortunes, the wife whom he loved. On hearing the sneering message of the Queen, her fiery Galla blood flamed with indignation. She rose and told Kassa that she loved the brave but abhorred the coward; and she could not remain any longer by his side if, after such an insult, he did not revenge it in blood. Her passionate words fell upon willing ears; vengeance filled the heart of Kassa, and as soon as he had sufficiently recovered he returned to Kouara and openly proclaimed his independence.

For the second time Ras Ali called him to his court; but the summons met with a stern refusal. Several generals were sent to enforce the command, but the young soldier easily routed these courtiers; whilst their followers, charmed with Kassa's insinuating manners and dazzled by his splendid promises, almost to a man enrolled themselves under his standard. His wife again exerted her influence, showing him how easily he might secure for himself the supreme power, and, as he hesitated, again threatened to leave him. Kassa resisted no longer; he advanced into Godjam, and carried all before him. The battle of Djisella, fought in 1853, decided the fate of Ras Ali. His army had been but for a short time engaged when, panic-stricken, the Ras left the field with a body of 500 horse, leaving the rest of his large host to swell the ranks of the conqueror. Victory followed victory, and after a few years, from Shoa to Metemma, from Godjam to Bogos, all feared and obeyed the commands of the Emperor Theodore; for under that name he desired to be crowned, after he had by the battle of Deraskié, fought in February, 1855, subdued Tigré, and conquered his most formidable opponent, Dejatch Oubié.

Shortly after the battle of Deraskié, Theodore turned his victorious arms against the Wallo Gallas, possessed himself of Magdala, and ravaged and destroyed so completely the rich Galla plain that many of the chiefs joined his ranks, and fought against their own countrymen. He had now not only avenged the long-oppressed Christians, so often victims of the Galla inroads, but curbed for a long time the haughty spirit of these clans. At the height of success, he lost his brave and loving wife. He felt the cruel blow deeply. She had been his faithful counsellor, the companion of his adventures, the being he most loved; and he cherished her memory while he lived. In 1866, when one of his artisans almost forced himself into his presence to request permission for me to remain a few days near the man's dying wife, Theodore bent his head, and wept at the remembrance of his own wife whom he had so deeply loved.

The career of Theodore may be divided into three very distinct periods:—First, from his early days to the death of his first wife; secondly, from the fall of Ras Ali to the death of Mr. Bell; thirdly, from this last event to his own death. The first period we have described: it was the period of promise. During the second—which extends from 1853 to 1860—there is still much to praise in the conduct of the Emperor, although many of his actions are unworthy of his early career. From 1860 to 1868 he seems little by little to have thrown off all restraint, until he became remarkable for reckless and wanton cruelty. His principal wars during the second period were with Dejatch Goscho Beru, governor of Godjam; with Dejatch Oubié, whom he conquered, as we have already stated, at the battle of Deraskié, and with the Wallo Gallas. He could, however, still be merciful, and though he imprisoned many of the feudal chiefs, he promised to release them as soon as the pacification of his empire should be complete.

In 1860 he advanced against his cousin Garad, the murderer of Consul Plowden, and gained the day; but he lost his best friend and adviser, Mr. Bell, who saved the Emperor's life by sacrificing his own. In January, 1861, Theodore marched with an overwhelming force against a powerful rebel, Agau Negoussi, who had made himself master of all northern Abyssinia; by cunning and skilful tactics, he easily overthrew his adversary but tarnished his victory by horrid cruelties and gross breach of faith. Agau Negoussi's hands and feet were cut off, and though he lingered for days, the merciless emperor refused him even a drop of water to moisten his fevered lips. His cruel vengeance did not stop there. Many of the compromised chiefs, who had surrendered on his solemn pledge of amnesty, were either handed over to the executioner or sent to linger for life, loaded with fetters, in some of the prison ambas. For the next three years Theodore's rule was acknowledged throughout the land. A few petty rebels had risen here and there, but with the exception of Tadla Gwalu, who could not be driven from the fastness of his amba in the south of Godjam, all the others were but of little importance, and did not disturb the tranquillity of his reign.

But though a conqueror, and endowed with military genius, Theodore was a bad administrator. To attach his soldiery to his cause, he lavished upon them immense sums of money; he was therefore forced to exact exorbitant tributes, almost to drain the land of its last dollar, in order to satisfy his rapacious followers. Finding himself at the head of a powerful host, and feeling either reluctant or afraid to dismiss them to their homes, he longed for foreign conquests; the dream of his younger days became a fixed idea, and he believed himself called upon by God to re-establish in its former greatness the old Ethiopian empire.

He could not, however, forget that he was unable to cope single-handed with the well-armed and disciplined troops of his foes; he remembered too well his signal failure at Kedaref, and therefore sought to gain his long-desired object by diplomacy. He had heard from Bell, Plowden, and others, that England and France were proud of the protection they afforded to Christians in all parts of the world; he therefore wrote to the sovereigns of those two countries, inviting them to join him in his crusade against the Mussulman race. A few passages selected from his letter to our Queen will prove the correctness of this assertion. "By his power (of God) I drove away the Gallas. But for the Turks, I have told them to leave the land of my ancestors. They refuse!" He mentions the death of Plowden and Bell, and then adds:—"I have exterminated those enemies (those who killed Bell and Plowden), that I may get, by the power of God, *your friendship*." He concludes by saying, "*See how the Islam oppress the Christian!*"

Theodore's army at this time consisted of some 100,000 or 150,000 fighting men; and if we take as the average four followers for every soldier, his camp must have numbered between 500,000 and 600,000 souls. Admitting, also, the population of Abyssinia to be nearly 3,000,000, about one fourth of the number had to be paid, fed, and clothed by the contributions of the remainder.

During a few years, such was Theodore's prestige that this terrible oppression was quietly accepted; at last, however, the peasants, half-starved and almost naked, finding that with all their sacrifices and privations they were still far from satisfying the daily increasing demands of their terrible master, abandoned the fertile plains, and under the guidance of some of the remaining hereditary chiefs, retired to high plateaus, or concealed themselves in secluded valleys. In Godjam, Walkait, Shoa, and Tigré, the rebellion broke out almost simultaneously. Theodore had for a while to abandon his ideas of foreign conquest, and did his utmost to crush the mutinous spirit of his people. Whole rebel districts were laid waste; but the peasants, protected by their strongholds, could not be reached: they quietly awaited the departure of the invader and then returned to their desolated homes, cultivating just enough for their maintenance; thus, with only a few exceptions, the peasants evaded the terrible vengeance of the now infuriate Emperor. His immense army soon suffered severely from this mode of warfare. Each year the provinces which the soldiers could plunder became fewer; severe famines broke out; large districts such as Dembea, the granary of Gondar and of central Abyssinia, lay waste and uncultivated.

The soldiers, formerly pampered, now in their turn half starved and badly clad, lost confidence in their leader; desertions were numerous; and many returned to their native provinces, and joined the ranks of the discontented.

The fall of Theodore was even more rapid than his rise. He was still unconquered in the battlefield, as, after the example of Negoussi's fate, none dared to oppose him; but against the passive warfare of the peasantry and the Fabian-like policy of their chiefs he could do nothing. Never resting, almost always on the march, his army day by day becoming reduced in strength, he went from province to province; but in vain: all disappeared at his approach. There was no enemy; but there was no food! At last, reduced by necessity, in order to keep around him some remnants of his former immense army, he had no alternative left but to plunder the few provinces still faithful to him.

When I first met Theodore, in January, 1866, he must have been about forty-eight years of age. His complexion was darker than that of the majority of his countrymen, the nose slightly curved, the mouth large, the lips so small as hardly to be perceived. Of middle size, well knit, wiry rather than muscular, he excelled as a horseman, in the use of the spear, and on foot would tire his hardiest followers. The expression of his dark eyes, slightly depressed, was strange; if he was in good humour they were soft, with a kind of gazelle-like timidity about them that made one love him; but when angry the fierce and bloodshot eye seemed to shed fire. In moments of violent passion his whole aspect was frightful: his black visage acquired an ashy hue, his thin compressed lips left but a whitish margin around the mouth, his very hair stood erect, and his whole deportment was a terrible illustration of savage and ungovernable fury.

Yet he excelled in the art of duping his fellow-men. Even a few days before his death he had still, when we met him, all the dignity of a sovereign, the amiability and good-breeding of the most accomplished "gentleman." His smile was so attractive, his words were so sweet and gracious, that one could hardly believe that the affable monarch was but a consummate dissembler.

He never perpetrated a deed of treachery or cruelty without pleading some specious excuse, so as to convey the impression that in all his actions he was guided by a sense of justice. For example, he plundered Dembea because the inhabitants were too friendly towards Europeans, and Gondar because one of our messengers had been betrayed by the inhabitants of that city. He destroyed Zagé, a large and populous city, because he pretended that a priest had been rude to him. He cast into chains his adopted father, Cantiba Hailo, because he had taken into his service a female servant he had dismissed. Tesemma Engeddah, the hereditary chief of Gahinte, fell under his displeasure because after a battle against the rebels he had shown himself "too severe," and our first head-jailor was taken to the camp and put in chains because he had "formerly been a friend" of the King of Shoa. I could adduce hundreds of instances to illustrate his habitual hypocrisy. In our case, he arrested us because we had not brought the former captives with us; Mr. Stern he nearly killed, merely for putting his hand to his face, and he imprisoned Consul Cameron for going to the Turks instead of bringing him back an answer to his letter.

Theodore had all the dislike of the roving Bedouin for towns and cities. He loved camp life, the free breeze of the plains, the sight of his army gracefully encamped around the hillock he had selected for himself; and he preferred to the palace the Portuguese had erected at Gondar for a more sedentary king, the delights of roaming about incognito during the beautiful cool nights of Abyssinia. His household was well-regulated; the same spirit of order which had introduced something like discipline into his army, showed itself also in the arrangements of his domestic affairs. Every department was under the control of a chief, who was directly responsible to the Emperor, and answerable for everything connected with the department entrusted to him. These officers, all men of position, were the superintendents of the tej makers, of the women who prepared the large flat Abyssinian bread, of the wood-carriers, of the water girls, &c.; others, like the "Balderas," had charge of the Royal stud, the "Azage" of the domestic servants, the "Bedjerand" of the treasury, stores, &c.; there were also the Agafaris or introducers, the Likamaquas or chamberlain, the Afa Negus or mouth of the King.

Strange to say, Theodore preferred as his personal attendants those who had served Europeans. His valet, the only one who stood by him to the last, had been a servant of Barroni, the vice-consul at Massowah. Another, a young man named Paul, was a former servant of Mr. Walker; others had at one time been in the service of Plowden, Bell, and Cameron. Excepting his valet, who was almost constantly near his person, the others, although they resided in the same inclosure, had more especially to take care of his guns, swords, spears, shields, &c. He had also around him a great number of pages; not that I believe he required their presence, but it was an "honour" he bestowed on chiefs entrusted with distant commands or with the government of remote provinces. Almost all the duties of the household were performed by women; they baked, they carried water and wood, and swept his tent or hut, as the case might be. The majority of them were slaves whom he had seized from slave-dealers at the time he made "manly" efforts to put a stop to the trade. Once a week, or more often as the case required, a colonel and his regiment had the honour of proceeding to the nearest stream, to wash the Emperor's linen and that of the Imperial household. No one, not even the smallest page, could, under the penalty of death, enter his harem. He had a large number of eunuchs, most of them Gallas, or soldiers and chiefs who had recovered from the mutilation the Gallas inflict on their wounded foe. The queen or the favourite of the day had a tent or house to herself, and several eunuchs to attend upon her; at night these attendants slept at the door of her tent, and were made responsible for the virtue of the lady entrusted to their care. As for the ordinary women, the objects of passing affections or of stronger passions that time had quenched, a tent or hut in common for ten or twenty, one or two eunuchs and a few female slaves for the whole, was all the state he allowed these neglected ladies.

Theodore was more bigoted than religious. Above all things he was superstitious; and that to a degree incredible in a man in other respects so superior to his countrymen. He had always with him several astrologers, whom he consulted on all important occasions —especially before undertaking any expedition,—and whose influence over him was unbounded. He hated the priests, despised them for their ignorance, spurned their doctrines, and laughed at the marvellous stories some of their books contain; but still he never marched without a tent church, a host of priests, defteras, and deacons, and never passed near a church without kissing its threshold.

Though he could read and write, he never condescended to correspond personally with any one, but was always accompanied by several secretaries, to whom he would dictate his letters; and so wonderful was his memory that he could indite an answer to letters received months, nay years, before, or dilate on subjects and events that had occurred at a far remote period. Suppose him on the march. On a distant hillock arose a small red flannel tent—it is there where Theodore fixed his temporary abode and that of his household. To his right is the church tent; next to his own the queen's or that of the favourite of the day. Then came the one allotted to his former lady friends, who travelled with him until a favourable opportunity presented itself of sending them to Magdala, where several hundreds were dwelling in seclusion, spinning cotton for their master's shamas and for their own clothes. Behind were several tents for his secretaries, his pages, his personal attendants, and one for the few stores he carried with him. When he made any lengthened stay at a place he had huts erected by his soldiers for himself and people, and the whole was surrounded by a double line of fences. Though not wanting in bravery, he never left anything to chance. At night the hillock on which he dwelt was completely surrounded by musketeers, and he never slept without having his pistols under his pillow, and several loaded guns by his side. He had a great fear of poison, taking no food that had not been prepared by the queen or her "remplacante;" and even then she and several attendants had to taste it first. It was the same with his drink: be it water, tej, or arrack, the cup-bearer and several of those present at the time had first to drink before presenting the cup to his Majesty. He made, however, an exception in our favour one day that he visited Mr. Rassam at Gaffat. To show how much he respected and trusted the English, he accepted some brandy, and allowing no one to taste it before him, he unhesitatingly swallowed the whole draught.

He was a very jealous husband. Not only did he take the precautions I have already mentioned, but (except in the last months of his life, when it was beyond possibility for him to do otherwise) he never allowed the queen or any other lady in his establishment to travel with the camp. They always marched at night, well concealed, with a strong guard of eunuchs; and woe to him who met them on the road, and did not turn his back on them until they had passed! On one occasion a soldier who was on guard crept near the queen's tent, and, taking advantage of the darkness of the night, whispered to one of the female attendants to pass him a glass of tej under the tent. She gave him one. Unfortunately, he was seen by a eunuch, who seized him, and at once brought him before his Majesty. After hearing the case, Theodore, who happened to be in good spirits that evening, asked the culprit if he was very fond of tej; the trembling wretch replied in the affirmative. "Well, give him two wanchas [Footnote: A wancha is a large horn cup.] full to make him happy, and afterwards fifty lashes with the girf [Footnote: A long hippopotamus whip.] to teach him another time not to go near the queen's tent." Evidently, Theodore, with a large experience of the *beau sexe* of his country, was profoundly convinced that his precautions were necessary. On one of his visits to Magdala, one of the chiefs of that amba made a complaint to him against one of the officers of the Imperial household, whom he had caught some time before in his lady's apartment.

Theodore laughed, and said to him, "You are a fool. Do I not look after my wife? and I am a king."

Theodore was always an early riser; indeed, he indulged in sleep but very little. Sometimes at two o'clock, at the latest before four, he would issue from his tent and give judgment on any case brought before him. Of late his temper was such that litigants kept out of his way; he nevertheless retained his former habits, and might be seen, long before daybreak, sitting solitary on a stone, in deep meditation or in silent prayer. He was also very abstemious in his food, and never indulged in excesses of the table. He rarely partook of more than one meal a day; which was composed of injera [Footnote: The pancake loaves made of the small seed of the teff.]

and red pepper, during fast days; of wât, a kind of curry made of fish, fowl, or mutton, on ordinary occasions. On feast days he generally gave large dinners to his officers, and sometimes to the whole army. At these festivals the "brindo" [Footnote: Raw beef] would be equally enjoyed by the sovereign and by the guests. At these public breakfasts and dinners the King usually sat on a raised platform at the head of the table. No one has ever been known, except perhaps Bell, to have dined out of the same basket at the same time as Theodore; but when he desired specially to honour some of his guests, he either sent them some food from his basket, or had others placed on the platform near him, or, what was a still higher honour, sent to the favoured one his own basket with the remains of his dinner.

Unfortunately Theodore had for several years before his death greatly taken to drink. Up to three or four o'clock he was generally sober and attended to the business of the day; but after his siesta he was invariably more or less intoxicated. In his dress he was generally very simple, wearing only the ordinary shama, [Footnote: A white cotton cloth, with a red border, woven in the country.] native-made trousers, and a European white shirt; no shoes, no covering to the head. His rather long hair—for an Abyssinian— was divided in three large plaits, and allowed to fall on his neck in three plaited tails. Of late he had greatly neglected his hair; for months it had not been plaited; and to show the grief he felt on account of the "badness" of his people, he would not allow it to be besmeared with the heavy coating of butter in which Abyssinians delight. On one occasion he apologized to us for the simplicity of his dress. He told us that, during the few years of peace that followed the conquest of the country, he used often to appear in public as a king should do; but since he had been by the bad disposition of his people obliged to wage constant war against them, he had adopted the soldier's raiments, as more becoming his altered fortune. However, after his fall became imminent, he on several occasions clad himself in gorgeous costumes, in shirts and mantles of rich brocaded silks, or of gold-embroidered velvet. He did so, I believe, to influence his people. They knew that he was poor, and though he hated pomp in his own attire, he desired to impress on his few remaining followers that though fallen he was still "the King."

During the lifetime of his first wife and for some years afterwards, Theodore not only led an exemplary life, but forbade the officers of his household and the chiefs more immediately around him to live in concubinage. One day in the beginning of 1860 Theodore perceived in a church a handsome young girl silently praying to her patron, the Virgin Mary. Struck with her beauty and modesty, he made inquiries about her, and was informed that she was the only daughter of Dejatch Oubié, the Prince of Tigré, his former rival, whom he had dethroned, and who was then his prisoner. He asked for her hand, and met with a polite refusal. The young girl desired to retire into a convent, and devote herself to the service of God. Theodore was not a man to be easily thwarted in his desires. He proposed to Oubié that he would set him at liberty, only retaining him in his camp as his "guest," should the Prince prevail on his daughter to accept his hand. At last Waizero Terunish ("thou art pure") sacrificed herself for her old father's welfare, and accepted the hand of a man whom she could not love. This union was unfortunate. Theodore, to his great disappointment, did not find in his second wife the fervent affection, the almost blind devotion, of the dead companion of his youth. Waizero Terunish was proud; she always looked on her husband as a "parvenu," and took no pains to hide from him her want of respect and affection. In the afternoon, Theodore, as it had been his former habit, tired and weary, would retire for rest in the queen's tent; but he found no cordial welcome there. His wife's looks were cold and full of pride; and she even went so far as to receive him without the common courtesy due to her king. One day when he came in she pretended not to perceive him, did not rise, and remained silent when he inquired as to her health and welfare; she held in her hand a book of psalms, and when Theodore asked her why she did not answer him, she calmly replied, without lifting up her eyes from the book, "Because I am conversing with a greater and better man than you—the pious King David."

Theodore sent her to Magdala, together with her new-born son, Alamayou ("I have seen the world"), and took as his favourite a widowed lady from Yedjow, named Waizero Tamagno, a rather coarse, lascivious-looking person, the mother of five children by her former husband; she soon obtained such an ascendancy over his mind that he publicly proclaimed "that he had divorced and discarded Terunish, and that Tamagno should in future be considered by all as the queen." Soon Waizero Tamagno had numerous rivals; but she was a woman of tact; and far from complaining, she rather encouraged Theodore in his debauchery, and always received him with a smile. One day she said to her fickle lord, who felt rather astonished at her forbearance, "Why should I be jealous? I know you love but me; what is it if you stoop now and then to pick up some flowers, to beautify them by your breath?"

Although Theodore had several children, Alamayou is the only legitimate one. The eldest, a lad of about twenty-two, called Prince Meshisha, is a big, idle, lazy fellow. Though at Zagé, Theodore introduced him to us, and desired us to make him a friend with the English, he did not love him: the young man was, indeed, so unlike the Emperor that I can well understand Theodore having had serious doubts of his being really his son.

The other children, five or six in number, the illegitimate offspring of some of his numerous concubines, resided at Magdala, and were brought up in the harem. He seems to have taken but very little notice of them: but every time he passed through Magdala he would send for Alamayou, and play with the boy for hours. A few days before his death he introduced him to Mr. Rassam, saying, "Alamayou, why do you not bow to your father?" and after the audience he sent him to accompany us back to our quarters.

Waizero Terunish, Almayou's mother, never made any complaint; though forsaken by her husband, she remained always faithful to him. She spent usually the long days of her seclusion reading the books she delighted in—the psalms, the lives of the saints and of the Virgin Mary—and bringing up by her side her only son, for whom she had a deep affection. Although she had never loved her husband, in difficult times she bravely stood by his side. When Menilek, the King of Shoa, made his demonstration before the amba, and treachery was feared, she sent out her son and made all the chiefs and soldiers swear fidelity to the throne. Two days before his death, Theodore sent for the wife he had not seen for years, and spent part of the afternoon with her and his son.

After the storming of Magdala, Waizero Terunish and her rival, Waizero Tamagno, were told to come to our former prison, where they would meet with protection and sympathy. It fell to my lot to receive them on their arrival; and I did my utmost to inspire them with confidence, to assuage their fears, and to assure them that under the British flag they would be treated with scrupulous honour and respect.

It was on the 13th of April, 1866, that Theodore, still powerful, had treacherously seized us in his own house; and strange to say, on the 13th of April, two years afterwards, his dead body lay in one of our huts, while his wife and favourite had to seek shelter under the roof of those whom he had so long maltreated.

Both his queens and Alamayou accompanied the English army on its march back, Waizero Tamagno left, with feelings of gratitude for the kindness and attention she had received at the hands of the English commander-in-chief, as soon as she could with safety return to her native land, Yedjow; but poor Terunish died at Aikullet. Her child, Alamayou, the son of Theodore, and grandchild of Oubié, has now reached the English shore, an orphan, an exile, but well cared for.

CHAPTER II

Abyssinia seems to have had a strange fascination for Europeans. The two first who were connected with the late Abyssinian affairs are Messrs. Bell and Plowden, who both entered Abyssinia in 1842. Mr. John Bell, better known in that country under the name of Johannes, first attached himself to the fortunes of Ras Ali. He took service with that prince, and was elevated to the rank of basha (captain); but it seems that Ras Ali never gave him much confidence, and tolerated him rather on account of his (Ras Ali's) friendship for Plowden, than for any liking for Bell himself. Bell shortly afterwards married a young lady belonging to one of the good families of Begemder. From this union he had three children: two daughters, afterwards married to two of the King's European workmen, and a son, who left the country together with the released captives. Bell fought by Ras Ali's side at the battle of Amba Djisella, which ended so fatally for that prince, and afterwards retired into a church, awaiting in that asylum the good pleasure of the victor. Theodore hearing of the presence of a European in the sanctuary, sent him word to come to him, giving him a most solemn pledge that he would be treated as a friend. Bell obeyed, and a strong friendship sprang up between the Emperor and the Englishman.

Bell had for many years quite identified himself with the Abyssinians both in dress and mode of life. He was a man of sound judgment, brave, well-informed, appreciated all that was great and good; and seeing in Theodore an ideal he had often conceived, he attached himself to him with disinterested affection—almost worshipped him. Theodore gave him the rank of likamaquas, and always kept him near his person. Bell slept at the door of his friend's tent, dined off the same dish, joined in every expedition, and would frequently remain for hours, at the Emperor's request, narrating to him all the wonders of civilized life, the advantages of military discipline, and the rules of good government. Theodore gave him on several occasions a few hundred young men to drill; but European tactics being distasteful to the unruly Abyssinians, he obtained such indifferent results that the Emperor soon relieved him from that hopeless task. Theodore ordered his friend to marry his wife "by the sacrament." Bell at once consented; but, strange to say, the family of his wife, out of dislike to Theodore, refused to give their consent. Whereupon the Emperor presented him with a Galla slave, to whom he was married, the Emperor officiating as father to the bride.

Bell was much beloved by all who knew him, and all Europeans who came into the country were sure to find in him a friend. Between him and Plowden the brotherly friendship that united them only increased with time; and on hearing of the murder of his friend, Bell took a solemn oath that he would avenge his death. About seven months afterwards the Emperor marched against Garad, and suddenly came upon him not far from the spot where Plowden fell. The Emperor was riding ahead, next to him came his faithful chamberlain; on their entering a small wood the two brothers Garad appeared in the middle of the road, only a few yards in front of them. Seeing the danger that threatened his master, Bell rushed forward, placed himself before the Emperor, so as to protect him with his body, and, with a steady aim, fired at his friend Plowden's murderer. Garad fell. Immediately the brother, who had been watching the Emperor's movements, turned upon Bell, and shot him through the heart. Theodore promptly avenged his faithful friend, for hardly had Bell fallen to the ground than his opponent was mortally wounded by the Emperor himself.

Theodore ordered the place to be at once surrounded, and all Garad's followers—some 1,600, I believe—were made prisoners and murdered in cold blood. Theodore mourned for several days the death of his faithful follower, in whom he lost more than a brave chief and a hardy soldier: I may almost say he lost his kingdom, for none dared honestly to advise and fearlessly to counsel him as Bell had done, and none ever enjoyed that confidence which rendered Bell's advice so acceptable.

Plowden seems to have been of a more ambitious turn of mind than his friend. Whilst Bell adopted Abyssinia as his home, and contented himself with service under the native princes, it is evident that Plowden strove to represent England in that distant land, and to be acknowledged by the rulers of Abyssinia as consuls are in the East,—a small *imperium in imperio*. He went the right way to work: induced Ras Ali to send presents to the Queen, and carried them himself; impressed upon Lord Palmerston the advantages of a treaty with Abyssinia; spoke a great deal about Mussulmans, slave-trade, oppressed Christians, &c.; and at length prevailed upon the Foreign Secretary to assent to his plans, and appoint him consul for Abyssinia. In justice to him, I must say, that from all accounts no man could have been better fitted for the post: he was beloved by all classes, and his name is still mentioned with respect. He did not, so much as Bell, identify himself with the natives; he always wore a European dress, and kept his house in a semi-English style. On the other hand, he was fond of show, and never travelled without being followed by several hundred servants, all well armed—a mere parade, as on the day of his death his numerous retinue did not afford him the slightest assistance.

Plowden returned to Abyssinia as consul in 1846. He was well received by Ras Ali, with whom he was a favourite, and he soon after concluded a paper treaty with that prince. Ras Ali was a weak-minded debauchee; all he asked for was to be left alone, and on the same principle he allowed every one around him to do pretty well as they liked. One day Plowden asked permission to erect a flag-staff. Ras Ali gave a willing consent, but added, "Do not ask me to protect it, I do not care for such things; but I fear the people will not like it." Plowden hoisted the Union Jack above his consulate; a few hours afterwards it was torn to pieces by the mob. "Did not I tell you so?" was all the satisfaction he could obtain from the ruler of the land. After the fall of Ras Ali, Bell, who had, as I have already mentioned, followed the fortunes of Theodore, wrote to his friend in enthusiastic terms, depicted in the eloquent language of admiring friendship all the good qualities of the rising man, and advised Plowden to present himself before the powerful chieftain who undoubtedly before long would be the acknowledged ruler of the whole of Abyssinia.

Plowden's first reception by Theodore was courteous in the extreme; but he had this time to deal with a very different kind of man to his predecessor. Theodore was all amiability, even offered money, but declined to recognize in him "the consul," or to ratify the treaty he (Plowden) had made with Ras Ali. For several years Plowden seemed to have joined his friend Bell in singing the praises of Theodore; he was to be the reformer of his country, had introduced a certain discipline in his army, and, to use Plowden's own words, "he is an honest man, and strives to be just, and, though firm, far from cruel."

During the last years of his life, Plowden's opinion had been greatly modified. Theodore did not like him; he feared him; and it was only on account of his friendship for Bell that he did not lay violent hands on him. Plowden, on one occasion, was told to accompany his Majesty to Magdala; arrived there, Theodore called for the Head of the mountain, who was at that time the son of the Galla queen, Workite, and asked him his advice as to whether he should put Plowden in chains or not. The prince, who had a great regard for Plowden, told his Majesty that if they watched him with the eye it was sufficient, and that he would be answerable for his prisoner. Plowden returned with Theodore some time afterwards to the Amhara country, but was constantly surrounded by spies. All his actions were reported to the Emperor, and for a long time, under some pretence or the other, he was refused leave to return to England. At last, broken in health, and disappointed, Plowden almost insisted on going. His Majesty granted his request, but at the same time informed him that the roads were infested with rebels and thieves, and strongly advised him to await his return. I was told on good authority that his Majesty only acquiesced in Plowden's wishes because he believed that it was quite impossible for him to leave.

However, Plowden, trusting in his popularity, and, perhaps, also in his retinue, started at once on his homeward journey. At a short distance from Gondar he was attacked and made prisoner by a rebel named Garad, a cousin of Theodore. It is probable that he would have been let off with a ransom, but for an unfortunate circumstance. Plowden, sick and tired, was resting under a tree, and while Garad was speaking to him, put his hand towards his belt, as his servant told us, to take out his handkerchief; but the rebel chief, believing that he intended to draw a pistol, immediately wounded him mortally with the lance he held in his hands. Plowden was ransomed by the Gondar merchants, but died a few days afterwards, in March, 1860, from the effects of the wound.

During our stay at Kuarata, at the time we were in high favour, office copies of Plowden's official letters for the year preceding his death, were brought to us. How altered his impression, how changed his opinion! He had begun to see through the fine words of the Emperor; he more than suspected that before long a hateful tyranny would replace the firm but just rule he had formerly so greatly admired. I remember well that at Zagé, when our luggage was returned to us a few hours after the arrest, with what haste and anxiety Prideaux, in whose charge the manuscript was at the time, opened his trunk behind his bed, so that the guards should not perceive the dangerous paper before he had time to destroy it.

If Bell and Plowden had been both living, it may be asked, would Theodore have dealt with them so as ultimately to call for the intervention of Government on Abyssinian affairs? I believe so. The King, as I have said, disliked Plowden personally; he repaid his ransom to the Gondar merchants, it is true, but it was only a political "dodge" of his; he knew well to whom he gave the money, and took it back "with interest," a few years later. Often he has been heard to sneer at the manner in which Plowden was killed, and say, "The white men are cowards: look at Plowden; he was armed, but he allowed himself to be killed without even defending himself." This was a malicious assertion on the part of Theodore, as he was well aware that Plowden was so sick at the time that he could hardly walk, and that though he carried a pistol, *it was not loaded*. Not long before his own death, Theodore spoke, on several occasions, in very harsh terms of Bell's eldest daughter, and on some of her friends representing to his Majesty that he should not forget that she was the daughter of the man who died protecting him, Theodore quietly replied, "Bell was a fool; he would never carry a shield!"

A few months after the news of Consul Plowden's death had reached England, Captain Charles Duncan Cameron was appointed to the vacant post, but for some reason or other, he reached Massowah only in February, 1862, and Gondar in July of the same year. Captain Cameron had not only served with distinction during the Kaffir war, and passed alone through more than 200 miles of the enemy's country, but had also been employed on the staff of General Williams, and had been for several years in the consular service. He was, in all respects, well fitted for his post; but, unfortunately for him, when he entered Abyssinia he had to deal with a fascinating, vainglorious, shrewd man, hiding his cunning under an appearance of modesty: in a word, with Theodore who had become an over-bearing despot. On his first arrival, Cameron was received with great honours, and treated by the Emperor with marked respect, and when he left in October, 1862, he was loaded with presents, escorted by the Emperor's servants, and almost acknowledged as a consul. Like so many others—I can say, like ourselves,—at first he had been so completely taken in by Theodore's manners that he did not discern the true character of the man he had to deal with, and but too late found out the worth of his gracious reception and the flatteries which had been so liberally bestowed upon him.

From Adowa Captain Cameron forwarded Theodore's letter to our Queen by native messengers, and proceeded to the province of Bogos, where he deemed his presence necessary. He found out during his stay that Samuel, the Georgis balderaba [Footnote: An introducer: generally given to foreigners in the capacity of a spy.] whom Theodore had given him—a clever, but rather unscrupulous Shoho—was intriguing with the chiefs of the neighbourhood, tributaries of Turkey, in favour of his imperial master. Captain Cameron thought it therefore advisable, in order to avoid future difficulties with the Egyptian Government, to leave Samuel behind with the Servants he did not require. Samuel was much hurt at not being allowed to accompany Cameron in his tour through the Soudan, and though he pretended to be well pleased with the arrangement, he shortly afterwards wrote a long letter to his master in which he spoke in very unfavourable terms of Captain Cameron. Arrived at Kassala, Captain Cameron one evening at a friend's house asked his Abyssinian servants to show the guests their native war-dance; some refused, others complied, but as it was not appreciated by the spectators, they were told to leave off. (I mention this fact as it was made a serious offence by Theodore, and is a sample of the pretences adopted by him when he desired to vindicate his conduct.) Arrived at Metemma, Cameron, who was at the time suffering from fever, wrote to his Majesty to inform him of his arrival, and requesting his permission to proceed to the missionary station of Djenda; which was granted.

Mr. Bardel, a Frenchman, had accompanied Cameron on his first voyage to Abyssinia; they disagreed, and Bardel left Cameron's service to enter the Emperor's. At the time Theodore sent Cameron with a letter to the Queen of England, he also entrusted one to Bardel for the Emperor of the French. During Bardel's absence M. Lejean, the French Consul at Massowah, arrived in Abyssinia; he was the bearer of credentials to the Emperor Theodore, and also brought with him a few trifles to be presented to his Majesty in the name of the Emperor Napoleon. M. Lejean was not allowed to leave before the arrival of Mr. Bardel; who returned to Gondar in September, 1863, with an answer from the French Secretary for Foreign Affairs, whom he described to Theodore as the mouthpiece (*afa negus*) of Napoleon. All the Europeans were summoned from Gondar to witness the reading of the letter; the King, seated at the window of the palace, had the letter read, and asked Bardel how he had been received.

"Badly," he replied. "I had an audience with the Emperor, when Mr. D'Abbadie whispered to him that your Majesty was in the habit of cutting off hands and feet; on that, without a word more, Napoleon turned his back upon me."

Theodore then took the letter, and, tearing it to pieces, said:—"Who is that Napoleon? Are not my ancestors greater than his? If God made him great, can he not make me also great?" After which his Majesty ordered a safe conduct to be given to M. Lejean, with orders that he should leave the country at once.

The Abouna, at that time in favour, afraid above all things of the Roman Catholics, urged the Emperor to let Lejean depart, lest the French should be afforded an excuse for taking possession of some part of the country, from whence their priests would endeavour to propagate their doctrines. But two days after Lejean's departure, Theodore, who had by that time regretted that he had let him go, sent to have him arrested on the road and brought back to Gondar.

In the autumn of 1863 the Europeans in Abyssinia numbered about twenty-five; they were, Cameron and his European servants, the Basle mission, the Scottish mission, the missionaries of the London Society for the Conversion of the Jews, and some adventurers.

In 1855 Dr. Krapf, accompanied by Mr. Flad, entered Abyssinia as pioneers for a mission which Bishop Gobat desired to establish in that country. The lay missionaries he intended to send were to be workmen, who would receive a small salary, if necessary, but were supposed to support themselves by their work: they were also to open schools, and seize every opportunity to preach the Word of God. Mr. Flad made several journeys backwards and forwards, and, at the time of the first trouble that befell the Europeans since the beginning of Theodore's reign, the lay missionaries, who had been joined by a few adventurers,—the whole of them better known by natives and Europeans under the name of the "Gaffat people" (on account of the name of the village they usually resided in), amounted to eight. Mr. Flad had some time previously abandoned the Basle Mission for the London Mission for the Conversion of the Jews.

The "Gaffat people" played an important part in all the transactions that, from 1863, took place between his Abyssinian Majesty and the Europeans residing in the country. Their position was not an enviable one; they had not only to please his Majesty, but, in order to keep themselves free from imprisonment or chains, to forestall his wishes, and to keep his fickle nature always interested in their work by devising some new toy suited to please his childish love for novelty. On their first arrival in the country they did their best to fulfil the instructions of their patron, the Bishop of Jerusalem. But on Theodore learning that these men were able workmen, he sent for them one day and told them, "I do not want teachers in my country, but workmen: will you work for me?" They bowed, and with good grace placed themselves at his Majesty's disposal. Gaffat, a small hillock about four miles from Debra Tabor, was assigned to them as a place of residence. There they built semi-European houses, established workshops, &c. Knowing that he would have a greater hold upon them, and that they would have more difficulty in leaving the country, Theodore ordered them to marry: they all consented. The little colony flourished, and Theodore for a long time behaved very liberally to them; gave them large sums of money, grain, honey, butter, and all necessary supplies in great abundance. They were also presented with silver shields, gold-worked saddles, mules, horses, &c.; their wives with richly embroidered burnouses, ornaments of gold and silver; and to enhance their position in the country they were allowed all the privileges of a Ras.

"His children," as Theodore called them, so far had nothing to complain of; but the Emperor soon got tired of carriages, pickaxes, doors, and such like; he was bent on having cannons and mortars cast in his country. He gently insinuated his desire; but they firmly refused, on the ground that they had no knowledge of such work. Theodore knew how to make them consent; he had only to appear displeased, to frown a little, and they awaited in trembling to have his good pleasure made known to them. Theodore asked for cannons; they would try. His Majesty smiled; he knew the men he had to deal with. After the guns, they made mortars; then gunpowder; then brandy;

again more cannons, shells, shots, &c. Some were sent to make roads, others erected foundries; a large number of intelligent natives were apprenticed to them, and with their assistance executed some really remarkable works. I, who happened to witness one day the harsh, imperative tone he took with them because he felt annoyed at a mere trifle, can well understand their complete submission to his iron will, and cannot blame them. They had given in at first, and accepted his bounty; they had wives and children, and desired to be left in quiet possession of their homes, and were only anxious to please their hard taskmaster.

Another missionary station had been established at Djenda. These gentlemen, most of them scripture-readers, not conversant with any trade, and striving but for one object, — the conversion of the Falashas, or native Jews, — declined to work for Theodore. The Emperor could not understand their refusal. According to his notions every European could work in some way or the other. He attributed their refusal to ill-will towards him, and only awaited a suitable opportunity to visit them with his displeasure. They and the Gaffat people were not in accord; though, for appearance' sake, a kind of brotherhood was kept up between the rival stations.

The Djenda Mission consisted of two missionaries, of the Scottish Society: a man named Cornelius, [Footnote: He died at Gaffat in the beginning of 1865.] brought to Abyssinia by Mr. Stern, on his first trip; of Mr. and Mrs. Flad, and of Mr. and Mrs. Rosenthal, who had accompanied Mr. Stern on his second journey to Abyssinia. The Rev. Henry Stern is really a martyr to his faith. A fine type of the brave self-denying missionary, he had already exposed his life in Arabia, where he had, with the recklessness of conviction, undertaken a dangerous, almost impossible, journey, in order to bring the "good tidings" to his oppressed brethren the Jews of Yemen and Sanaa. He had just escaped almost by a miracle from the hands of the bigoted Arabs, when he undertook a first voyage to Abyssinia, in order to establish a mission in that country, where thousands of Jews were living.

Mr. Stern arrived in Abyssinia in 1860, was well received and kindly treated by his Majesty. On his return to Europe he published a valuable account of his tour, under the title of *Wanderings amongst the Falashas of Abyssinia*. In that book Mr. Stern gives a very favourable account of Theodore; but, as becomes a true historian, gave some details of the Emperor's family, which were, to a certain extent, the cause of many of the sufferings he had afterwards to undergo. About that time several articles appeared in one of the Egyptian newspapers, purporting to have issued from the pen of Mr. Stern, and reflecting rather severely on the marriage of the Gaffat people. Mr. Stern has always denied having been the author of these articles; and though I, and every one else who knows Mr. Stern, will place unlimited confidence in his word, still the Gaffat people would not accept his denial: to the very last they believed him to have written the obnoxious articles, and harboured bitter feelings against him, in consequence.

Mr. Stern undertook a second journey to Abyssinia in the autumn of 1862, accompanied this time by Mr. and Mrs. Rosenthal. He and his party reached Djenda in April, 1863.

As soon as the Gaffat people heard of the arrival of Mr. Stern at Massowah, they went in a body to the Emperor and begged him not to allow Mr. Stern to enter Abyssinia. His Majesty gave an evasive answer, but did not comply with the request; on the contrary, he seems to have rejoiced at the idea of an enmity existing between the Europeans in his country, and chuckled at the prospect of the advantages he might reap from their jealousy and rivalry. Mr. Stern soon perceived the great change that had already taken place in the deportment of Theodore, and saw but too plainly, during his several missionary tours, abundant proofs of the cruelty of the man he had so shortly before admired and praised. The Abouna (Abyssinian bishop) at the time in frequent collision with the Emperor, spoke but too openly of the many vices of the ruling sovereign, and as he had always been friendly disposed towards Mr. Stern, this gentleman frequently visited him, even made some short stays in his house. This friendship was construed by the Emperor as implying an understanding between the bishop and the English priest unfavourable to himself, and with a view to the cession of the church lands for a certain sum of money, which was to be placed in Egypt at the Abouna's disposal.

To sum up, this was the state of the different parties when the storm at last burst on the head of the unfortunate Mr. Stern:—Bell and Plowden, the only Europeans who might have had some influence for good over the mind of the Emperor, were dead. The Gaffat people worked for the King, were frequently near his person, and entertained anything but friendly feelings towards Mr. Stern and the Djenda Mission. While Captain Cameron and his party were watched in Gondar, and in no way mixed up with the differences that unfortunately divided the other Europeans.

CHAPTER III

Such was the state of affairs when Mr. Stern obtained leave to return to the coast. Unfortunately it was impossible for him to avail himself at once of this permission. On Mr. Stern at last taking his departure he had to remain at Gondar a few days, and, but too late, thought of presenting his respects to his Majesty. He also accepted during his short stay there the hospitality of the bishop. On the 13th October Mr. Stern, accompanied for a short distance by Consul Cameron and Mr. Bardel, started on his homeward journey. On arriving on the Waggera Plain he perceived the King's tent. What followed is well known: how that unfortunate gentleman was almost beaten to death; and from that hour, almost without remission, loaded with chains, tortured, and dragged from prison to prison, until the day of his deliverance from Magdala by the British army.

When speaking of Theodore's treatment of foreigners, I will endeavour to explain the real cause of the misfortunes that befell Mr. Stern. That he was only the victim of circumstances, is a fact beyond any doubt. The extracts from his book and the notes from his diary, brought as charges against him, were only discovered several weeks *after* many cruelties had been inflicted upon him. But I believe that many small, apparently trifling, incidents combined to make him the first European victim of the Abyssinian monarch. The Emperor could not endure the thought that Europeans in his country should do aught else but work for him. On his first interview with Mr. Stern, after this gentleman's return to Abyssinia, Theodore, on being informed as to the motives of Mr. Stern's journey, said, in an angry mood, "I have enough of your Bibles." Theodore also believed that by ill-using Mr. Stern he would please his "Gaffat children," therefore, immediately after Mr. Stern's imprisonment, he wrote to them saying, "I have chained your enemy and mine."

That the crisis was at last brought on by malicious representations to his Majesty of trifling incidents, was proved to us quite accidentally on our way down. At Antalo I had a few friends at dinner, amongst them Mr. Stern, when, in the evening, Peter Beru, an Abyssinian who had received his education at Malta and had been one of the interpreters of Mr. Stern's book at the famous public trial at Gondar, came into the tent, and, being a little excited, told Mr. Stern that three things had called down upon him the King's displeasure: first, the enmity of the Gaffat people against him; secondly, his (Mr. Stern's) intimacy with the Abouna; thirdly, his not having called upon his Majesty during his last stay at Gondar.

On the 22nd of November Mr. Laurence Kerans arrived at Gondar. He came for the purpose of joining Captain Cameron in the capacity of private secretary. He brought with him some letters for Captain Cameron; amongst them one from Earl Russell ordering the consul back to his post at Massowah. Of all the captives none deserves greater sympathy than poor Kerans. Quite a youth when he entered Abyssinia, he suffered four years of imprisonment in chains, for no reason whatever except that he arrived at an inauspicious time. It is true that, according to his wonted habit, his Majesty charged him with having intended to insult him by offering him a carpet representing Gerard the lion-killer. Gerard, in his Zouave costume, Theodore said, represented the Turks, the lion was himself, upon whom the infidel was firing, the attendant a Frenchman; but he added, "I do not see the Englishman who ought to be by my side." Poor Kerans remained only a few weeks in semi-liberty at Gondar; he had presented on his own account a rifle to his Majesty (the carpet was supposed to have been sent by Captain Speedy, who had previously been in Abyssinia); and every morning Samuel, who was the balderaba of the Europeans, would present himself, with supposed compliments from his Majesty, adding, "The Emperor desires to know what you would like?" Kerans answered, "A horse, a shield, and a lance." The next morning Samuel would ask, from his Majesty, what kind of horse he preferred, and so on, until at last the poor lad, who was obliged every day to bow to the ground in thankfulness for the supposed gift, began to suspect that all was not right.

Consul Cameron, a few days after the arrival of Kerans, was called to the King's camp and told to remain there until further orders. He was already so far a prisoner that he was not allowed to return to Gondar, when, on the plea of bad health, he applied for permission to do so. Cameron waited until the beginning of January, daily expecting a letter for the Emperor, but at last, as none came, he considered himself bound to obey his instructions, and accordingly, informed his Majesty that he had received orders from his Government to return to Massowah, and begged that he might be allowed to leave in a few days.

The next morning, 4th January, Cameron, his European servants, the missionaries from Gondar, and Messrs. Stern and Rosenthal (both since some time already in chains), were all sent for by his Majesty. They were ushered into a tent close to the Emperor's inclosure, with two loaded twelve-pounders placed in front of it and pointed in that direction. The place was crowded with soldiers; everything was so arranged as to make resistance impossible. Shortly after Cameron's arrival Theodore sent several messages, asking, "Where is the answer to the letter I gave you? Why did you go to my enemies the Turks? Are you a consul?" At last the messages ceased with this last one: "I will keep you a prisoner until I get an answer, and see if you are a consul or not." On that Cameron was very rudely handled by the soldiers; he was knocked down, his beard torn off, and heavy fetters hammered on him. The captives were all placed in a tent near the Emperor's inclosure; for a time they were well supplied with rations, and, apart from the fetters, not otherwise ill used.

On the 3rd of February Mr. Bardel returned from a mission the Emperor had intrusted to him, viz., to spy the land, and report about the doings of an Egyptian general, who, at the head of a considerable force, had been for some time staying at Metemma, the nearest post to Abyssinia on the north-west frontier. The following day the Gaffat people were called by the Emperor to consult about the liberation of the European captives. On their recommendation, two missionaries of the Scottish society, two German hunters, Mr. Flad and Cornelius, were freed from their fetters, and allowed to remain at Gaffat with the workmen. The head of the Gaffat people then told Captain Cameron that he would request Theodore to release the whole of them and allow them to depart, if Captain Cameron would give a written document to the effect that no steps would be taken by England to avenge the insult inflicted upon her in the person of her representative. Cameron, not considering himself justified in taking upon himself such a responsibility, declined. A few days afterwards Mr. Bardel having offended his Majesty, or rather being of no more use to him, was sent to join those whom he had been greatly instrumental in depriving of their liberty.

The Rev. Mr. Stern has ably described the painful captivity which he and his fellow-sufferers experienced up to their first release on the arrival of our mission in the beginning of 1865; how they were dragged from Gondar to Azazo; the horrid torture inflicted upon them on the 12th of May: their long march in chains from Azazo to Magdala; their confinement in chains on that amba in the common jail; and the horrid tale of sufferings and misery they had for so many months to endure. Suffice it to say, that on the date of Captain Cameron's note—14th of February, 1864—which gave the first intimation of their imprisonment, the captives, eight altogether, were Captain Cameron and his followers (Kerans, Bavdel, McKilvie, Makerer, and Pietro), Messrs. Stern and Rosenthal.

Much of what I have said, and a great deal of what I have still to narrate, would appear unintelligible if I were not to describe the conduct Theodore had adopted towards foreigners. It is plain, from facts that I will now adduce, that Theodore had for several years systematically insulted them. He did so partly to dazzle the people with his power, and partly because he believed that complete impunity would always attend his grossest misdeeds.

In December, 1856, David, the Coptic Patriarch of Alexandria, arrived in Abyssinia, bearer of certain presents for Theodore, and the expression of the good-will of the Pasha of Egypt. The fame of Theodore had spread far and wide in the Soudan; and probably the Egyptian authorities, in order to save that province from being plundered, or unwilling to engage at the time in an expensive war with their powerful neighbour, adopted that expedient as the best suited to appease the ire of their former foe. As usual, Theodore found an excuse for the ill treatment he inflicted upon the aged Patriarch, on the ground that a diamond cross presented to him was only intended as an insult: it meant, he said, that they considered him as a vassal; and on the Patriarch proposing that he should send a letter to the Pasha, accompanied with suitable presents, and that the Pasha would in return send him fire-arms, cannons, and officers to drill his troops, his Majesty exclaimed, "I see, they now desire me to declare myself their tributary."

Most probably Theodore, always jealous of the power of the Church, took advantage of the presence of its highest dignitary to show to his army whom they had to fear and obey. On the pretexts above mentioned he caused one day a hedge to be built around the Patriarch's residence, and for several days the eldest son of the Coptic Church kept his father in close confinement. Theodore had some time previously been excommunicated by the Bishop; he therefore enjoyed very much the disreputable quarrel which took place on that matter, as he induced the Patriarch, through fear, to take off the excommunication of his inferior. After a while, however, Theodore apologized, and allowed the terrified old man to depart. The Patriarch on his return told his tale, but the fame for justice and wisdom of the would-be descendant of Solomon was so great that, far from being credited, the Turkish Government, who attributed the failure of the negotiation to the unfitness of their agent, soon after despatched a mission on a larger scale, together with numerous and costly presents, under the orders of an experienced and trusty officer, Abdul Rahman Bey.

The Egyptian envoy reached Dembea in March, 1859. At first Theodore, gratified at receiving such beautiful gifts, treated the ambassador with all courtesy and distinction; but on account of the unsafe condition of the country at the time, he took his guest with him, and considering Magdala a proper and suitable place of residence, left him there. He soon ignored him entirely, and the unfortunate man had to remain nearly two years, a semi-prisoner, on that amba. At last, on the reception of several strongly worded and threatening letters from the Egyptian Government, he allowed him to depart, but caused him to be plundered of all he had near the frontier, by the Shum of Tschelga. Theodore, after the departure of Abdul Rahman Bey, wrote to the Egyptian Government, denying any knowledge of the plunder, and accusing the envoy of serious crimes. Hearing of this, the unfortunate Bey, fearing that his denials would not stand against the charge brought against him by the pious Emperor, poisoned himself at Berber.

His third victim was the Nab of Arkiko. He had accompanied the Emperor to Godjam, when, without reason given, the Emperor cast him into prison and loaded him with chains. It was only on the representation of several influential merchants, who, fearing that the Nab's relations would retaliate on the Abyssinian caravans, impressed upon his Majesty the prudence of letting him depart, that the Emperor allowed his vassal to return to his country.

The same day on which he imprisoned the Nab of Arkiko, M. Lejean, a member of the French diplomatic service, disgusted with Abyssinia and the many discomforts of camp life, presented himself before the Emperor to apply for leave to depart. Theodore could not grant the desired interview, but M. Lejean persisted in his demand, and sent a second time, representing that, as his Majesty was *en route* for Godjam, each day would increase the difficulty of his return. Such presumption could not be tolerated. Theodore had defied Egypt; he would now defy France. Lejean was seized, and had to remain in full uniform for twenty-four hours in chains. He was only released on his making an humble apology, and desisting from his desire to leave the country. He was sent to Gaffat, and ordered to abide there until the return of Mr. Bardel.

Theodore scoffed at and imprisoned the Patriarch of Alexandria; the Egyptian ambassador he kept a semi-prisoner for several years; the Nab he chained; the French consul he chained, insulted, and kicked out of the country. Nothing came of all this: on the contrary, in his own camp his influence was greater. Under these circumstances, any barbarian would have done and thought exactly as Theodore did. He came to the conviction that, either through fear of his power or the impossibility of reaching him, whatever ill treatment he might inflict on strangers, no punishment could possibly overtake him. That such was his impression is evident from the gradually increasing brutality of his conduct, always most severe, but never so outrageous as in the case of the British captives. The savage, barbarous treatment he inflicted on Messrs. Stern, Cameron, Rosenthal, and their followers, is without precedent in modern history. Theodore at last took no trouble to hide his contempt for Europeans and their governments.

He knew in August, 1864, that before a month an answer to his letter to the Queen had arrived at Massowah. "Let them wait my good pleasure," was the only observation he made on the subject. It is probable that he would never have taken any notice of her Majesty's letter or of the mission sent to him, if his rapid fall—at that time beginning—had not influenced his conduct. When we arrived at Massowah in July, 1864, Theodore was still powerful, at the head of a large army, and master of the greater part of the country. His campaign to Shoa in 1865 was most disastrous. He lost by it, not only that prosperous kingdom, but a large portion of his army; the Gallas seizing the occasion to annoy him greatly on his return. He foresaw his fall, and it probably struck him that the friendship of England might be useful to him; or should he doubt its possibility, he might seize us as hostages, in order to make capital out of us; therefore, but with apparent reluctance, he granted us the long-expected permission to enter his country.

We have now the solution of a part of this difficult problem; we can understand, to a certain degree, the strange character of this man so remarkable in many ways. Imbued with a few European notions, he longed to obtain some of the advantages he had heard of: but how? England and France would only return his friendship by words—he wanted deeds; sweet phrases he would not listen to. He soon became convinced that he might with impunity insult foreigners or envoys from friendly states; and at last it struck him that, while he insulted and ill used Europeans, he might as well keep in his hands an important man like a consul, as a hostage.

CHAPTER IV

In the spring of 1864 it was vaguely rumoured that an African potentate had imprisoned a British consul; the fact appeared so strange, that few credited the assertion. It was soon ascertained, however, that a certain Emperor of Abyssinia, calling himself Theodore, had cast into prison and loaded with chains, Captain Cameron, the consul accredited to his court, and several missionaries stationed in his dominions. A small pencil note from Captain Cameron at last reached Mr. Speedy, the acting vice-consul at Massowah, giving the number and names of the captives, and suggesting that their release depended entirely on the receipt of a civil letter in answer to the one the King had forwarded some months before.

There is no doubt that much difficulty presented itself in order to meet the request expressed by Consul Cameron. Little was known about Abyssinia, and the conduct of its ruler was so strange, so contrary to all precedents, that it became a matter of grave consideration how to communicate with the Abyssinian Emperor without endangering the liberty of others.

In the official correspondence on Abyssinian affairs there is a letter from Mr. Colquhoun, her Majesty's Agent and Consul-General in Egypt, dated Cairo, 10th May, 1864, in which that gentleman informs Earl Russell "that it is difficult to get at Theodore." He was expecting to learn what means the Bombay Government could place at his disposal, as from Egypt none were available; he adds, "except from Aden I really can see no measures feasible, and such could only be of a mild nature, for from the character we have had of late of the King, he would appear to become subject to fits of rage which almost deprive him of reason, and would *render all approach dangerous.*"

On June 16th the Foreign Office selected for the difficult and dangerous task of Envoy to Theodore, Mr. Hormuzd Bassam, Assistant Political Resident at Aden; instructions were at the same time forwarded to that gentleman to the effect that he should hold himself in readiness to proceed to Massowah, and, if needful, to Abyssinia, with a view of obtaining the release of Captain Cameron and other Europeans detained in captivity by King Theodore. A letter from her Majesty the Queen of England, one from the Coptic Patriarch of Alexandria for the Abouna, and one from the same to King Theodore, were forwarded to Mr. Rassam, in order to facilitate his mission. Mr. Rassam was to be conveyed to Massowah in a ship-of-war;

he was at once to inform Theodore of his arrival, bearing a letter to him from the Queen of England, and also forward, by the same messenger, the letters from the Patriarch to the Abouna and to the Emperor. He was to await a reply at Massowah, before deciding whether he should proceed himself, or forward the Queen's letter to Captain Cameron for delivery. The instructions added that Mr. Rassam might, however, adopt any other course which might appear to him more advisable; but he should take special care not to place himself in a position that might cause further embarrassment to the British Government.

It so happened that at the time Mr. Rassam received an intimation that he was selected for the duty of conveying a letter from the Queen to the Emperor of Abyssinia, I had gone with him on a visit to Lahej, a small Arab town about twenty-five miles from Aden. We talked a great deal about that strange land, and on my expressing my desire to accompany Mr. Rassam to the Abyssinian Court, that gentleman proposed to Colonel Merewether, the Political Resident at Aden, to allow me to go with him as his companion: a request that Colonel Merewether immediately granted, and which was shortly afterwards sanctioned by the Governor of Bombay and the Viceroy of India.

We had to wait a few days, as the Queen's letter had been detained in Egypt, in order to have it translated, and it was only on the 20th of July, 1864, that Mr. Rassam and myself left Aden for Massowah in her Majesty's steamer *Dalhousie*.

On the morning of the 23rd, at a distance of about thirty miles from the shore, we sighted the high land of Abyssinia, formed of several consecutive ranges, all running from N. to S., the more distant being also the highest; some of the peaks, such as Taranta, ranging between 12,000 and 13,000 feet.

As the outline of the coast became more distinct, the sight of a small island covered with white houses surrounded by green groves, reflecting their welcome shadows in the quiet blue water of the bay, gave us a thrill of delight; it seemed as if at last we had come to one of those enchanted spots of the East, so often described, so seldom seen, and to the longing of our anxious hearts the quick motion of the steamer seemed slow to satisfy our ardent wishes. But nearer and nearer as we approached the shore, one by one all our illusions disappeared; the pleasant imagery vanished, and the stern reality of mangrove swamps, sandy and sunburnt beach, wretched and squalid huts, stared us in the face. Instead of the semi-Paradise distance had painted to our imagination, we found (and, alas! remained long enough to verify the fact) that the land of our temporary residence could be described in three words—sun, dirt, and desolation.

Massowah, latitude 15.36 N., longitude 39.30 E., is one of the many coral islands that abound in the Red Sea; it is but a few feet above high-water mark, about a mile in length, and a quarter in breadth. Towards the north it is separated from the mainland by a narrow creek about 200 yards in breadth, and is distant from Arkiko, a small town situated at the western extremity of the bay, about two miles. Half-a-mile south of Massowah, another small coral island, almost parallel to the one we describe, covered with mangroves and other rank vegetation, the proud owner of a sheik's tomb of great veneration, lies between Massowah and the Gedem peak, the high mountain forming the southern boundary of the bay.

The western half of the island of Massowah is covered with houses: a few two stories high, built of coral rock, the remainder small wooden huts with straw roofs. The first are inhabited by the wealthier merchants and brokers, the Turkish officials, and the few Banians, European consuls; and merchants whose unfortunate fate has cast them on this inhospitable shore. There is not a building worth mentioning: the Pasha's residence is a large, ungainly mansion, remarkable only for its extreme filthiness. During our stay the offensive smell from the accumulation of dirt on the yards and staircases of the palace was quite overwhelming: it is easier to imagine than to describe the abominable stench that pervaded the whole place. The few mosques are without importance—miserable whitewashed coral buildings. One, however, under construction promised to be a shade better than the others.

The streets—if by this name we may call the narrow and irregular lanes that run between the houses—are kept pretty clean; whether with or without municipal intervention I cannot say. Except in front of the Pasha's residence, there is no open space worthy of the name of square. The houses are much crowded together, many even being half built over the sea on piles. Land is of such value on this spot so little known, that reclamation was at several points going on; though I do not suppose that shares and dividends were either issued or promised.

The landing-place is near the centre of the island, opposite to the gates of the town, which are regularly shut at eight P.M.; why, it is difficult to say, as it is possible to land on any part of the island quite as easily, if not more so, than on the greasy pier. On the landing-place a few huts have been erected by the collector of customs and his subordinates; these, surrounded by the brokers and tallow-scented Bedouins, register the imports, exacting such duties as they like, before the merchandise is allowed to be purchased by the Banians or conveyed to the bazaar for sale. This last-named place— the *sine qua non* of all Eastern towns—is a wretched affair. Still, the Bedouin beau, the Bashi-bazouk, the native girls, and the many *flaneurs* of the place, must find some attractions in its precincts, for though redolent with effluvia of the worst description, and swarming with flies, it is, during part of the day, the rendezvous of a merry and jostling crowd.

The eastern half of the island contains the burial-ground, the water-tanks, the Roman Catholic mission-house, and a small fort.

The burial-ground begins almost with the last houses, the boundary between the living and the dead being merely nominal. To improve the closer relationship between the two, the water-tanks are placed amongst the graves! but there are but few tanks still in good condition. After heavy showers, the surface drainage finds its way into the reservoirs, carrying with it the detritus of all the accumulated filth of the last year or two, and adding an infusion of human bodies, in all stages of decomposition. Still, the water is highly prized, and, strange to say, seems to have no noxious effects, on the drinkers. At the north and south points of this part of the island two buildings have been erected—the one the emblem of good-will and peace; the other, of war and strife—the mission-house and the fort. But it is difficult to decide which of the two means the most mischief; many are inclined to give the palm to the worthy fathers' abode. The fort appears formidable, but only at a great distance; on near approach it is found to be but a relic of former ages, a crumbled-down ruin, too weak to bear any longer its three old rusty guns now lying on the ground: it is the terror, not of the neighbourhood, but of the unfortunate gunner, who has already lost an arm whilst endeavouring to return a salute through their honeycombed tubes. On the other hand, the mission-house, garbed in immaculate whiteness, smiles radiantly around, inviting instead of repulsing the invader. But within, are they always words of love that fill the echoes of the dome? Is peace the only sound that issues from its walls? Though the past speaks volumes, and though the history of the Roman Church is written in letters of blood all over the Abyssinian land, let us hope that the fears of the people have no foundation, and that the missionaries here, like all Christian missionaries, only strive to promote one object—the cause of Christ.

Massowah, as well as the immediate surrounding country, is mainly dependent on Abyssinia for its supplies. Jowaree is the staple food; wheat is little used; rice is a favourite amongst the better classes. Goats and sheep are killed daily in the bazaar, cows on rare occasions; but the flesh of the camel is the most esteemed, though, on account of the expense, rarely indulged in except on great occasions.

The inhabitants being Mussulmans, water is the ordinary beverage; *tej* and araki (made from honey) can, however, be purchased in the bazaar. The limited supply of water obtained from the few remaining tanks is quite inadequate to meet the wants of even a small portion of the community; water is consequently brought in daily from the wells a few miles north of Massowah, and from Arkiko. The first is brought in leather bags by the young girls of the village; the latter conveyed in boats across the bay. The water in both cases is brackish, that from Arkiko highly so. For this reason, and also on account of the greater facility in the transport, it is cheaper, and is purchased only by the poorer inhabitants.

To avoid useless repetitions, before speaking of the population, climate, diseases, &c., a short account of the immediate neighbourhood is necessary.

About four miles north of Massowah is Haitoomloo, a large village of about a thousand huts, the first place where we meet with sweet water; a mile and a quarter further inland we came upon Moncullou, a smaller but better built village. A mile westward of the last place we find the small village of Zaga. These, with a small hamlet east of Haitoomloo, constitute all the inhabited portions of this sterile region. The next village, Ailat, about twenty miles from Massowah, is built on the first terrace of the Abyssinian range, 600 feet above the level of the sea. All these villages are situated in the midst of a sandy and desolate plain; a few mimosas, aloes, senna plants, and cactuses struggle for life in the burning sand. The country residences of the English and French consuls shine like oases in this desert, great pains having been taken to introduce trees that thrive even in such a locality.

The wells are the wealth of the villages—their very existence. Most probably, huts after huts have been erected in their vicinity until the actual prosperous villages have arisen, surrounded as they are on all sides by a burnt and desert tract. The wells number about twenty. Many old ones are closed, but new ones are frequently dug, so as to keep up a constant supply of water. The reason old wells are abandoned is, that after a while the water becomes very brackish. In a new well the water is almost sweet. The water obtained from these wells proceeds from two different sources: First, from the high mountains in the vicinity. The rain filters and impregnates the soil, but not being able to soak beyond a certain depth, on account of the volcanic rocks of the undersoil, forms a small stratum always met with at a certain depth. Secondly, from the sea by filtration. The wells, though about four miles from the shore, are only from twenty to twenty-five feet deep, and consequently on or below the level of the sea.

The proof of an undercurrent of water, due to the presence of the high range of mountains, becomes more apparent as the traveller advances into the interior; though the soil is still sandy and barren, and little vegetation can as yet be seen, trees and shrubs become more plentiful, and of a larger size. A few miles farther inland, even during the summer months, it is always possible to obtain water by digging to the depth of a few feet in the dried-up bed of a water-torrent.

It often struck me that what artesian wells have done for the Sahara they could equally accomplish for this region. The locality seems even more favourable, and there is every hope that, like the great African desert, the now desolate land of Samhar could be transformed into a rich date-bearing land.

Taken as they are; these wells could certainly be improved. On our arrival at Moncullou, we found the water of the well belonging to the consular residence scarcely used, on account of its very brackish taste; we had the well emptied, a large quantity of saltish sand removed, and we dug deeper until large rocks appeared. The result was that we had the best well in the place, and requests for our water were made by many, including the Pasha himself. Unfortunately, the forefathers of the present Moncullites never did such a thing to their wells, and as all innovations are distasteful to a semi-civilized race, the fact was admired, but not imitated.

Arkiko, at the extremity of the bay, is much nearer the mountains than the villages situated north of Massowah, but the village is built almost on the beach itself; the wells, not a hundred yards from the sea, are also much more superficial than those on the northern side, consequently the sea-water, having a much shorter distance to filter through, retains a greater proportion of saline particles, and I believe, were, it not for the presence of a small quantity of sweet water from the hills, it would be quite unpalatable.

In the neighbourhood of Maasowah there are several hot mineral springs. The most important are those of Adulis and Ailat. In the summer of 1865 we made a short trip to Annesley Bay, to inspect the locality. The ruins of Adulis are several miles from the shore, and, with the exception of a few fragments of broken columns, contain no traces of the former important colony. The place was even hotter than Massowah; there was no vegetation, no trace of habitations on that desolate shore. Fancy our surprise, on reaching the same spot in May, 1868, to find piers, railways, bazaars, &c.—a bustling city had sprung out of the wilderness.

The springs of Adulis [Footnote: A short time before our departure for the interior, some of the water of the hot springs of Adulis was collected and forwarded to Bombay for analysis.] are only a few hundred yards from the sea-shore, surrounded by a pleasing green patch covered with a vigorous vegetation, the rendezvous of myriads of birds and quadrupeds, who, morning and evening, swarm thither to quench their thirst.

At Ailat [Footnote: Water collected and sent to Bombay, November, 1864.] the hot spring issues from basaltic rocks on a small plateau between high and precipitous mountains. At the source itself the temperature is 141 Fahrenheit, but as the water flows down the different ravines, it gradually cools until it differs in no way from other mountain streams. It is palatable, and used by the inhabitants of Ailat for all purposes: it is also highly esteemed by the Bedouins. On account of its medicinal properties, numbers resort to the natural baths, formed of hollowed volcanic roots, for the relief of every variety of disease. From what I could gather, it appears to prove beneficial in chronic rheumatism and in diseases of the skin. Probably in these cases any warm water would act as well, considering the usual morbid condition of the integument in those dirty and unwashed races.

The population of Massowah, including the surrounding villages (as far, at least, as I could ascertain), amounts to 10,000 inhabitants. The Massowah race is far from pure; being a mixture of Turkish, Arab, and African blood. The features are generally good, the nose straight, the hair in many instances short and curly; the skin brown, the lips often large, the teeth even and white. The men are of the middle height; the women under it. So much for their physical appearance. Morally they are ignorant and superstitious, having apparently retained but few of their forefathers' virtues, but a great many of their vices. A very good distinction can be made, in the male portion of the community, between those who wear turbans and long white shirts, and those hard-working wretches who, girded with a single leather skin, roam about with their flocks in search of pasture and water. The first live I know not how. They call themselves brokers! It is true that three or four times a year caravans arrive from the interior, but as a rule, with the exception of a skin or two of honey, and a few bags of jowaree, nothing is imported. What possible business can about 500 brokers have? How ten dollars' worth of honey and fifty of grain can give a brokerage sufficient to clothe and feed, not only themselves but also their families, is a problem I have in vain endeavoured to solve!

In the East, children, instead of being a burden to poor people, are often a source of wealth: at Massowah they certainly are. The young girls of Moncullou, &c., bring in a pretty good income to their parents. I know big, strong, but lazy fellows who would squat down all day in the shade of their huts, living on the earnings of two or three little girls, who daily went once or twice to Massowah laden with a large skin full of water. The water-girls vary in age from eight to sixteen. The younger ones are rather pretty, small, but well made, the hair neatly braided and falling on the shoulders. A small piece of cotton reaching from the waist to the knee is generally the only garment of the poorest. Those better off wear also a piece of plaid thrown gracefully across the shoulders. The right nostril is ornamented with a small copper ring; as a substitute, a shirt-button is much esteemed, and during our stay our buttons were in constant demand.

If we take into consideration that Massowah is situated within the tropics, possessing no running stream, that it is surrounded by burning deserts, and that rain seldom falls, the conclusion we could beforehand have arrived at is, that the climate is essentially hot and dry.

From November to March the nights are cool, and during that period the day, in a good house or tent, is pleasant enough. From April to October the nights are close, and often very oppressive. During those hot months, both in the morning before the sea-breeze springs up and in the evening when it has died away, all animal creation falls into a torpid state. The perfect calm that then reigns is fearful in its stillness and painful in its effects.

From May to August sand-storms frequently occur. They begin usually at four P.M. (though occasionally they appear in the morning), and last from a few minutes only to a couple of hours. Long before the storm is felt, the horizon towards the N.N.W. is quite dark; a black cloud extends from the sea to the mountain range, and as it advances the sun itself is obscured. A few minutes of dead calm, and then suddenly the dark column approaches; all seems to disappear before it, and the roar of the terrible hurricane of wind and sand now coursing over the land is almost sublime in its horrors. Coming after the moist sea breeze, the hot and dry wind appears quite cool, though the thermometer rises to 110 or 115 degrees. After the storm a gentle land breeze follows, and often lasts all night. The amount of sand carried by the wind in these storms can be imagined by the mere mention of the fact that we could not discern, at a short distance from us, such a large object as a tent.

It seldom rains; occasionally there are a few showers in August and November.

As far as Europeans are concerned, climates like the one we have just described cannot be considered as unhealthy; they debilitate and weaken the system, and predispose to tropical diseases, but seldom engender them. I expected to find many cases of scurvy, due to the brackish condition of the water and to the absence of vegetables; but either scurvy did not exist to a great extent or did not come under my observation, as during my stay I did not meet with more than three or four cases. Fevers affect the natives after a fall of rain, but though some cases are of a very pernicious type, the majority belong to the simple intermittent or remittent, and yield rapidly to a proper treatment.

Small-pox now and then makes fearful ravages. When it breaks out, a mild case is chosen, and from it a great many are inoculated. The mortality is considerable amongst those who submit to the operation. On several occasions during the summer I received vaccine lymph, and inoculated with it. In no case did it take; owing, I suppose, to the extreme heat of the weather. During, the cold season I applied again, but could not obtain any. The greatest mortality is due to childbirth—a strange fact, as in the East confinements are generally easy. The practice in use here has probably much to do with this unfavourable result. After her confinement the woman is placed upon an alga or small native bed; underneath which, fire with aromatic herbs is so arranged as almost to suffocate the newly-delivered woman. Diarrhoea was frequent during the summer of 1865, and dysentery at the same period proved fatal to many. Diseases of the eyes are seldom met with, except simple inflammation caused by the heat and glare of the sun. I suffered from a severe attack of ophthalmia, and was obliged in consequence to proceed to Aden for a few weeks. I have met with no case of disease of the lungs, and bronchial affections seem almost unknown. I had occasion to attend upon cases of neuralgia, and one of gouty rheumatism.

For several years locusts have been committing great damage to the crops. In 1864 they occasioned a scarcity and dearness of the first necessaries of life, but in 1865 the whole of Tigré, Hamasein, Bogos, &c. had been laid waste by swarms of locusts, and at last no supplies whatever reached from the interior. The local Government sent to Hodeida and other ports for grain, and rice, and thus avoided the horrors of a complete famine. As it was, numbers died, and many half-starved wretches were ready victims for such a disease as cholera. This last-named scourge made its appearance in October, 1865, at the time we were making our preparations to proceed into the interior. The epidemic was severely felt. All those who had been suffering from the effects of insufficient or inferior food became an easy prey; few, indeed, of those who contracted the disease rallied; almost all died. During our residence at Massowah, out of the small community of Europeans five died, two from heat apoplexy, two from debility, and one from cholera. (None came under my care.) The Pasha himself was several times on the point of death, from debility and complete loss of tone of the digestive organs. He was at last prevailed upon to leave, and saved his life by a timely trip to sea.

The Bedouins of the Samhar, like all bigoted and ignorant savages, have great confidence in charms, amulets and exorcisms. The "medicine man" is generally an old, venerable-looking Sheik—a great rascal, for all his sanctified looks. His most usual prescription is to write a few lines of the Koran upon a piece of parchment, wash off the ink with water, and hand it over to the patient to drink; at other times the writing is enclosed in small squares of red leather, and applied to the seat of the disease. The Mullah is no contemptible rival of his, and though he also applies the all-efficacious words of the revealed "cow," he effects more rapid cures by spitting several times upon the sick person, muttering between each ejection appropriate prayers which no evil spirit could withstand, should his already sanctified spittle not have been sufficient to cast them off. Massowah boasts, moreover, of a regular medical practitioner, in the shape of an old Bashi-bazouk. Though superior in intelligence to the Sheik and the Mullah, his medical knowledge is on a par with theirs. He possesses a few drugs, given to him by travellers; but as he is not acquainted with their properties or doses, he wisely keeps them on a shelf for the admiration of the natives, and employs simples, with which, if he effects no wonderful cures, he still does no harm. Our *confrère* is not at all conceited, though he no doubt imposes upon the credulity of the aborigines; when we met in "consultation," he always, with becoming meekness, acknowledged his ignorance.

Massowah, as I have already stated, is built on a coral rock; the same formation exists on many parts of the coast, and forms cliffs, some of them thirty feet above the level of the sea. Further inland, towards Moncullou and Haitoomloo, volcanic rocks begin to appear, scattered here and there as if carelessly thrown on the sandy plain; at first isolated landmarts over the level space, they soon become more united, increasing in number, size, and importance, until the mountains themselves are reached, where almost every stone declares the predominance of the volcanic formation.

The flora is scanty, and belongs, with but few exceptions, to the *Leguminosae*. Several varieties of antelopes roam over the desert. Partridges, pigeons, and several species of the *Natatores* at certain seasons, arrive in great numbers. Apart from these, nothing useful to man is met with amongst the other members of the animal creation, consisting principally of hosts of hyenas, snakes, scorpions, and innumerable insects.

We remained at Massowah from the 23rd of July, 1864, to the 8th of August, 1865, the date of our departure for Egypt, where we went in order to receive instructions, when a letter at last reached us from the Emperor Theodore. Massowah offered no attractions: the heat was so intense at times that we could hardly breathe; and we ardently longed for our return to Aden or India, as we had given up all hopes regarding the acceptance of our mission by the Abyssinian Emperor. No pains were spared, no stone was left unturned, no possible chance left untried to obtain information as to the condition of the captives, to supply them with the necessaries of life, or induce the obstinate potentate to call for the letter it was said he was so anxious to receive. The very day of our arrival at Massowah, efforts were made to engage messengers to proceed to the Abyssinian court and inform his Ethiopian Majesty that officers had arrived at the coast with the answer to his letter to the Queen of England. But such was the dread of his name, that it was with great difficulty, and only on the promise of a large reward, that any could be obtained. On the evening of the 24th, the day after our arrival, the messengers were despatched with the letters to the Abouna and the Emperor from the Patriarch, one from Mr. Rassam to the Abouna, and one to the Emperor, the messengers promising to be back in the course of a month or so.

Mr. Rassam, in his letter to the Emperor Theodoros, informed him, in courteous language, that he had arrived at Massowah the day before, bearing a letter from H.M. the Queen of England to his address, and that he was desirous of delivering it into his Majesty's hands. He also informed him that he would await the answer at Massowah, and requested, should his Majesty send for him, kindly to provide him with an escort. He, however, left to Theodore the option of sending the prisoners down with a trustworthy person to whom he could deliver the letter from the Queen of England. He concluded by advising his Majesty that his embassy to the Queen had been accepted, and should it reach the coast before his (Mr. Rassam's) departure for Aden, he would take the necessary steps to see that it reached England in safety.

A month—six weeks—two months, passed in hourly expectation of the return of the messengers. All suppositions were exhausted: perhaps the messengers had not reached; possibly the King had detained them; or they might have lost the packet whilst crossing some river, etc.; but as no reliable information could moreover be obtained, as to the exact condition of the captives, it was impossible to remain any longer in such a state of uncertainty. Mr. Rassam, therefore, despatched with considerable difficulty two more messengers, with a copy of his letter of July 24, accompanied by an explanatory note. Private messengers were, at the same time, sent to the Emperor's camp to report on his treatment of the captives, and to different parts of the country, from whence we supposed information might possibly be obtained. A short time afterwards, having succeeded in securing the names of some of the Gaffat people who had formerly been in communication with Consul Cameron, we wrote to them in English, French, and German, not knowing what language they understood, earnestly requesting that they would inform us as to what steps they considered most advisable in order to obtain the release of the captives.

Again we waited on the desert shore of Massowah for that answer so long expected; none came, but on Christmas-day we received a few lines from Messrs. Flad and Schimper, the two Europeans with whom we had communicated. All they had to say was, that the misfortunes which had befallen the Europeans were due to the Emperor's letter not having been answered, and they advised Mr. Rassam to send the letter he had brought with him to his Majesty. However, Mr. Rassam thought it unbecoming the British Government to force upon the Emperor a letter signed by the Queen of England, when, by his refusing even to acknowledge its presence at Massowah, he clearly showed that he had changed his mind and did not care any more about it.

In the meanwhile some of the prisoners' servants had arrived with letters from their masters; other messengers despatched from Massowah were also equally successful; stores, money, letters were now regularly forwarded to the captives, who, in return, kept us informed as to their condition and the movements of the King. So far our presence at Massowah was of the utmost importance, since without the supplies and money we were able to provide them with, their misery would have been increased tenfold, if even they had not at last succumbed to privation and want.

The friends of the captives and, to a great extent, the public, unaware of the efforts made by Mr. Rassam to accomplish the object of his mission, and of the great difficulties that were to be contended with, attributed the apparent failure to causes far removed; many suggestions were advanced, a few even tried, but no result followed. It was said that one of the reasons his Majesty did not vouch us an answer was, that the mission was not of sufficient importance; that his Majesty considered himself slighted, and therefore would not condescend to acknowledge us. To remedy this, in February, 1865, Government decided on adding another military officer to our party, and, as the press reported at the time, it was confidently expressed that great results would follow this step. Hence, Lieut. Prideaux, of her Majesty's Bombay Staff Corps, arrived in Massowah in May. As might reasonably be expected, his presence at the coast did not in the least influence Theodore's mind. The only advantage gained by the addition of this officer to the mission was a charming companion, who was doomed to spend with me in a tent on the sea-beach the hot months of hot Massowah. More months elapsed: still no answer! the condition of the prisoners was very precarious; they saw with great apprehension another rainy season about to set in; their letters were written in a most desponding tone; and though we had done our utmost to supply them with money and a few comforts, the distance and the rebellious state of the country made it difficult to provide more abundantly for their wants.

At last, in March, we determined on a last effort; should it fail we would request our recall. We had heard of Samuel, how he had been in many respects mixed up in the affair, and we knew that he enjoyed in some degree the confidence of his master; so when we were informed that one of his relations was willing to convey a letter and he assured us of an answer before forty days, once more our hopes were excited and we trusted in the possibility of success. The forty days expired, then two, then three months; but we heard nothing!! It seemed as if a kind of fatality attended our messengers: from whatever class they were taken—simple peasants, followers of the Nab, or relatives of one of the Emperor's courtiers—the result was invariably the same; not only they did not bring back any answer from the Emperor, but not even one returned to us.

The prolonged delay of Mr. Rassam's mission at Massowah without any apparent good results having been achieved, was so contrary to all expectations, that it was at last decided to resort to other means.

In February, 1865, a Copt, Abdul Melak, presented himself at the consulate of Jeddah, pretending to have just arrived from Abyssinia with a message from the Abouna to the Consul-General, purporting that if he could bring from H.M.'s Consul-General in Egypt a written declaration to the effect that, should the Emperor allow the Europeans in chains to depart, no steps would be taken to punish the offence, he, the Abouna, would engage himself to obtain their liberation, and become their security. That impostor, who had never been in Abyssinia at all, gave such wonderful details that he completely imposed upon the Consul of Jeddah and the Consul-General. The fact that he pretended to have passed through Massowah without entering into communication with Mr. Rassam was by itself suspicious; but had these gentlemen possessed the slightest knowledge of Abyssinia, they would at once have discovered the deception when he purchased some "suitable" presents for the Abouna, before proceeding on the mission that had been intrusted to him. In Abyssinia tobacco is considered "unclean" by the priests; none ever smoke; and even admitting that in his privacy the Abouna might have now and then indulged in a weed, he would have taken great care to keep the matter as quiet as possible. Therefore to present him with an *amber mouthpiece* would have been a gratuitous insult to a man who was supposed to have rendered an important favour. It was, indeed, the very last testimonial any one in the slightest degree conversant with Abyssinian priesthood would ever have selected. As it is, the man started, and lived for months amongst the Arab tribes between Kassala and Metemma, on the strength of a certificate that described him as an ambassador and recommended him to the protection of the tribes that lay on his road. We met him not for from Kassala; he acknowledged the deceit he had practised, and was delighted when he heard that we had no intention of requesting the Turkish authorities to make him a prisoner.

Government at last decided on recalling us, and appointed Mr. Palgrave, the distinguished Arabian traveller, in our stead.

In the beginning of July we went for a short trip to the Habab country, situate north of Massowah; on our return, we were met in the desert of Chab by some of the Naib's relations, who informed us that Ibrahim (the relative of Samuel) had returned with an answer from his Majesty, and was expected daily; that all our former messengers had obtained leave to depart; but what was still more gratifying was the intelligence, brought down by them, that Theodore, to show his regard for us, had liberated Consul Cameron and his fellow-captives. On July 12, Ibrahim arrived. He gave full details about the release of the Consul; a story which was corroborated a few days afterwards by another relative of his, also one of our former messengers. I believe, from what I afterwards learnt, that Theodore himself was party to the lie, as he publicly, in presence of the messengers, gave orders to some of his officers to go and remove the Consul's fetters; only the messengers improved on it by stating that they had seen the Consul after the chains had been removed.

The reply Theodore had at last granted to our repeated demands was not courteous, nor even civil—it was neither signed nor sealed; he ordered us to proceed through the distant and unhealthy route of the Soudan, and, once arrived at Metemma, to inform him of our arrival there, and that he would then provide us with an escort. We did not like the letter; it seemed more the production of a madman than of a reasonable being. I select a few extracts from this letter, as they are really curiosities in their way. He said:—

"The reason I do not write to you in my name, because of Abouna Salama, the so-called Kokab (Stern) the Jew, and the one you called Consul, named Cameron (who was sent by you). I treated them with honour and friendship in my city. When I thus befriended them, on account of my anxiety to cultivate the friendship of the English Queen, they reviled me.

"Plowden and Johannes (John Bell), who were called Englishmen, were killed in my country, whose death, by the power of God, I avenged on those who killed them; on account these (the three above mentioned) abused me, and denounced me as a murderer.

"Cameron, who is called Consul, represented to me that he was a servant of the Queen. I invested him with a robe of honour of my country, and supplied him with provisions for the journey. I asked him to make me a friend of the Queen.

"When he was sent on his mission, he went and stayed some time with the Turks, and returned to me.

"I spoke to him about the letter I sent through him to the Queen. He said, that up to that time he had not received any intelligence concerning it. What have I done, said I, that they should hate me, and treat me with animosity? By the power of the Lord my creator, I kept silent."

Although the steamer *Victoria* only arrived in Massowah on the 23rd of July, we had as yet received no letters from Consul Cameron, nor from any of the captives. By the *Victoria* we were informed that Mr. Rassam was recalled and Mr. Palgrave appointed. Under the new aspect matters had suddenly taken, Mr. Rassam could but refer to Government for instructions. We therefore at once started for Egypt, where we arrived on the 5th of September.

Through her Majesty's Agent and Consul-General, Government was apprised of the receipt of a letter from Theodore, granting us permission to enter Abyssinia; that the letter was uncourteous, and not signed; that Cameron was released, and though Cameron had always insisted on our not proceeding into the interior with or without safe-conduct, we were ready to go at once, should Government consider it advisable. Mr. Palgrave was told to remain, Mr. Rassam and his companions to go; a certain sum of money was allowed for presents; letters for the governors of the Soudan were obtained; and, our necessary stores and outfit being purchased; we returned to Massowah, where we arrived on the 25th of September.

There we heard that messengers had arrived from the prisoners; that they had been taken to Aden by a man-of-war; and that they had verbally reported, that far from having been released, hand-chains had been added to the captives' previous fetters. As we could not find anybody to accompany us through the Soudan (on account of its unhealthiness at that time of the year) before the middle of October, we thought it advisable to proceed at once to Aden, in order to gain correct information from the captives' letters, as to their actual condition, and to confer with the Political Resident of that station, as to the expediency of complying with the Emperor's requests, under the totally different aspect matters now presented.

Although Captain Cameron, in several of his former communications, had repeatedly insisted that on no account we should enter Abyssinia, in the note just received he implored us to come up at once, as our declining to do so would prove of the utmost danger to the prisoners. The Political Resident, therefore, taking into consideration Captain Cameron's earnest appeal for Mr. Rassam to acquiesce with Theodore's request, advised us to proceed and hope for the best.

After a short stay at Aden we again returned to Massowah, and, with the utmost diligence, made all our arrangements for the long journey that lay before us. Unfortunately cholera had broken out, the natives were unwilling to cross the plains of Braka and Taka, on account of the malarious fever, so deadly at that time of the year, and it required all the influence of the local authorities to insure our speedy departure.

CHAPTER V

On the afternoon of the 15th October, all our preparations being apparently complete, the mission, composed of Mr. H. Rassam, Lieut. W.F. Prideaux, of her Majesty's Bombay Staff Corps, and myself, started on its dangerous enterprise. We were accompanied by a nephew of the Naib of Arkiko; and an escort of Turkish Irregulars had been graciously sent by the Pasha to protect our sixty camels, laden with our personal luggage, stores, and presents for the Ethiopian monarch. We also took with us several Portuguese and other Indian servants, and a few natives of Massowah as muleteers.

On a first march something is always found wanting. On this occasion many of the cameleers were unprovided with ropes: boxes, portmanteau-bags, were strewed all over the road, and night was far advanced before the last camel reached Moncullou. A halt was in consequence absolutely necessary, so that the actual start was only made on the afternoon of the 16th.

From Moncullou our route lay N.W. across the desert of Chab, a dreary wilderness of sand, intersected by two winter torrents, generally dry: but by digging in their sandy beds it is possible at all seasons to obtain some muddy water. The rapidity with which these torrents fill up is most astonishing.

During the summer of 1865, we had made a trip to Af-Abed, in the Hababs' country. On our return, whilst crossing the desert, we experienced a very severe storm. We had just reached our encamping-ground on the Southern bank of one of these water-courses, and half the camels had already crossed the dry bed of the river, when, on a sudden, a tremendous roar was heard, shortly afterwards followed by a fearful rush of water. In the former empty bed of the torrent now dashed a mighty stream, tearing down trees and rocks, so that no human being could possibly cross. Our luggage and servants were still on the opposite bank, and although we were only a stone's throw from the party so suddenly cut off from us, we had to spend the night on the bare ground, with no other covering than our clothing.

In the very centre of the desert of Chab, arises, Amba Goneb, a conical basaltic rock several hundred feet high, an advanced sentry detached from the now approaching mountains. On the evening of the 18th, we reached

Ain, and from the glaring and dreary desert passed into a lovely valley, watered by a small winding stream, cool and limpid, shaded by mimosas and tamarinds, and glowing with the freshness and luxuriance of topical vegetation. [Footnote: The distance from Massowah to Ain is about forty-five miles.]

We were fortunate enough to leave the cholera behind us. Apart from a few cases of diarrhoea, easily checked, the whole party was in excellent health; every one in high spirits at the prospect of visiting almost unknown regions, and above all at having at last bid adieu to Massowah, where we had spent in anxious expectation long and dreary months.

From Ain to Mahaber [Footnote: From Ain to Mahaber (direction E. by N.) about twenty miles.] the road is most picturesque; always following the winding of the small river Ain, here and there compressed to only a few yards by perpendicular walls of trachyte, or basalt; further on expanding into miniature green plateaus, bordered by conical hills, covered to the very summit by mimosas and huge cactuses, alive with large hordes of antelopes (the agazin), which, bounding from rock to rock, scared by their frolics the countless host of huge baboons. The valley itself, graced by the presence of gaudy-feathered and sweet-singing birds, echoed to the shrill cry of the numerous guinea-fowls, so tame, that the repeated reports of our fire-arms did not disturb them in the least.

At Mahaber we were obliged to remain several days awaiting fresh camels. The Hababs, who had now to supply us, frightened by the presence of the hairy nephew of the Nab and the Bashi-hazouks, made themselves scarce, and it was only after much parley and the repeated assurance that every one would be paid, that the camels at last made their appearance. The Hababs are a large pastoral tribe, inhabiting the Ad Temariam, a hilly and well-watered district, about fifty miles north-west of Massowah, included between longitude 38.39 and latitude 16 to 16.30. They represent the finest type of the roving Bedouins; of middle height, muscular, well made, they claim an Abyssinian origin. With the exception of a darker hue of the skin, certainly in other respects they do not differ from the inhabitants of the table-land, and have but few characteristics of the aboriginal African races. Some fifty years ago they were a Christian tribe—nominally, at least—but were converted to Mohammedanism by an old Sheik, still alive, who resides near Moncullou, and is an object of great veneration all over the Samhar. Once their doubts removed, their suspicions lulled, the Hababs proved themselves friendly, willing, and obliging.

Gratitude is no common virtue in Africa, at least as far as my own experience goes. Its rarity brings back to my memory a fact that I will here record. On our previous trip to the Ad Temariam, I had seen several patients, amongst them a young man, suffering from remittent fever, and I gave him some medicine. Hearing of our arrival at Mahaber, he came to thank me, bringing as an offering a small skin of milk. He apologized for the absence of his aged father, who also, he said, wished to kiss my feet, but the distance (about eight miles) was too much for the old man's strength.

I may as well mention here that a young commercial traveller, Mr. Marcopoli, had accompanied us from Massowah. He was going to Metemma, *viâ* Kassala, to be present at the annual fairs held at that place in winter. He took advantage of our short stay at Mahaber, to proceed to Keren, in the Bogos, where he was called by business, intending to join again our party a few stages ahead. We looked at our map, and estimated the distance from our halting-place to the Bogos at the utmost eighteen miles. As he was provided with excellent mules, in four or five hours he naturally expected to reach his destination. He accordingly started at daybreak, and never halted once; but night was far advanced before he perceived the lights of the first village on the Bogos plateau: so much for travellers' maps. The poor man's anxiety had been great. Soon after dark he perceived—or, as I suspect, imagination worked to a high pitch of excitement through fear, conjured to his fancy the phantom of some huge animal—a lion, a tiger, he did not know very exactly; but, at all events, he saw some horrid beast of prey, glaring at him through the brushwood, with fiery and bloodshot eyes, watching all his movements for a suitable opportunity to fall upon his helpless prey. However, he reached Keren in safety.

He found that we were expected by the Bogos people, who believed that we were proceeding by the upper route. Flowers were to be strewed in our path, and our entrance was to be welcomed by dances and songs in our praise; the officer in command of the troops was to receive us with military honours, the civil governor intended to entertain us on a large scale: in a word, a grand reception was to be offered to the English friends of the mighty Theodore. The disappointment was no doubt great when Mr. Marcopoli informed the Bogosites that our route lay in an opposite direction to their fair province. On that the military commander decided on accompanying Mr. Marcopoli back, and paying us his respects at our halting-place. Marcopoli was delighted; he had a too vivid recollection of *his lion* not to be overjoyed at the idea of having companions with him.

Late in the evening they started, the Abyssinian officer and his men having before marching indulged in deep draughts of tej to keep out the cold. On their way down, the "warriors" cantered about in the most frantic manner; now riding at a full gallop up to poor Marcopoli, the lance in rest, and dexterously wheeling round when the weapon almost touched his breast; then charging upon him at full speed and firing off their loaded pistols quite close, and only a few feet above his head. Marcopoli felt very uncomfortable in the society of his bellicose and drunken escort, but not knowing their language, he had nothing to do but to appear pleased.

Early in the morning, at our second stage from Mahaber, these specimens of Abyssinian soldiers made their appearance, and a batch of more villanous-looking scoundrels I have never seen during my stay in Abyssinia: evidently Theodore was not very particular as to whom he selected for such distant outposts, unless he considered the roughest and most disorderly the fittest for such duties. They presented us with a cow they had stolen on the road, and begged us not to forget to mention to their master that they had come all the distance from Bogos to pay their respects to his guests. After having refreshed themselves with a few glasses of brandy and partaken of a slight collation, they kissed the ground in acknowledgment of the pleasant things they had received in return for their gift, and departed—to our great satisfaction.

On that 23rd we started from Mahaber, going due west, and following for eight miles longer the charming valley of Ain. Afterwards, we diverged to the left, going in a south-west direction, until we reached the province of Barka; when again our route lay west by north, until we came to Zaga. From this point to Kassala the general direction is west by south. [Footnote: The distance from Mahaber to Adart on the frontier of Barka is about fifty miles; from Adart to Kassala about 130 miles.] From Mahaber to Adart the road is very pleasant; for several days we continually ascended, and the more we advanced into the mountainous region the more agreeable and pleasant did we feel it, and we enjoyed the sight of splendid and luxuriant vegetation.

On the 25th we crossed the Anseba, a large river flowing from the high lands of Bogos, Hamasien, and Mensa, and joining the river Barka at Tjab. [Footnote: Tjab, lat. 17 10', long. 37 15'.]

We spent a pleasant day in the beautiful Anseba valley, but aware of the danger of remaining after sunset near its flowery but malarious banks, we pitched our tent on a rising ground at some distance, and the next morning proceeded to Haboob, the highest point we had to gain before descending into the Barka through the difficult pass of Lookum. After this abrupt descent of more than 2,000 feet, the roads generally slope towards the low land of Barka.

From Ain to Haboob [Footnote: The Anseba, at the point we crossed, is about 4,000 feet above the level of the sea; Haboob about 4,500.] the country is well wooded, and watered by innumerable small streams. The soil is formed of the detritus of the volcanic rocks, specially of feldspar; pumice abounds in the ravines. The channels of the rivulets are the only roads for the traveller. This mountain chain is, on the whole, a pleasant spot, more delightful for the reason that it rises between the arid shores of the Red Sea and the flat, hot, and level plains of the Soudan. The province of Barka is a boundless prairie, about 2,500 feet above the level of the sea, covered at the time of our journey with half-dried grass some five or six feet high, and dotted here and there with small woods of stunted mimosas.

From Barka to Metemma we find alluvium as the general formation.

Water is scarce; even a month after the rainy season all the rivers are dried up, and water is only obtained by digging in the sand of the dry beds of the river Barka and its tributaries. When we passed through these plains many spots were still green; but a few months later we should have crossed a parched-up prairie little better than the desert itself.

Our pretty songsters of Ain were no more to be seen. The guinea-fowl was seldom met with, and only a few tiny antelopes wandered over the solitary expanse. Instead, we were aroused by the roar of the lion, the laugh of the hyena, and we had to protect our sheep and goats, as the spotted leopard was lurking around our tents.

On the 31st of October we reached Zaga, a large sloping plain situated at the junction of the Barka and the Mogareib. Water can be obtained at that spot by digging wells in the dried-up beds of the rivers, in sufficient quantity to have induced the Beni Amer to make it their winter encamping-ground.

We had that day made a very long march, on account of the absence of water on the road. Starting at two P.M., we only reached our halting ground (the bed of a dried-up winter torrent, a few hundred yards below the Beni Amer's camp), a couple of hours before daybreak. We were so sleepy and tired that during the latter part of the stage it had been with great difficulty that we managed to keep in the saddle; and no sooner did our guide give us the grateful intelligence that we had arrived, than we stretched on the ground the piece of tanned cowhide we carried with us, and covering ourselves with our cloaks, lay down to rest until daybreak. I offered to Mr. Marcopoli to share my "bedding," as his own had not arrived, and in a few minutes we both fell into that deep slumber that follows the exhaustion of a long weary march. I remember my disgust at being violently shaken by my bed companion; who, in a faint and trembling voice, whispered into my ear: "Look there!" I understood at once his look of anguish and terror, for two splendid lions, not more than twenty paces from us, were drinking near the wells that had been sank by the Arabs. I thought, and told my companion, that as we had no fire-arms with us; the wisest plan was to go to sleep and remain as quiet as possible. I set him the example, and only woke up late in the morning, when the sun was already high up and pouring its burning rays over my uncovered head. Marcopoli, with an absent terrified look impressed on his countenance, was still sitting near me. He told me that he had not slept, but kept watching the lions: they had remained for a long time, drinking, roaring and beating their sides with their tails; and even when they departed he kept listening to their dreadful roar, sounding more distant as the first rays of day appeared.

We had, no doubt, had a narrow escape, as that night a lion had carried away a man and a child who had strayed from the Arab encampment. The Sheik of the Beni Amer, during the few days we remained at Zaga, with true Arab hospitality, always placed at night a strong guard around our tent, to watch the large fires that they kindle in order to keep at a respectful distance these unwelcome night rovers.

We had agreed with the Hababs that we would exchange camels at this spot, but none could be obtained for love or money. It was lucky for us that the Bedouins had by this time found out that all white men are not Turks, otherwise we should have been cast helpless in the very centre of Barka. The Beni Amers could never be induced even to acknowledge that they had camels, though more than 10,000 were grazing under our very eyes.

The Beni Amers are Arabs, speak the Arab language, and have preserved up to the present day all the characteristics of their race. A roving Bedouin of the Yemen and a Beni Amer are so much alike that it seems hardly credible that the Beni Amers possess no record of their advent on the African coast, or of the causes that induced them to leave the land of their ancestors. Their long, black, silky hair has not acquired the woolly texture of that of the sons of Ham, and the small extremities, the well-knit limbs, the straight nose and small lips, the dark bronzed complexion, distinguish them alike from the Shankallas and the Barias, and from the mixed races of the plateaus. They wear a piece of cloth a few yards in length, folded round the body, with an elegance peculiar to the savage. Even with this dirty rag, they must be admired, like the Italian beggar, not only for their beautiful forms, but also for the look of impudence and roguery displayed in the bright glare of their dark eyes. The Beni Amers retain to a high degree that nuisance so well described by a distinguished traveller in the East, and, like their brethren of the Arabian shore, they are *une race bavarde et criarde*. They pay a nominal tribute to the Egyptian Government, and the reason we could not obtain camels was that, troops being moved about, they feared that on their arrival at Kassala they would be pressed into the Government service, and not only receive no pay, but most likely in the end lose the greater number of their camels. This tribe roams along the banks of the Barka and its many tributaries. Zaga is only their winter station; at other times they wander over the immense plains north of Barka in search of pasture and water for their innumerable flocks. All over the district of Zaga camps appeared in every direction; the herds of cattle, especially camels, seemed without number: this all indicates that they form a wealthy, powerful tribe.

We encamped near their head-quarters, where resides the Sheik of all the Beni Amers, Ahmed, surrounded by his wives, children, and people. He is a man of middle age, conspicuous among his cunning followers by a shrewd and crafty look. He was friendly to us, and presented us with a few sheep and cows. His camp covered several acres of ground, the whole enclosed by a strong fence; the wigwams are built in a circle a few feet from the hedge; the open space in the centre being reserved for the cattle, always driven in at night. The chief's small circular wood and grass huts contrasted favourably with the dwellings of his followers. The latter, constructed in a circle, are formed by thrusting into the ground the extremities of small branches; a few pieces of coarse matting thrown over them complete the structure. They cannot be more than four feet high, and their average circumference is twelve feet; nevertheless, some eight or ten unwashed faces were seen peeping through the small door, staring with their black, frightened eyes at the strange white men. Small-pox was raging at the time with great virulence; fever also was daily claiming many victims. I gave medicine to several of the sufferers, and good hygienic advice to Sheik Ahmed. He listened with all becoming respect to the good things that fell from the Hakeem's lips: he would see; but they had never done so before, and with Mussulman bigotry and superstition he put an end to the conversation by an "Allah Kareem." [Footnote: "God is merciful"]

On the 3rd of November we were again on the march. On the 5th we arrived al Sabderat, the first permanent village we had met with since leaving Moncullou. This village—in appearance similar to those of the Samhar—is built on the side of a large granitic mountain, cleft in two from the summit to the base. Numerous wells are dug in the dried-up bed of the water-course that separates the village. The inhabitants of this divided village often contend between themselves for the possession of the precious fluid; and when the rushing waters have disappeared, human passions too often fill with strife and warfare the otherwise quiet bed of the stream.

On the morning of November 6 we entered Kassala. The Nab's nephew had preceded us, to inform the governor of our arrival, and present him with a letter recommending us to the care of the authorities, written by the Pasha of Egypt. To honour us according to his masters firman, the governor sent all the garrison to meet us a few miles from the town, with a polite apology for his absence, due to sickness. The senior partner of the Greek firm of Paniotti also came to welcome us, and afforded us the hospitality of his house and board.

Kassala, the capital of Takka, a walled town near the River Gash, containing about 10,000 inhabitants, is on the model of most modern Egyptian towns, public as well as private buildings being alike of mud. The arsenal, barracks, &c. are the only structures of any importance. Beautiful gardens have been made at a short distance from the town, near the Biver Gash, by the European portion of the community. Just before, and immediately after the rains, the place is very unhealthy. During those months malarious fever and dysentery prevail to a great extent.

Kassala, formerly a prosperous city, the centre of all the trade of the immense tract of country included from Massowah and Suakin to the Nile, and from Nubia to Abyssinia, was, at the date of our arrival, almost deserted, covered with ruins and rank vegetation, destitute of the most common necessaries of life, the spectre of its former self, haunted by its few remaining ghost-like and plague-stricken citizens. Kassala had just gone through the ordeal of a mutiny of Nubian troops. Pernicious fevers, malignant dysenteries and cholera had decimated both rebels and loyalists; war and sickness had marched hand in hand to make of this fair oasis of the Soudan a wilderness painful to contemplate. The mutiny broke out in July. The Nubian troops had not been paid for two years, and when they claimed a portion of their arrears, they only met with a stern refusal. Under these circumstances, it is not astonishing that they became ready listeners to the treasonable words and extravagant promises made to them by one of their petty chiefs, named Denda, a descendant of the former Nubian kings. They matured their plot in great secresy, and every one was horrified one morning to learn that the black troops had broken out in open mutiny and murdered their officers, and, no longer restrained, had followed their natural inclinations to revel in carnage and plunder. A few Egyptian regulars had, luckily, possession of the arsenal, and held it against these infuriated savages until troops could arrive from Kedaref and Khartoum. The Europeans and Egyptians gallantly defended their part of the town. They erected walls and small earthworks between themselves and the mutineers, and continually on the alert, though few in number, they repulsed with great gallantry the assault of the fiends thirsting for their lives and property. Egyptian troops poured in from all directions and relieved the besieged city. More than a thousand of the mutineers were killed near the gates of the town; nearly a thousand more were tried and executed; and those who attempted to escape the vengeance of the merciless pasha and fled for safety to the wilderness, were hunted down like beasts by the roving Bedouins. Though order was now restored, it was no easy matter to obtain camels. It required all the power and persuasion of the authorities to induce the Shukrie-Arabs to enter the town and convey us to Kedaref.

We heard at Kassala the miserable end of Le Comte de Bisson's mad enterprise. It appears that the Comte, formerly an officer in the Neapolitan army, had married at an advanced age a beautiful, accomplished and rich heiress, the daughter of some contractor; it was "a mariage de convenance," a title bought by wealth and beauty. In the autumn of 1864, De Bisson reached Kassala accompanied by some fifty adventurers, the scum of the outcasts of all nations, who had enrolled themselves under the standard of the ambitions Comte, "on the promised assurance that power and wealth would be, before long, their envied portion." De Bisson's idea seems to have been to personify a second Moses: he came not only to colonize, but also to convert. The wild roving Bedouin of the Barka plains would, he believed, not only at once and with gratitude acknowledge his rule, but would soon, abandoning his false creed, fall prostrate before the altar he intended to erect in the wilderness. About a hundred town Arabs were induced to join the European party,—a useless set of vagabonds, who adorned themselves with the regimental uniform, accepted the rifle, pistol, and sword, drew their rations, were punctual in their attendance and always ready to salaam, but showed much dislike to the drill and other civilized notions the Comte and his officers endeavoured to impress upon them.

Their departure from Kassala for the land of milk and honey was quite theatrical; in front rode on a camel, a gallant captain (who had taken his discharge from the Austrian service,) playing on the bugle a parting "fanfare;" behind him, the second in command, mounted on a prancing charger, and followed by the European part of the force, who with military step, and shoulder to shoulder, marched as men for whom victory is their slave. Behind came Le Comte himself, clad in a general's uniform, his breast covered with the many decorations which sovereigns had only been too proud to confer on such a noble spirit; next to him rode gracefully his beautiful wife, looking handsomer still in the picturesque kepi and red uniform of a French zouave; behind, closing the march, the well-knit Arabs, with plunder written in their dark bright eyes, marched with a quick elastic step and as much regularity as could be expected from men who abhorred order and had been drilled for so short a time. Need I say that the expedition failed utterly? The Arabs of the plains declined to accept another pontiff and king in the person of the gallant and noble Comte. They were even vicious enough to induce those of their brethren who had accepted service, to return to their former occupations, and *forget to leave* behind them on their departure the arms, clothes, etc., which had been dealt out to them on their entering the Comte's service.

The return to Kassala was humble: there was no trumpet this time; the brilliant uniforms had given way to soiled and patched raiments: even the general adopted a civilian's dress; the lady alone was still smiling, laughing, beautiful as ever; but no Arab in gaudy attire closed the hungry-looking and worn out cortege. De Bisson had failed: but why?—Because the Egyptian Government had not only afforded none of the assistance that had been promised to him, but all at once stopped the supplies he considered himself entitled to expect. A claim of I do not know how many millions was at once made on the Egyptian Government. A commissioner was sent out, who it appears took a very different view of the question, as he declared the "Comte's" pretensions absurd and unreasonable. The Comte soon afterwards, with his wife, returned to Nice, leaving at Kassala the remnant of his European army; the few who had not succumbed to fever or other malarious diseases.

At the time of the mutiny of the Nubian troops, a few not in hospital or on their way to Khartoum or Massowah, fought well; two even paid with their lives their gallant attempt at a sortie, and they had gained for themselves, by their bravery in those difficult times, the respect they had lost during the long days of inaction.

De Bisson was instrumental in spreading the most fallacious reports as to the condition of the captives held by Theodore, and even when an army was already marching to their rescue, "correct" accounts appeared of the repulse of the British by Theodore; at another time a mendacious report was spread that a great battle had been fought in Tigré between Theodore and a powerful rebel—a battle which was said to have lasted three days without any marked success having been gained by either side; and that Theodore, having perceived in the enemy's camp some Europeans, had sent orders for our immediate execution; the fulfilment of the sentence resting with the Empress, who was residing at Gondar, and that his (De Bisson's) agent was using his influence to stay the execution. Absurd and ridiculous as were these reports, they were not the less productive of great distress to the families and friends of the captives.

During the five days we spent at Kassala, I am happy to say that I was able to relieve many sufferers; amongst them our host himself, and one of his guests, a young, well-educated Egyptian officer, laid at death's door by a severe attack of dysentery.

A Nubian colonel called on us one morning; he strongly advised us to stop before it was too late. He had heard much about Theodore's doings, and assured us that we would meet but with deceit and treachery at his hands. On our telling him that we were officers and bound to obey, he said, nothing more, but bid us good-by in a sorrowful voice.

CHAPTER VI

On the afternoon of the 10th November we started for Kedaref. Our route now lay in a more southerly direction. On the 13th we crossed the Atbara, a tributary of the Nile, bringing to the father of rivers the waters of Northern Abyssinia. On the 17th we entered Sheik Abu Sin, the capital of the province of Kedaref. [Footnote: From Kassala to Kedaref is about 120 miles.] Our cameleers belonged to the Shukrie-Arabs. They are a semi-pastoral, semi-agricultural tribe, and reside principally in the neighbourhood of and along the course of the Atbara, or wander over the immense plains that extend almost without limit from this river to the Nile. They are more degenerated than the Beni-Amers, having mixed more with the Nubian and other tribes that dwell around them. They speak an impure Arabic. Many have retained the features and general appearance of the original race, whilst others might be looked upon as half-castes, and some can with difficulty be distinguished from the Nubians or Takruries.

From Kassala to Kedaref we crossed interminable plains, covered with high grass, speckled here and there with woods of mimosas, too scanty to afford the slightest shade or protection during the fearful heat of the mid-day sun. Here and there on the horizon appeared a few isolated peaks; the Djbel Kassala, a few miles south of the capital of Takka. Eastward, the Ela Hugel and the Abo-Gamel were in sight for many days, whilst towards the west, lost almost in the misty horizon, appeared in succession the outlines of Derkeda and Kassamot.

The valley of the Atbara, luxuriant in vegetation, inhabited by all varieties of the feathered tribe, visited by the huge thirsty quadruped of the savannah, presented a spectacle so grand in its savage beauty that we could with difficulty tear ourselves from its shady groves; had it not been that "Forward" was our watchword, we would, braving malaria, have spent a few days near its green and fragrant banks.

Sheik Abu Sin is a large village; the houses are circular and built of wood and covered with straw; A small hut belonging to the firm of Paniotti, our host of Kassala, was placed at our disposal. We shortly afterwards received the visit of a Greek merchant, who came to consult me for a stiff joint brought on by a gun-shot wound. It appears, that some years before, whilst riding a camel on an elephant-hunting expedition, the gun, a large half-ounce bore, went off by itself, he never knew how. All the bones of the fore-arm had been smashed, the cicatrice of a dreadful flesh-wound showed what sufferings he had undergone, and it was indeed a wonder for me that, residing as he did in such a hot unhealthy climate, deprived of all medical advice, he had not succumbed to the effects of the wound, still more that he had been able to save the limb. I considered the cure so extraordinary, that, as there was nothing to be done, I advised him to leave well alone.

The governor also called upon us, and we returned his civility. Whilst sipping our coffee with him and other grandees of the place, we were told that Tisso Gobazé, one of the rebels, had beaten Theodore and made him a prisoner. He said he believed the news to be correct, but advised us to inquire into it on our arrival at Metemma, and should we find it untrue, to return on our steps and on no account to enter Abyssinia if Theodore was still the ruler. He then gave us some examples of the Emperor's cruelty and treachery; but we did not put much credence in his word, as we knew that of old a bad feeling existed between the Abyssinian Christians and their Mussulman neighbours of the plain. At Metemma that rumour was not even known; however, we had no choice, and never thought one instant of anything else but of accomplishing the mission intrusted to us, in face of all perils and dangers.

At Kedaref we were lucky enough to arrive on a market-day, consequently had no difficulty in exchanging camels. That very evening we were *en route* again, still towards the south, but this time making almost an angle with our former route, marching towards the rising sun.

Between Sabderat and Kassala, between that town and the Gash, we had for the first time seen some cultivation; but it was nothing compared to the immense vista of cultivated fields, beginning a day's journey from Sheik Abu Sin, and extending, almost without interruption, throughout the provinces of Kedaref and Galabat. Villages appeared in all directions, crowning every rounded hillock. As we advanced, these eminences increased in size until they gave place to hills and mountains, which ultimately blend with the uninterrupted chain of high peaks forming the Abyssinian table-land, now again, after so many days, rising before us.

We arrived at Metemma on the afternoon of the 21st of November. In the absence of Sheik Jumma, the potentate of these regions, we were received by his *alter ego*, who put one of the Imperial residences —a wretched barn— at the disposal of the "great men from England." If we deduct the seven days we were obliged to halt *en route*, on account of the difficulty we had in obtaining camels, we performed the whole journey between Massowah and Metemma, a distance of about 440 miles, in thirty days. Our journey on the whole was extremely dreary and fatiguing. Apart from a few pretty spots, such as from Ain to Haboob, the valleys of the Anseba and Atbara, and from Kedaref to Galabat, we crossed only endless savannahs, saw not a human being, not a hut, only now and then a few antelopes, or the tracks of elephants, and heard no sound but the roar of wild beasts. Twice our caravan was attacked by lions; unfortunately we did not see them, as we were on both occasions riding ahead, but every night we heard their awful roar, echoing like distant thunder in the still nights of those silent prairies.

The heat of the day was at times really painful. In order that the camels might start in time, our tents were packed early; sometimes we would sit for hours waiting the good pleasure of the cameleers under the scanty shade of a mimosa, vainly endeavouring to find in its dwarfed foliage a relief from the burning rays of the sun. Night after night, be it moonlight or starlight, on we went; the task was before us, and duty urged us on to reach the land where our countrymen were lingering in chains. Often in the saddle between three and, four P.M., we have jogged along on our wearied mules until the morning star had disappeared before the first rays of day. For several days we had no water but the hot and filthy fluid we carried in leathern skins; and even this nauseous decoction was so scanty and precious, that we could not afford to soothe the sun-burnt skin and refresh the exhausted frame by a timely ablution.

Notwithstanding the discomfort, inconveniences, nay, danger of crossing the Soudan in that unhealthy season of the year, by care and attention we reached Metemma without having had a single death to lament. Several of the followers and native servants, even Mr. Rassam, suffered more or less from fever. They all eventually recovered, and when a few weeks later we started for Abyssinia, the whole party was in better health than when we left the hot and sultry shores of the Red Sea.

Metemma, the capital of Galabat, a province situated on the western frontier of Abyssinia, is built in a large valley, about four miles from the Atbara. A small rivulet runs at the foot of the village, and separates Galabat from Abyssinia. On the Abyssinian side there is a small village, inhabited by the few Abyssinian traders who reside there during the winter months; at which period a large traffic is carried on with the interior. The round, conical hut is here again the abode of all classes the size and better state of repair being the only visible difference between the dwelling of the rich and that of his less fortunate neighbour. Sheik Jumma's palaces are inferior to many of his subjects' huts, probably to dispel the credited suspicion that he is rich, and that incalculable treasures are buried under the ground. The huts put at our disposal were, as I have already stated, his property; they are situated on one of the small hills that overlook the town; the Sheik removes there with his family during the rainy season, as it is in some degree less unhealthy than the swampy ground below.

Though following the creed of the Medina prophet, the capital of Galabat cannot boast of a single mosque.

The inhabitants of Galabat are Takruries, a negro race from Darfur. They number about 10,000; of these 2,000 reside in the capital, the remainder in the many villages that arise in all directions amidst cultivated fields and green meadows. The whole province is well adapted for agricultural purposes. Small rounded hillocks, separated by sloping valleys watered by many rivulets, impart a pleasing aspect to the whole district; and if it was not for the extreme unhealthiness of the place, it is possible to understand the selection made by the Darfur pilgrims: though it is no compliment paid to their own native land. The pious Darfur Mussulmans, on their way to Mecca, observed this favoured spot, and fancied it realized, *minus* the houris, some of the inferior Paradises of Mohammed. At last some remained; Metemma was built; other pilgrims followed the example; and soon, though a lazy and indolent race, owing to the extreme fertility of the soil, they formed a prosperous colony.

At the outset they acknowledged the Sultan of Darfur, paid him tribute, and were governed by one of his officers. But the Galabat colony soon found out that the Egyptians and Abyssinians were more to be feared than their distant sovereign, who could neither protect nor injure them; accordingly, they quietly murdered the viceroy from Darfur, and elected a Sheik from amongst themselves. The ruler at once made terms with both Egyptians and Abyssinians, and tendered yearly tribute to both. This wise but servile policy met with the best results; the colony increased and prospered, trade flourished, Abyssinians and Egyptians flocked to the well-supplied market, and the tribute of a few thousand dollars to each party fell lightly on the now rich and cunning negroes.

From November to May, on Mondays and Tuesdays, the market is held on a large open space in the centre of the village. Abyssinians bring horses, mules, cattle, and honey; the Egyptian merchant displays in his stall, calico, shirtings, hardware, and gaudy prints. Arabs and Takruries arrive with camels laden with cotton and grain. The market-place is now a crowded and exciting scene: horses are tried by half-naked jockeys, who, with whip and heel, drive at a furious pace their diminutive steeds, reckless as to the limbs and lives of the venturous spectators.

Here cotton is being loaded on donkeys, and will soon find its way to Tschelga and Gondar; here some fat Nubian girls, redolent with rancid castor-oil flowing from their woolly heads down their necks and shoulders, issue grinning from a Frank's store, holding in their hands red and yellow kerchiefs, the long-desired object of their dreams. The whole scene is lively; good-humour prevails; and though the noise is fearful, the bargaining being long and clamorous, and every one is armed with lance or club, still, all is peaceful: no blood is ever shed on these occasions but that of a few cows, killed for the many visitors from the high country who enjoy their raw beefsteak under the cool shadow of the willows that border the stream.

On Friday the scene changes. On that day the whole community is seized with martial ardour. Having no mosque, the Takruries devote their holy day to ceremonies more suited to their taste, and resort to the market-place, now transformed into a parade-ground, a few to drill, the greater number to admire. Some Takruries, having served for a time in the Egyptian army, returned to their adopted land full of the value of disciplined troops, and of the superiority of muskets over lances and sticks. They prevailed on their countrymen to form a regiment on the model of "master's," Old muskets were purchased, and Sheik Jumma had the glory to see during his reign the 1st, or Jumma's Own, rise to existence. A more ludicrous sight could not, I believe, be witnessed. About a hundred flat-nosed, woolly, grinning negroes march around the parade-ground in Indian file, out of step, for about ten minutes. Line is then formed, but not being as yet well up to the proper value of the words of command, half face on one side, half on the other. Still the crowd admires; white teeth are displayed from ear to ear. The yellow-eyed monsters now feel confident that with such support nothing is impossible, and no sooner is "stand at ease" proclaimed, than the spectators rush, forward to admire more closely, and to congratulate, the future heroes of Metemma.

Sheik Jumma is an ugly specimen of an ugly race: he is about sixty years of age, tall and lank, with a wrinkled face, very black, having a few grey patches on the chin, and the owner of a nose so flat that it requires time to see that he has one at all; He is generally drunk, and spends the greater part of the year carrying the tribute either to the Abyssinian Lion, or to his other master the Pasha of Khartoum. A few days after our arrival at Metemma he returned from Abyssinia, and politely paid us a visit, accompanied by a motley and howling train of followers. We returned his call; but he had got drunk in the interval, and was at least uncivil, if not positively rude.

During our stay we had occasion to witness the great yearly, festival of the re-election of the Sheik. Early in the morning a crowd of Takruries came pouring in from all directions, armed with sticks or spears, a few mounted, the majority on foot, all howling and screeching (I believe they call it singing), so that before even the dust raised by a new party could be seen, the ear was deafened by their clamour. Every Takrurie warrior—that is, every one who can howl and carry a bludgeon or lance—is entitled to a vote; for this privilege he pays a dollar. The polling consists in counting the money, and the amount decides the ruler's fate. The re-elected Sheik (such was the result of the election we witnessed) killed cows, supplied jowaree loaves, and, above all, immense jars of merissa (a kind of sour toast-and-water, intoxicating for all that), and feasted for two days the whole body of the electors. It is difficult to say which of the two is out of pocket, the elector or the Sheik. There is no doubt that every Takrurie will eat and drink to the full amount of his dollar; is content with paying his homage, and wishes to have the worth of his money. Bribery is unknown! The drums, the sign of royalty, have been silent for three days (during the interregnum), but the cows are no sooner slaughtered and the merissa handed round by black maidens or fair Galla slaves, than their monotonous beat is again heard; soon to be drowned under the howling chorus of two thousand intoxicated negroes.

The following morning the whole assembled "by orders" on a place some distance from the town. Arranged in a large crescent, Sheik Jamma addressed his warriors in these words: "We are a strong and mighty people, unequalled in horsemanship and in the use of the club and the spear!" Moreover, (said he), they had increased their power by adopting the system of fire-arms, the real strength of the Turks. He was all-confident that the very sight of their gunmen would strike terror into every neighbouring tribe. He ended by proposing a raid into Abyssinia, and said: "We will take cows, slaves, horses, and mules, and please our master the great Theodore by plundering his enemy Tisso Gobazé!" A wild *feu-de-joie*, and a terrible roar, from the excited crowd, informed the old Sheik that his proposal was accepted. That very same afternoon they started on their expedition, and probably surprised some peaceful district, as they returned after a few days, driving before them several thousand heads of cattle.

Metemma, from May to November, is very unhealthy. The principal diseases are continued, remittent, and intermittent fevers, diarrhoea, and dysentery. The Takruries are a tough race, and resist well the noxious influences of the climate; but not so the Abyssinian, or the white man: the first is almost certain to die should he attempt to spend the dreaded months in the malarious low country, the second most probably will suffer much in health, but resist for a season or two. During our stay, I had many demands for medicine. Large, cake-like spleens were greatly reduced by local applications of tincture of iodine, and the internal administration of small doses of quinine and iodine of potassium. Chronic diarrhoea yielded readily to a few doses of castor oil, followed by opium and tannic acid. Acute and chronic dysentery was treated by ipecacuanha, followed by astringents.

One of my patients was the son and heir of the Sheik. He had been suffering for the last two years from chronic dysentery; and although under my care he entirely recovered, his ungrateful father never even thanked me for all my trouble. Simple ophthalmia, skin diseases, and glandular swellings were also common.

The Takruries have no knowledge whatever of medicine: charms are here, as throughout the Soudan, the great remedy. They are also used as preventatives to keep off the evil eye, bad spirits, and genii of different sorts; for these reasons almost every individual— nay, cattle, mules, and horses, are covered with amulets of all shapes and sizes.

The day after our arrival at Metemma we despatched two messengers with a letter to the Emperor Theodore, to inform him that we had reached Metemma, the place he had himself fixed upon, and were only waiting for his permission to proceed to his presence. We feared that the fickle despot might change his mind, and leave us for an unlimited period in the unhealthy Galabat. More than a month had elapsed, and we were giving way to despair, when, to our great joy, on the 25th of December (1865), the messengers we had despatched on our arrival, also those sent from Massowah at the time of our departure, returned, bringing for us civil and courteous answers from his Majesty. Sheik Jumma was also ordered by his Abyssinian master to treat us well, and to provide us with camels up to Wochnee. At that village, Theodore informed us, we should be met by an escort and by some of his officers, by whom arrangements would be made to convey our luggage to the imperial camp.

CHAPTER VII

Heartily sick of Metemma, and longing to climb the high range so long a forbidden barrier to our hopes and wishes, we soon made our preparations, but were delayed a few days on account of the camels. Sheik Jumma, probably proud of his late achievements seemed to take his orders pretty coolly, and, had we not been more anxious ourselves to penetrate into the tiger's den than the Sheik to comply with the King's request, we should no doubt have remained many a day longer at the court of that negro potentate. By dint of courteous messages; promises, and threats, the required number of camels was at last forthcoming, so that on the afternoon of the 28th December, 1865, we passed the Ethiopian Rubicon, and halted for the night on Abyssinian ground. On the morning of the 30th we arrived at Wochnee, and pitched our tents under some sycamores at a short distance from the village. This, our first stage in Abyssinia, led us through woods of mimosas, acacias, and incense-trees; the undulating ground, waving like the ocean after a storm, was covered with high and still green grass. As we advanced, the ground became more irregular and broken, and we crossed several ravines, having each its small running rivulet of crystal water. By-and-by the rounded hillocks acquired a more abrupt and steep appearance; the grass was no longer tall and green, but fine and dry; the sycamore, the cedar, and large timber-trees began to appear. As we approached Wochnee, our route was a succession of ascents and descents more precipitous and very fatiguing, as we trudged through deep ravines and climbed the almost perpendicular sides of the first range of the Abyssinian mountains.

At Wochnee we found no one to welcome us. The cameleers, having unladen their camels, were going to depart, when a servant of one of the officers sent to receive us by his Majesty arrived. He brought us compliments from his master, who could not join us for a few days, as he was collecting bearers; he told us that we must proceed another stage by the camels, as no bearers could be obtained in the district of Wochnee. A serious altercation then took place between the governor of Wochnee and the cameleers. They declined to proceed any further, and after a short consultation between themselves, each man seized his camel and walked away. But the governor and the officer's servant had also been consulting together: seeing the cameleers departing, they went to the village, and, as it happened to be market-day, soon collected a good number of soldiers and peasants. As the cameleers were passing close to the village, on a given signal, the whole of the camels were seized. I regret to say, for the honour of the Arabs and Takruries, that, though well armed, they did not show fight, but on the contrary, ran away in every direction. Unwilling to lose their precious beasts of burden, the owners returned by twos and threes. More consultations followed: at last, on the promise of an extra dollar for each, and a cow for all, peace and harmony were satisfactorily restored. After a couple of hours' march, we reached Balwaha. I can understand the difficulties the cameleers raised, as the road is exceedingly bad for camels, passing as it does over two high and steep mountains and across two narrow ravines densely overgrown with tall bamboos.

At Balwaha we encamped in a small natural enclosure, formed by beautiful foliaged trees. Three days after our arrival, two of the officers sent by Theodore to meet us at last made their appearance, but no bearers. We had unfortunately arrived during the last days of the long feast before Christmas, and we must, said the chief of the escort, have patience till the feast was over.

On the 6th January about twelve hundred peasants were assembled, but the confusion was so great that no start could be made before the following day, and even then we only made the short stage of four miles. The greater part of the heavy baggage was left behind, and it required a reinforcement from Tschelga to allow us to proceed on our journey. On the 9th we made a better stage, and halted for the night on a small plateau opposite the high hill fort of Zer Amba.

We were now fairly in the mountains, and had often to dismount to descend some precipitous declivity, wondering how our mules could climb the opposite steep, wall-like ascent. On the 10th the same awful road, only worse and worse as we advanced; and when at last we had ascended the almost perpendicular precipice that leads to the Abyssinian plateau itself, and admired the grand vista that lay at our feet, we congratulated ourselves upon having at last reached the land of promise. We halted a few miles from the market town of Tschelga, at a place called Wali Dabba. Here we had to exchange bearers and consequently to wait several days till the new ones arrived, or anything like order could be introduced. From that day my troubles began.

I was at all hours of the day surrounded by an importuning crowd, of all ages and sexes, afflicted by the many ills that flesh is heir to. I had no more privacy, and no more rest. Did I leave our camp with my gun in search of game, a clamorous crowd followed me. On the march, at every halt from

Wali Dabba to Theodore's camp in Damot, I heard nothing else from sunrise to sunset but the incessant cries of "*Abiet, abiet; medanite, medanite.*" [Footnote: "Lord Master, medicine, medicine."] I did my best; I attended at any hour of the day those who would benefit from a few doses of medicine. But this did not satisfy the great majority, composed of old syphilitic cases, nor the leper, nor those suffering from elephantiasis, the epileptic, the scrofulous, or those who had been mutilated at the hands of the cruel Gallas. Day after day the crowd of patients increased; those who had met with refusal remained in the hope that on another day the "Hakeem's" boxes of unheard-of medicine might be opened, for them also. New ones daily poured in. The many cures of simple cases that I had been able to accomplish spread my fame far and wide, and even reached my countrymen at Magdala, who heard that an English Hakeem had arrived, who could break bones and instantly set them, so that the individual operated upon walked away like the paralytic in Holy Writ. At last the nuisance became intolerable, and I was obliged to keep my tent closed all day long; whenever I left it I was surrounded by an admiring crowd. The officers of the escort were obliged to place a guard round my tent, and only allowed their relatives and friends to approach. Still, these were often countless, and it was not till the dread of the despot overcame even their love of life and health, that successful and unsuccessful postulants returned to their homes.

On the 13th January we began our march towards the Emperor's camp, and passed successively through the provinces of Tschelga, part of Dembea, Dagossa, Wandigé, Atchefur, Agau Medar, and Damot, leaving the Tana Sea on our left. The three first-named provinces had a few years before fallen under the wrath of the despot; every village had been burnt, every crop destroyed, and the inhabitants had either perished from famine or been absorbed into the Imperial army. A few had just then returned to their broken-down homes, on hearing of the pardon proclaimed by the Emperor; who, after three years, had relented, and allowed those who still wandered in distant provinces, destitute and homeless, to return again to the land of their fathers. Here and there, amongst the ruins of former prosperous villages, some half-starved and almost naked peasants were seen erecting small sheds on the ashes of their ancestral huts, near the land they were going again to cultivate. Alas, they knew not how soon the same merciless hand would be stretched upon them! Atchefur had also been plundered at the same date; but their "crime" not having been so great, the "father of his people" had been content to strip them of all their property, and did not call fire in aid to complete his vengeance. The villages of Atchefur are large and well built; some, such as Limju, can rank with small towns; but the people had a poor and miserable appearance. The small amount of cultivation indicated but too plainly that they expected another plunder, and just tilled the soil enough to meet their immediate wants.

The Agau Medars were always pets of the Emperor; he never plundered them, or, what is the same, he never made any lengthened "friendly stay" among them. The rich and abundant harvest ready for the sickle, the numerous herds of cattle grazing in the flower-speckled meadows, the large and neat villages, the happy look of the peasants, clearly proved what Abyssinia can do for its children if their rich and fertile soil was not laid waste in wanton destruction, and themselves driven by warfare and bloodshed to perish from misery and hunger.

Theodore's camp was at this time in Damot. He had already burnt, plundered, and slaughtered to his heart's content; it is therefore not astonishing that from Agau to his camp we saw, apart from our escort and bearers, not a human being: no sleek cattle, no smiling hamlet—a dire, contrast to the happy Agau that "St. Michael protects."

The 25th of January was our last stage. We had halted the night before at a short distance from the Imperial camp. The black and white tents of Theodore, pitched on a high conical hill, stood out in bold relief as the setting sun made the dark background darker still. A faint, distant hum, such as one hears on approaching a large city, came now and then to us, carried by the soft evening breeze, and the smoke that arose for miles around the dark hill crowned by its silent tents, left us no, doubt that we should before long find ourselves face to face with the African despot, and that we were even then almost in the midst of his countless host. As we approached, messenger after messenger came to meet us; we had to halt several times, march on again for a while, and then halt anew; at last the chief of the escort told us that it was time to dress. A small rowtie was accordingly pitched; we put on our uniforms, and, mounting again, we had hardly proceeded a hundred yards, when, coming to a sudden turn in the road, we saw displayed before us one of those Eastern scenes which brought back to our memory the days of Lobo and of Bruce.

A conical wooded hill, opposite to the one honoured by the Imperial tents, was covered to the very summit by the gunners and spearmen of Theodore; all in gala dress; they were clad in shirts of rich-coloured silks, the black, brown, or red lamd [Footnote: A peculiar mantle of fur or velvet.] falling from their shoulders, the bright iron of the lances glancing in the light of the midday sun which poured its rays through the dark foliage of the cedars. In the valley between the hills a large body of cavalry, about 10,000 strong, formed a double line, between which we advanced. On our right, dressed in gorgeous array, almost all bearing the silver shield and the Bitwa, their horses adorned with richly plated bridles, stood the whole of the officers of his Majesty's army and household, the governors of provinces and of districts, &c. All were mounted, some on really noble-looking animals, tribute from the plateaus of Yedjow and the highlands of Shoa. On our left, the corps of cavalry was darker, but more compact, than its aristocratic *vis-à-vis*. The horses, though on the whole, perhaps, less graceful, were strong and in good condition; and seeing their iron ranks, we could well understand how panic-stricken the poor scattered peasants must have been when Theodore, at the head of his well-armed and well-mounted band of ruthless followers, suddenly appeared among their peaceful homes, and, before his very presence was suspected, had come, destroyed, and gone.

In the centre opposite to us stood Ras Engeddah, the Prime Minister, distinguished from all by his gentlemanly appearance and the great simplicity of his attire. Bare-headed, the shama girded in token of respect, he delivered the Imperial message of welcome, translated into Arabic by Samuel, who stood by him, and whose finely chiselled features and intellectual countenance at once proclaimed his superiority over the ignorant Abyssinian. Compliments delivered, the Ras and ourselves mounted, and advanced towards the Imperial tents, preceded by the body of mounted grandees, and followed by the cavalry. Arrived at the foot of the hill, we dismounted, and were conducted to a small red flannel tent pitched for our reception on the ascent itself. There we rested for a while, and partook of a slight collation. Towards three o'clock we were informed that the Emperor would receive us; we ascended the hill on foot, escorted by Samuel and several other officers of the Imperial household. As soon as we reached the small plateau on the summit, an officer brought us renewed greetings and compliments from his Majesty. We advanced slowly towards the beautiful durbar-tent of red and yellow silk, between a double line of gunners, who, on a signal, fired a salute very creditable to their untaught skill.

Arrived at the entrance of the tent, the Emperor again inquired after our health and welfare. Having acknowledged with due respect his courteous inquiries, we advanced towards the throne, and delivered into his hands the letter from her Majesty the Queen. The Emperor received it civilly, and told us to sit down on the splendid carpets that covered the ground. The Emperor was seated on an alga, wrapped up to the eyes in a shama, the sign of greatness and of power in Abyssinia. On his right and left stood four of his principal officers, clad in rich and gay silks, and behind him watched one of his trusty familiars, holding a double-barrelled pistol in each hand. The King made a few complaints about the European prisoners, and regretted that by their conduct they had interrupted the friendship formerly existing between the two nations. He was happy to see us, and hoped that all would be well again. After a few compliments had been exchanged, on the plea that we must be tired, having come so far, we were allowed to depart.

The letter from the Queen of England, which we had handed over to his Abyssinian Majesty, was in English, and no translation had been affixed to it. His Majesty did not break the seal before us, probably on account of the presence of his high officers; as he would not have liked them to witness his disappointment had the letter not suited his views. As soon as we had reached our tent, the letter was sent to us to be translated; but as we had with us no European who understood the language of the country, it had to be rendered first by Mr. Rassam into Arabic to Samuel, and by him from that language into Amharic. There is much reason to regret that none of the Europeans in the country who were conversant with the Amharic language were sent for before that important document was made over to his Majesty; for I believe that not only the translation was—in many respects—a bad one, but, moreover, incorrect. A simple phrase was rendered into one of deep importance to the success of the mission—one of such serious meaning, considering Theodore's position, that I am still inclined to believe that it was introduced in the Amharic translation by Theodore's instructions. The English ran thus:—"And so, not doubting that you will receive our servant Rassam in a favourable manner, and give entire credit to all that he shall say to you on our part." This was rendered:—"He will do for you whatever you require," or words to that effect. His Majesty was greatly pleased, so his confidential servants said, with the Queen's letter; and intimated that he would before long release the captives.

On the following morning Theodore sent for us. He had no one near him except Ras Engeddah. He was standing at the entrance of his tent, leaning gracefully on his lance. He invited us to enter the tent; and there, before us, he dictated to his secretary, in presence of Ras Engeddah, Samuel, and our interpreter, a letter to the Queen,—an humble, apologizing letter, which he never intended to despatch.

In the afternoon we had the honour of another interview, in order to make over to him the presents we had brought with us. He first asked if the gifts came from the Queen or from Mr. Rassam himself. Having been informed that they had been purchased in the name of the Queen, he accepted them; remarking, at the same time, that he did so not for their value, but as a token from a friendly Power whose renewed friendship he was so happy to acknowledge. Amongst the presents there was a large looking-glass. Mr. Rassam, on presenting it, told his Majesty that he had intended it for the Queen. On that his Majesty looked rather serious; but calmly replied that he had not been happy in his married life, and that he was on the point of marrying another lady, to whom he would offer the splendid mirror. Soon after our arrival, cows, sheep, honey, tej, and bread were sent in abundance, and ourselves and followers were daily supplied with all necessaries of life from the Imperial kitchen.

His Majesty accompanied us several stages towards the Tana Sea, Kourata having been fixed upon as our place of residence until the arrival of our countrymen from Magdala. On the first day's march we were left behind, on account of our luggage, and had a good opportunity of experiencing what it is to travel with an Abyssinian army. The fighting men were in front with the king, but the camp-followers (numbering on that occasion about 250,000), encumbered as they were with the tents and provisions of the soldiers, came more slowly behind. It is almost impossible to describe the crush and confusion that frequently took place when a small river had to be forded, or when a single footpath led along a steep, incline of almost naked rocks. Thousands heaped together pushed, screamed, and vainly endeavoured to penetrate the living mass, which always increased as the mules and donkeys became more frightened, and the muddy banks of the stream more slippery and broken. Several times, driven to despair by hours of patient waiting, we went in search of another road, or some other ford, where the crush and crowd might be less. It was only late in the afternoon that we reached our encamping-ground: we had been the whole day upon a march that the Emperor accomplished in an hour and a half.

Theodore, having heard to what inconvenience we had been put, had the heavy luggage conveyed as before; but ourselves, with a few light articles, were allowed the privilege of riding with him in front of the army. During the few days he accompanied us we made but short stages, never more than ten miles a day. Theodore travelled with us for several reasons: he wanted to take us by a short cut by the Tana Sea, and as the country was depopulated, he was obliged to have our luggage carried by his soldiers. He had not as yet plundered that part of Damot; the inhabitants had fled, but the harvest ready for the sickle remained, and at a sign from the Emperor was reaped by thousands of hands. Whilst the greater part of his soldiers were thus employed, and the sword was practically used as an implement of peace, the King, with a large body of cavalry, left the camp, and shortly afterwards the smoke that arose far and wide proclaimed their merciless errand.

A few incidents that occurred during our short stay with Theodore deserve to be recorded, as they will illustrate his character during his friendly moods. On our second day's march with his Majesty, (February 1st,) the Blue Nile was crossed not far from its source; the banks were steep and slippery, the crush was fearful, and many a child or woman would have been drowned or otherwise killed had not Theodore sent some of the chiefs, who waited on him, to make steps on the slope with their spears, whilst he remained there until the last camp-follower had passed. When we arrived his Majesty sent us word not to dismount. We crossed the water on our mules; but the moment we reached the opposite bank we alighted, and climbed to the spot where his Majesty was standing. The road was so precipitous and slippery that Mr. Rassam, who was in front, had some difficulty in reaching the summit; Theodore; seeing his position, advanced, took him by the hand, and said, in Arabic, "Be of good cheer, do not be afraid."

The following day, during the march, Theodore sent Samuel backwards and forwards with questions,—such as: "Is the American war over? How many were killed? How many soldiers had they? Did the English fight with the Ashantees? Did they conquer them? Is their country unhealthy? Is it like this? Why did the King of Dahomey kill so many of his subjects? What is his religion?" He then gave one of his *excuses* for not having sent for us sooner. He had been disappointed, he said, with all the Europeans that had entered his country. None were good but Bell and Plowden; and he wanted to know, by report, if the Englishman who had landed at Massowah was like all the rest. His patience was such that he had believed him to be a good man, and had, therefore, decided upon sending for him.

On the 4th he again sent for us. He was alone, sitting in the open air. He made us sit down on a carpet near him,—and spoke at length about his former career. He told us how he dealt with the rebels: first he sent them word to pay tribute; if they refused, he went himself and plundered their, country. On the third refusal, to use his own words, "he sent their bodies to the grave; and their souls to hell." He also told us that Bell had spoken to him so much about our Queen, that for many years he had intended sending her an embassy; he had even everything ready when; Captain Cameron made him an enemy of his former friend. He had ordered, he said, some tokens of his regard to be made for us, as he had nothing with him fit to offer us; he had been pleased to see us, and considered us as "three brothers." The interview was long; when at last his Majesty dismissed us, he informed us that the following day he would send us to Kourata to await there the arrival of our countrymen from Magdala. Shortly after reaching our tent, Mr. Rassam received a polite note, informing him that he would receive 5,000 dollars, which he might spend as he liked, but always *in a manner agreeable to the Lord*. A verbal message was also sent to me to inquire if I knew anything about smelting iron, casting guns, etc.: to which I answered, in pursuance of friendly advice, that I was ignorant of everything except my own medical profession.

CHAPTER VIII

On the 6th of February his Majesty sent us word to depart. We did not see him, but before we left he sent us a letter informing us that as soon as the prisoners joined us he would take steps to send us out of his country in "honour and safety." The officer ordered to proceed to Magdala to deliver the captives, and conduct them to us, was one of our escort; we were the bearers of an humble apology from Theodore to our Queen: all smiled upon us; and rejoiced beyond expression by the apparently complete success of our mission, we retraced our steps with a light and thankful heart through the plains of Agau Medar. On the afternoon of the 10th of February, we encamped on the shore of the Tana Sea, a large fresh-water lake, the reservoir of the Blue Nile. The river enters at the south-west extremity of the lake, and issues again at its south-east extremity, the two branches being only separated by the promontory of Zagé.

The spot we pitched our camp upon was not far from Kanoa, a pretty village in the district of Wandigé, Kourata being almost opposite to us, bearing N.N.E. We had to wait several days while boats were constructed for ourselves, escort, and luggage. These boats—of the most primitive kind of construction still in existence—are made of bulrushes, the papyrus of the ancients. The bulrushes are tied together so as to form a flat surface some six feet in breadth and from ten to twenty feet in length. The two extremities are then rolled up and tied together. The passengers and boatmen sit upon a large square bundle of bulrushes forming the essential part of the boat, which the outward cage serves only to keep in place, and by its pointed extremities to favour progression. To say that these boats leak is a mistake; they are full of water, or rather, like a piece of cork, always half submerged: their floating is simply a question of specific gravity. The manner in which the boats are propelled adds greatly to the discomfort of the traveller. Two men sit in front, and one behind. They use long sticks, instead of oars, beating the water alternately to the right and left; at each stroke they send in front and from behind jets of spray like a shower-bath, and the unfortunate occupant of the boat, who had beforehand taken off his shoes and stockings and well tucked up his trousers, finds that he would have been wiser had he adopted a more simple costume still, and followed the example of the naked boatmen.

The Abyssinian navy does not weigh heavily on the estimates, nor does it take years to construct a fleet; two days after our arrival fifty new vessels had been launched, and several hundreds had joined from Zagé and the Isle of Dek.

The few days we spent on the shore of the Tana Sea were among the small number of happy ones we have seen in this country. Samuel, now our balderaba (introducer) and chief of the escort, did not allow the former crowds to invade my tent. Being an intelligent man, and his relatives and friends less numerous than those of his predecessor, he only brought to me those he knew would benefit by a few doses of medicine, or whom he was compelled to introduce; for by refusing the petty chiefs and important men of the several neighbouring districts he would have made serious enemies. It was now a recreation, instead of a fatigue; a study of the diseases of the country; a fact almost impossible, before, when I could only defend myself against the importunities of a crowd, and in peace not examine a single case. The remainder of my time was spent in shooting. Aquatic birds, ducks, geese, &c., were in abundance, and so tame that the survivors did not move away, but remained bathing, feeding, and cleaning their bright feathers around the dead bodies of their mates and companions.

On the morning of the 16th we started for Dek, the largest and most important island of the Tana Lake; it is situated about half-way from our starting-place and Kourata. We were shower-bathed for about six hours; our speed was about two and a half knots, so that the distance must be about fifteen miles. Dek is a very pretty island indeed; a long, flat volcanic rock, surrounded by conical hillocks, forming so many island pearls around a coronet. The whole island is well wooded, covered with the most luxuriant vegetation, dotted with numerous and prosperous villages, and proudly boasts of four old and revered churches—the shrines of many devoted pilgrims. We spent the night in the heart of the picturesque island—the ideal of an earthly abode. Alas! we knew only some time afterwards that the passage of the white men caused tears and distress among the Arcadian inhabitants of that peaceful land. The inhabitants of the island had been ordered to supply us with 10,000 dollars. The chiefs, almost despairing of being able to raise so large a sum, made a powerful appeal to their friends and neighbours; painted in true colours the wrath of the despot should he learn that his request had not been complied with, and the wilderness that would then replace their rich and happy isle. The eloquence of some, and the threats of others, were equally successful. All the savings of years were brought to the chiefs; silver rings and chains—the dower and fortune of many a young maiden—were added to the newly spun shama of the matron: all were reduced to poverty, and were trembling; though they smiled whilst making the sacrifice of all their worldly goods. How they must have cursed, in the bitterness of their grief, the poor white strangers who were the innocent cause of all their misfortunes!

The following morning we started for Kourata, the distance and inconvenience being about the same as on the preceding day. Once again on *terra firma*, we hailed with delight the end of our short and disagreeable passage. On the beach we were received by the clergy, who had turned out in full canonicals to welcome us with all the pomp usually accorded only to royalty; for such had been the Imperial command. Two of the wealthiest merchants of the place claimed us as their guests, in the name of their royal master, and, mounted on beautiful mules, we ascended the hill on which Kourata is built; the privilege of riding through the sacred streets having been conferred on, the honoured guests of the sovereign of the land.

Kourata is, after Gondar, the most important and wealthy city of Abyssinia; it is a town of priests and merchants, built on the sides of a conical hill and bathed by the waters of the Tana Sea. The houses, many of them built of stone, are superior to any we saw in Abyssinia. The church erected by the Queen of Socinius is held in such sanctity that the whole town is considered sacred, and none but the bishop or the emperor are allowed to ride through its narrow and steep lanes. From the sea it is almost impossible to see the town, so close and compact are the towering dark cedars and sycamores— the just pride of the inhabitants. The whole hillock is so completely covered with vegetation of every description, that the spot from a distance seems more like a luxuriant waste untouched by man's hand, than the abode of thousands, and the central mart of Western Abyssinia. For a few days we resided in the town, where several of the best houses had been put at our disposal; but the countless host of unmentionable insects fairly drove us away. We obtained permission to pitch our tents on the sea beach, on a pleasant spot only a few hundred yards from the town, where we enjoyed the double luxury of fresh air and abundance of water.

A few days after our arrival at Kourata we were joined by the "Gaffat people." The Emperor had written to them to come and remain with us during our stay, as he feared that we might feel lonely and unhappy in his country, separated from our own people. Agreeably to the instructions they had received, on arriving at a short distance from our encampment, they sent to inform us of their arrival, and requested permission to present themselves before us. I was never so much taken aback as at the sight of these Europeans wearing the Abyssinian gala dress, silk shirts of gaudy colours, trousers of the same material, the shama thrown over the left shoulder, many with naked feet, several without covering to their head. They had been so long in Abyssinia that I doubt not they considered themselves very smart; and, if we did not admire them, the natives certainly did. They pitched their camp a little distance in rear of ours. A few days later their wives and children arrived, and on more intimate acquaintance we soon perceived that several amongst them were well-educated and well-informed men—not at all despicable companions in that distant laud.

On the 12th of March our poor countrymen, so long in chains and misery, at last arrived. We provided tents for those who had none, and they remained in our inclosure. They all, more or less, bore traces of the many sufferings they had endured; but Messrs. Stern and Cameron more than the others. We endeavoured to cheer them up by the prospect of a speedy return to Europe, and only regretted that we could not show them more kindness; as Mr. Rassam did not think it advisable, on account of Theodore's suspicious character, to appear to be on too intimate terms with them. They knew the Emperor better than we did, and now and then expressed doubts as to the favourable issue of the affair. They had heard *en route* that they would have to make boats for Theodore, and were always anxious and nervous each time a messenger arrived from the Imperial camp.

Theodore, after plundering Metcha, the fertile province at the southern extremity of Lake Tana, destroyed the large and populous town of Zagé, and pitched his camp on a small strip of land connecting the promontory of Zagé with the mainland. The Emperor was very attentive; he sent us 5,000 dollars more, supplies in abundance, and put thirty milch cows at our disposal; he also sent us lion cubs, monkeys, &c., and almost every second day wrote civil and courteous letters to Mr. Rassam. All our interpreters, all the messengers, even Mr. Rassam's butler, went one after the other to Zag to be invested with "the order of the shirt." To the messenger who had brought us down the false intelligence of Captain Cameron's release, he gave a marguf (silk-bordered) shama, a title, and the government of a district; and requested Mr. Rassam to love him, and cause him to be loved by our Queen, as his stratagem had fortunately succeeded, and had induced us to come to him. When one of our interpreters, Omar Ali, a native of Massowah, went in his turn to be decorated, he found his Majesty sitting near the beach making cartridges. He told him, "You see my occupation; but I am not ashamed of it. I cannot make up my mind to let Stern and Cameron go; but, for the sake of your masters, I will. I like them because they are always so well behaved, hold their caps in their hand as soon as they approach my presence, and are respectful before me, whilst Cameron used to pull his beard about all the time."

If I mention these apparent trifles, it is to show that Theodore was still doubtful in his mind whether he would allow any one to depart or not. As he was still wavering, he might, perhaps, have allowed himself to be guided by his better qualities, had not a few incidents that occurred at the time worked upon his suspicious nature.

Theodore, always fond of showing himself as a just man before his people, desired a kind of trial of the former captives to take place, before him and us, and in presence of his soldiers; when, had they acknowledged that they were wrong, and begged his Majesty's pardon, he would probably have gone through the form of a public reconciliation, and after presenting them with a few gifts, allowed them to depart.

Mr. Rassam, on the contrary, believed it to be advisable that his Majesty should not see the former captives, as their sight might put him in a passion; and as everything appeared to progress so favourably, he considered it more prudent to do his utmost to avoid a meeting between the two.

Shortly after the arrival of the Magdala prisoners, who had been joined at Debra Tabor by those who had been detained there on parole, his Majesty, at Mr. Rassam's instigation, instead of calling them to him as he had intended, sent several of his officers, his secretary, etc., to Kourata, and requested us to have certain charges read publicly to the captives, who would declare whether he or they were in the wrong.

All the captives, the Gaffat people, and the Abyssinian officers, being assembled in Mr. Rassam's tent, the scribe read the charges. The first was against Captain Cameron. Theodore began by stating that Cameron, on his representing himself to be a messenger from the Queen, was received with all due honour and respect, and welcomed to the best of his ability. He accepted with humility the presents the Queen sent to him, and on Cameron explaining that an exchange of consuls between the two countries would be greatly to the interest of Abyssinia, Theodore, to use his own words, said, "I was glad on hearing this, and said, very well!" He continued by stating that he impressed upon the consul that the Turks were his enemies, and requested him to protect the mission and presents he intended to send to the Queen; that he gave him a friendly letter, and sent him away, but Cameron, instead of delivering the letter, went to the Turks who hated him, and before whom he insulted and lowered him; that on Cameron's return, he asked him, "'Where is the answer to the friendly letter I entrusted you with? what have you come for?' He answered: 'I do not know;' so I said to him, 'You are not the servant of my friend the Queen, as you had represented yourself to be,' and by the power of my creator I imprisoned him. Ask him if he can deny this."

The second charge was against Mr. Bardel; but he had evidently got tired of the affair, as the charges against Stern, Rosenthal, &c. are not specified;

though on former occasion he several times referred to his grievances against them. They are included in a general charge which runs as follows:—

"The other prisoners have abused me, I am well aware, I used to love, and honour them. A friend ought to be a shield to his friend, and they ought to have shielded me. Why did they not defend me? On this account I disliked them.

"Now, by the power of God! for the sake of the Queen, and the British people, and yourselves, I cannot continue my dislike against them. I wish you to make between us a reconciliation from the heart. If I am in fault, do you tell me and I will requite them; but if you find that I am wronged, I wish you to get them to requite me."

After the charges had been read, the captives were asked if they had done wrong or not. It would have been absurd for them not to have acknowledged their faults, and begged for pardon. We knew that they were innocent, injured men, and that any errors of judgment they might have committed were so trivial compared to the sufferings they had undergone, that they could, under any other circumstances, have applied for the requital he offered them. In acknowledging that they were wrong they acted wisely: it was what we counselled, nay ordered.

The sitting concluded with the public reading of the Amharic translation of the Queen's letter, and of the reply which Theodore said he would send by us.

Though all seemed smooth and favourable, no doubt a storm was imminent; and shortly afterwards, though everything was as yet friendly, we should have been far less confident had our knowledge of Theodore been greater.

On our way to Kourata we had been asked indirectly by his servants whether we knew anything about boat-making? We replied in the negative. As I have stated, some of the escort had told Captain Cameron, that at Kourata he would be employed in ship-building. There was no doubt that his Majesty had made up his mind to have a small navy, and I believe that the real reason we were sent to Kourata, and the Gaffat people to keep us company there, was that Theodore imagined that we knew more about making boats than we wished to say, and hoped to coax us into undertaking the work. The Gaffat people, were told to make boats; they replied that they knew nothing about it, but would work with any one who could direct them: at the same time they intimated that his Majesty ought to take advantage of Mr. Rassam's friendship to ask him to write for some proper person and instruments; that they had no doubt that on Mr. Rassam making the application, his Majesty would obtain anything he required.

A few days later Theodore wrote to Mr. Rassam requesting him to write for workmen, and to await their return. Until that date all had been plain sailing. I acknowledged that the letter was rather a "damper" on Mr. Rassam. Two courses were left open to him: to decline, in courteous terms, on the ground that his instructions did not warrant his making such a request; or accept, on condition that the former captives should be allowed to depart, himself remaining with one of his companions until the workmen arrived. Instead of that Mr. Rassam took a half-way course; he told Theodore that it would be better for him if he was allowed to depart, as at home he could better represent the desires of his Majesty, but if the Emperor insisted upon it he would write.

Theodore was so far confirmed in the impression conveyed to him by his workmen that through the intervention of Mr. Rassam he could obtain anything he liked, that the only thing which for a few days longer remained undecided by him was—should he endeavour to gain his object by flatteries or by bullying? He at once went to work, and did the best to succeed by amicable measures. For this purpose he sent us a polite invitation to come and spend a day with him at Zagé, ordering at the same time his workmen to accompany him. On the 25th of March we proceeded by native boats and reached Zagé after a four-hours' shower-bath; at a short distance from the landing-place we dressed ourselves in uniform, and were met on our arrival by Ras Engeddah (Commander-in-Chief), the Master of the Horse, and several other high officials of the Imperial household. His Majesty had sent us by the Ras polite greetings, and mounting the beautiful mules sent from the royal stable, we proceeded to the Emperor's inclosure. We were at first conducted to some silk tents, which had been pitched at a short distance from his banqueting-hall, so that we might rest awhile and partake of the collation his Queen had forwarded to us. In the afternoon the Emperor sent us word that he would come and see us.

We shortly afterwards went out to meet him, and to our astonishment saw him coming towards us, his cloth folded and the right arm uncovered: a sign of inferiority, of high respect—an honour Theodore was never known to have paid to any man. He was all smiles, all amiability, sat down a few minutes on Mr. Rassam's couch, and when he left he shook hands in the most friendly manner with him. A little later we returned his call. We found him in the audience-hall, seated on a carpet; he gracefully saluted us, and made us sit down by his side. To his left stood his eldest son Prince Meshisha, and Ras Engeddah; his workmen were also present standing in the centre of the hall in front of him. He had before him quite an arsenal of guns and pistols; he spoke about and showed those we had brought with us, guns that had been made to order by the brother of a gunmaker in his service, a manufacturer at St. Etienne, near Lyons. He conversed on various topics, about the different ranks in his army, presented us to his son, and ordered him at the conclusion of the audience, together with the Gaffat people, to escort us back to our tent.

The following day Theodore sent repeated kind messages; but we did not see him. In the morning he called, all his chiefs together, and asked them to advise him as to whether he should allow the Europeans to depart or not. All exclaimed, "Let them go;" one only remarking that if once out, and they wanted to fight, "let them come, we will then have God on our side." As soon as he had dismissed his chiefs, he called the Gaffat people and asked them also what he should do. They told us that they had strongly advised him to let us depart. It was reported that on returning to his house; his valet said to him, "Every one tells you to let them go; you know that they are your enemies, and what will you have in your hands?" In the evening his Majesty was rather excited: he sent for the Gaffat people, and taking hold of the rude pillar of his hut, said: "Is that the dwelling fit for a king?" What conversation passed between them at the time, I cannot say; but a few days afterwards one of them told me that his Majesty was much put out, as Mr. Rassam had not mentioned to him the objects he had so dear at heart, viz.: the artisans and instruments, and that on our applying to be allowed to return to Kourata, his Majesty looked very black at first, and refused, and that they had had great fears that he might have forcibly detained us.

On our return to Kourata the correspondence between Theodore and Mr. Rassam began afresh. The letters, as a rule, contained nothing of importance, but the messages brought backwards and forwards were highly special, and had significant reference to the former captives, with whom Theodore was bent on having a reconciliation before their departure. Apprehensive that Theodore might get into a passion at the sight of them, Mr. Rassam endeavoured: by all means to avoid a meeting he so much dreaded; and, at last, his Majesty seemed to have been convinced by his friend's reasonings, and to all appearance gave in to him. Some of the former captives were naturally anxious, and would have much preferred the risk of having to bear a few harsh words rather than excite Theodore's suspicions. It was too late. He had already made up his mind to detain us forcibly, and at the time he pretended to agree not to see the former captives, he was all the while, building a fence for their reception.

Mr. Rassam, to divert the Emperor's mind, proposed to him to institute an order to be called the "Cross of Christ and Solomon's Seal;" the rules and regulations were drawn out, one of the workmen made a model of the badges according to Mr. Rassam's direction, his Majesty approved of them, and nine were ordered—three of the first, three of the second, three of the third orders. Mr. Rassam, together with Ras Engeddah and Prince Meshisha, were to be made knights of the first order; the English officers of the mission were to be second class; as for the third, I do not know for whom they were destined, unless for such as Bappo, his butler.

Quite unaware of all that was going on behind the scenes, we fancied that we had nothing more to fear, and that all obstacles had been cleverly removed; we were building castles in the air—seeing in imagination dear friendly faces once more, and, thinking we were homeward bound, we laughed at the scorching heat of the Soudan's hottest months: when suddenly all our plans, hopes, and expectations were cruelly crushed.

CHAPTER IX

On the 13th of April we made our third experiment of the bulrush boats, as the Emperor desired once more to see his dear friends before they left. The European workmen of Gaffat accompanied us. All the Magdala and Gaffat prisoners started the same day, but by another route; the whole party was to rendezvous at Tankal, near the north-west extremity of the lake, where the luggage was also to be conveyed by boats.

On our arrival at Zagé, we were received with the usual marks of respect. Ras Engeddah and several high officers came to meet us on the beach, and richly harnessed mules were provided for us from the royal stables. We dismounted at the entrance of his Majesty's inclosure, and were conducted at once to the large audience-hall, erected quite close to the Emperor's private fence. On entering, we were surprised to see the large hall lined on both sides by Abyssinian officers in their gala dress. The throne had been placed at the extremity of the hall, but was empty, and the large circular space around it was filled with the highest officers of the realm. We had only advanced a few stages, preceded by Ras Engeddah, when he bowed and kissed the ground, we thought out of respect for the throne; but it was the signal for an act of base treachery. No sooner had the Ras prostrated himself, than nine men, posted for the purpose, rushed upon each of us, and in less time than I can express it our swords, belts, and caps were cast to the ground, our uniforms torn, and the officers of the English mission, seized by the arm and neck, were dragged, to the upper part of the hall, degraded and reviled before the whole of Theodore's courtiers and grandees!

We were allowed to sit down, our captors sitting next to us. The Emperor did not appear, but questions were brought to us by the Ras Engeddah, Cantiba Hailo (the Emperor's adopted father), Samuel, and the European workmen. Some of the questions asked by his Majesty were, to say the least, childish: "Where are the prisoners? Why have you not brought them to me? You had no right to send them without my permission. I wished you to reconcile me with them. I intended also to give to those who had no mule a mule, and to those who had no money some money for the road. Why have you given them fire-arms? Did you not come with a friendly letter from the

Queen of England? Why have you sent letters to the coast?" and such like rubbish.

Many of the highest officers several times expressed openly their approval of our answers—a rare proceeding in an Abyssinian Court. They evidently did not like, nor could they justify, the treacherous conduct of their master. Between the questions, a paper was partially read, referring to his Majesty's pedigree. As it had nothing to do with, our alleged offences, I could not understand its object, except that it was a certain weakness of this *parvenu* to glory in his supposed ancestors. His Majesty's last message was: "I have sent for your brethren, and when they arrive, I will see what I shall do."

The assembly having been dismissed, we waited a little while, whilst a tent was pitched for us near the Emperor's inclosure. At the time we were undergoing our trial, all the luggage we had brought with us was personally examined by his Majesty. All arms, money, papers, knives, &c., were confiscated; the remainder being sent to us after we had been escorted to the tent; We had hardly entered our new abode, and had not yet recovered from our surprise at the turn the Abyssinian *imbroglio* had just taken, when cows and bread in abundance were sent to us by Theodore a strange contrast to his recent dealings.

At about the same hour which witnessed this reverse in our fortunes, the released captives were also destined to meet with a fearful disappointment. Their fate was even worse than ours. After about two hours' ride they came to a village, and were resting under the shade of a few trees, until their tents should be pitched, when they were called for, and told to enter the house of the chief of the village. As soon as they were all collected, a number of soldiers entered, and the chief of the escort, showing them a letter, asked them if it was his Majesty's seal. On their replying in the affirmative, they were told to sit down. They were rather perplexed, but imagined that perhaps his Majesty had sent them a letter to bid them farewell, and that they were allowed to sit down as they were tired. However, their conjectures were soon set at rest. On a signal given by the chief of the escort, they were seized by the soldiers who lined the room. The letter from Theodore was then read to them. It was addressed to the chief of the escort, and ran thus:—"In the name of the Father, the Son, and the Holy Ghost, to Bitwaddad Tadla. By the power of God, we, Theodore, the king of kings, are well. We are angry with our friends, and with the Europeans, who say, 'We are going to our country,' and we are not yet reconciled. Until we consult as to what we shall do, seize them; but do not make them uncomfortable or afraid, and do not hurt them."

In the evening they were chained two by two, their servants were watched, and but two allowed to each individual to prepare his food; the following morning they were taken to Kourata. There they heard of our arrest, and even reports to the effect that we had been killed. The wives of the Gaffat people treated them very kindly: they themselves were in great anguish, as they were quite ignorant of the fate of their relatives. On the morning of the 15th they were taken over by boat to Zagé. On their arrival they were received by guards, who conducted them to a fenced space; mules had been brought for Captain Cameron, Mrs. Rosenthal, and Mrs. Flad, and shortly afterwards the Emperor sent them cows, sheep, bread, &c., in abundance.

The three days we spent in the small tent at Zagé were days of great anxiety. We had until then seen but the good side, the amiable mood of our host, and we were not as yet accustomed to his sudden bursts of temper, to his violence and treachery. As soon as our luggage was returned, we destroyed every letter, paper, note, diary, in our possession, and repeatedly questioned Samuel as to our future prospects. On the morning of the second day Theodore sent us his compliments, and told us that as soon as the captives arrived, everything would be all right. We sent him some shirts that had been made for him during our stay at Kourata; he received them, but declined the soap that accompanied them, as, he said, we should require it for the road. In the afternoon we watched him through the links of the tent, whilst he was sitting for hours on a raised platform in front of his inclosure. He appeared calm, and remained, for a long time, in conversation with his favourite, Ras Engeddah, who stood below.

We were guarded night and day, and could not move a few steps outside the tent without being followed by a soldier; at night, if we had to go out, we were told to carry a lantern with us. Our guards were all old confidential chiefs of the Emperor, men of rank and position, who executed their orders, but did not abuse their position to make us feel still more our disgrace. On the evening of the 15th a small farce was played that amused me at the time. I was going out a short distance, a servant carrying a lantern before me. We had only advanced a few steps when a soldier roughly seized my servant; immediately the officer on guard ran up towards us, and pretending to be very indignant at the soldier's conduct, told him to let my servant go, and lifting up his stick, gave him a few strokes on the back, exclaiming, "Why do you stop him? These are not prisoners; they are the friends of the King." On turning round; I saw the chief and the soldier having a good laugh together. The following morning the reconciliation was to take place. Theodore desired to impress us with the idea that we might be still his friends, and that we had better give in to him with good grace, as the arrest of the 13th would prove to us that he could also treat us as enemies. His plan was not a bad one; at all events it succeeded.

On the 17th we received a message from his Majesty, telling us to go to him, as he desired to try before us the Europeans who had, he said, formerly insulted him. Theodore knows well how to make a display; and on this occasion he did his utmost to impress all, Europeans as well as natives, with an idea of his power and greatness. He was seated on an alga in the open air, in front of the audience-hall. All the great officers of state were stationed on his left hand in front; on his right were the Europeans, and around these more important individuals, the petty chiefs and soldiers formed an almost complete circle.

As soon as we approached, his Majesty rose and saluted us; received us, in short, as though we were still his honoured guests, and not the heralds from a great Power he had recently so grossly insulted. We were told to sit down. A few minutes of silence followed, and we saw advancing from the outer gate our countrymen guarded as criminals, and chained two by two. They were arranged in a line in front of his Majesty, who, after observing them for a few seconds, "kindly" inquired after their health, and how they had spent their time. The captives acknowledged these compliments by repeatedly kissing the ground before that incarnation of the Evil One, who all the time grinned in delight at the sight of the misery and humiliation of his victims. Captain Cameron's and Mr. Bardel's fetters were then opened, and they were told to come and sit down near us. All the other captives remained standing in the sun, and had to answer to the Emperor's questions. He was collected, and calm; only once, when addressing us, did he appear in any way excited.

He asked them, "Why did you wish to leave my country before you took leave of me?" They answered that they had only acted according to Mr. Rassam's orders, to whom they had been made over. He then said, "Why did you not ask Mr. Rassam to bring you to me, and be reconciled before you left?" and turning towards Mr. Rassam, said, "It is your fault. I told you to reconcile me with them; why did you not do so?" Mr. Rassam replied: that he had believed the written reconciliation that followed the trial of the charges he had sent against them to be sufficient. The Emperor then said to Mr. Rassam, "Bid I not tell you I wanted to give them mules and money, and you answered me that you had bought mules for them, and that you had money enough to take them to their country? Now, on your account, you see them in chains. From the day you told me that you desired to send them by another road I became suspicious, and imagined that you did so in order that you might say in your country that they were released through your cunning and power."

The former captives' supposed crimes are well known, and its the remainder of the trial was only a repetition of the one of Gondar, it would be a mere waste of time to speak of it here; suffice it to say that these unfortunate and injured men answered with all humility and meekness, and endeavoured by so doing to avert the wrath of the wretch in whose power they were.

The Emperor's pedigree was then read: from Adam to David all went on smoothly enough; from Solomon's supposed son Menilek to Socinius few names were given—perhaps they were patriarchs in their own way; but when it came to Theodore's father and mother the difficulty increased, indeed it became serious; many witnesses were brought forward to testify to their royal descent, and even the opinion of the puppet-Emperor Johannes was recorded in favour of Theodore's legal right to the throne of his ancestors.

We were then called forward, and the scene of the 18th enacted over, again. After we had been told to sit down, Theodore called his workmen before him, and asked them if he ought to get "kassa?" (meaning a reparation for what he had suffered at the hands of the Europeans). Some did not audibly reply; whilst others loudly proclaimed that "kassa was good." In conclusion, his Majesty said, addressing himself to us "Do you want to be my masters? You will remain with me; and wherever I go, you will go; wherever I stay, you will stay." On that we were dismissed to our tents, and Captain Cameron was allowed to accompany us. The other Europeans, still in chains, were sent to another part of the camp, where several weeks before a fence had been erected, no one knew why.

The following day we were again called before Theodore, but this time it was quite a private affair. The prisoners were first conducted to our tent, and released from their fetters. We were then called into his presence; the former captives followed us, and the Gaffat people shortly afterwards entered, and were told to sit at the Emperor's right. As soon as the released prisoners entered; they bowed their heads to the ground and begged for pardon. His Majesty told them to rise, and after informing them that they had never done anything wrong, and that they were his friends, bowed his head to the ground, and in his turn begged for pardon. He remained in that attitude until they had repeatedly told him, "For God's sake, we forgive you!" Captain Cameron then read aloud Dr. Beke's letter and the petition of the prisoners' relatives. The reconciliation effected, the Emperor dictated a letter for our Queen, and Mr. Flad was selected to convey it. We then all had our tents pitched in a large enclosure, fenced that very morning under his Majesty's supervision. We were once more all united; but this time all prisoners. Mr. Flad left; we expected that his mission would be unsuccessful, and that England, disgusted with so much treachery, would not condescend to treat further, but enforce her demands. The day Mr. Flad left, his wife accompanied the workmen, who were ordered back to Kourata; with them we had much less intercourse than before, as they were at all times timid, and very careful not to have many dealings with doubtful friends of the King.

Zagé was one of the principal towns of the formerly prosperous and populous district of Metsha, but when we came we saw nought but ruins; and had we not been told that the guicho and coffee-covered hill was only a few weeks before the abode of thousands, we could not have credited it; nor that the small circular patches, now green with grass and weeds, had been the homes of a thriving and industrious population.

A few days after the reconciliation—the very morning Flad left for England—his Majesty returned us our arms, and a portion of our money; he also presented us at the same time with silver-mounted shields, spears, and mules, and a few days later with horses. We saw him on several occasions: twice he came to see us in our tents; one day we went with him to assist at the trial of some guns made by his European workmen; once duck-shooting with him on the lake; another time to see him play the national game of goucks. He endeavoured to appear friendly, supplied us with abundant rations, and twice a day sent his compliments; he even fired a salute and gave a feast on our Queen's birthday. Nevertheless, we felt unhappy: our cage was gilt, but still a cage; and the experience we had had of the King's treachery made us constantly fear a recurrence of it. When we met him in Damot, and when we visited him before at Zagé, we had only seen the actor in his smiling mood; now all restraint was thrown off: women were flogged to death close to our tents, and soldiers laden with chains or beaten to death on the most trivial pretexts. The true character of the tyrant became daily more apparent, and we felt that our position was most dangerous and critical.

Theodore was still bent on building boats; seeing that everybody seemed reluctant to help him he went to work himself; he made an immense flat-bottomed bulrush boat of great thickness, and to propel it made two large wheels worked by hand: in fact he had invented a paddle steamer, only the locomotive agent was deficient. We saw it several times on the water; the wheels were rather high up and it required at least a hundred men on it to make them dip sufficiently. Strange to say he spent his time in that frivolous way and never took notice of a large rebel force not four miles from his camp.

Cholera had been making havoc in Tigré; we were not surprised, therefore, to hear that it had spread over other provinces, and that several cases had already broken out at Kourata. The King's camp was pitched in a very unhealthy situation, on a low, swampy ground; fevers, diarrhoea, and dysentery had prevailed to a great extent. Informed of the approach of cholera, his Majesty wisely decided upon moving his camp to the highlands of Begemder. Mrs. Rosenthal was at the time very unwell, and could not stand the journey by land; she was therefore allowed to proceed by water to Kourata, accompanied by her husband, myself, and Captain Cameron, also in delicate health. We started on the evening of the 31st of May, and reached Kourata early the next morning. A gale of wind was blowing at the time, and we had to make frequent stoppages on the lee of the land, as the heavy sea frequently threatened to swamp our frail boats. Without exaggeration, this last passage was in all respects the *ne plus ultra* of discomfort.

CHAPTER X

At Kourata a few empty houses were put at our disposal, and we went to work to make these dirty native dwellings inhabitable. It was rumoured that Theodore intended to spend the rainy season in the neighbourhood, and on the 4th he made a sudden visit; he was only accompanied by a few of his chiefs. He came and returned by water. Ras Engeddah arrived about an hour before him. I was advised to go and meet him on the beach; I therefore accompanied the Gaffat people, who also went to present him their respects. His Majesty, on seeing me, asked me how I was, if I liked the place, &c. No one ever knew why he came. I believe, to judge for himself if the cholera was raging there at the time or not, as he made many inquiries on the subject.

On the 6th of June Theodore left Zagé with his army; Mr. Rassam and the other prisoners accompanied him; all the heavy baggage had been sent by boat to Kourata. On the 9th, his Majesty encamped on a low promontory south of Kourata. Cholera had by this time broken out in the camp, and hundreds were dying daily. In the hope of improving the sanitary condition of the army, the Emperor moved his camp to some high ground a mile or so north of the town; but the epidemic continued to rage with great virulence both in the camp and in the town. The church was so completely choked up with dead bodies that no more could be admitted, and the adjoining streets offered the sad sight of countless corpses, surrounded by the sorrowful relatives, awaiting for days and nights the hallowed grave in the now crowded cemetery. Small-pox and typhus fever also made their appearance, and claimed the victims cholera had spared.

On the 12th June we received orders to join the camp, as Theodore intended to leave on the following day for the higher and more healthy province of Begemder. On the 13th, at early morning, the camp was struck, and we encamped in the evening on the banks of the Gumaré, a tributary of the Nile. The next day the march was resumed. We had been more or less ascending since our departure from Kourata, and Outoo (a beautiful plateau, our halting-place of the 14th) must have been several thousand feet higher than the lake; nevertheless, cholera, small-pox, and typhus fever continued unabated. His Majesty inquired what was usually done in our country under similar circumstances. We advised him to proceed at once to the higher plateau of Begemder, to leave his sick at some distance from

Debra Tabor, to break up as far as possible his army, and distribute it over the whole province, selecting a few healthy and isolated localities where every fresh case that broke out should be sent. He acted upon this advice, and before long had the satisfaction of seeing the several epidemics lose their virulence, and, before many weeks, disappear entirely.

On the 16th we made a very long march. We started at about 6 A.M. and never halted once until we arrived at Debra Tabor at about 2 P.M. As soon as we reached the foot of the hill on which the Imperial houses arise, we received a message from his Majesty telling us not to dismount, and shortly afterwards he rode towards us, accompanied by a few of his bodyguard. We all started for Gaffat, the European station, about three miles east of Debra Tabor. *En route* we were overtaken by the most severe hailstorm I have ever seen or experienced; such was its violence, that Theodore was several times obliged to halt. The hail poured down in such thick masses, and the stones were of such an enormous size, that it was indeed quite painful to bear. At last we reached Gaffat, frozen and drenched to the skin; but the Emperor, seemingly quite unaffected by the recent shower, acted as our cicerone, and took us about the place, explaining to us the foundry, workshops, water-wheels, &c. A few planks were transformed into seats, and a fire lighted by his order, and we remained with him alone for more than three hours, discussing the laws and customs of England. Some carpets and cushions had been left behind at Debra Tabor, and he sent back Ras Engeddah to have them conveyed. As soon as he returned with the bearers, Theodore led the way up the hill to Gaffat, and with his own hands spread the carpets, and placed the throne in the house selected for Mr. Rassam. Other houses were distributed to the other Europeans, after which his Majesty left.

On the 17th June the European workmen, who had remained behind at Kourata, arrived at Debra Tabor. We are not aware that they made any objection to our occupying their houses, but the Emperor perceived by their demeanour that they were not pleased; he therefore accompanied them to Gaffat, and in a few hours had the foundry, by means of shamas, gabis, and carpets, transformed into a very decent abode. The throne was also conveyed there, and when all was ready we were called. His Majesty, after apologizing for the accommodation he was obliged to give us for a few days, returned to Debra Tabor, promising that the next day he would see for a more suitable dwelling for his guests. Accordingly, the following morning he arrived, and had several native houses on a small hill opposite Gaffat cleared out for our reception. As Mr. Rassam's house was rather small, that gentleman took advantage of the circumstance to request that the Emperor would withdraw the honour of placing the throne in his room. His Majesty acquiesced, but had the place well carpeted, and the walls and ceiling lined with white cloth. After all these daily changes we thought that we were settled for the rainy season. Cholera and typhus fever had made their appearance at Gaffat, and from morning to night I was in constant attendance on the sick. One of my patients, the wife of one of the Europeans, greatly occupied my time: she had first been attacked with cholera, and was afterwards laid for many days at death's door with typhus fever.

On the morning of the 25th of June we received a message from the Emperor, to the effect that Mr. Rassam, his companions, the priests, and any one he would like to take with him, should repair to Debra Tabor, to be present at a political trial. The European workmen, Cantiba, Hailo, and Samuel accompanied us. Arrived at Debra Tabor, we were surprised at not being received with the usual salutations, and instead of being at once conducted to the presence of Theodore, we were ushered into a black tent pitched in the King's inclosure. We surmised that the political trial concerned ourselves. We had been seated but a few minutes, when the European workmen were sent for by his Majesty. After a while they returned, with Cantiba Hailo, Samuel, and an Afa Negus (mouth of the King), who delivered the Imperial messages.

The first and most important was, "I have received a letter from Jerusalem, in which I am told that the Turks are making railways in the Soudan, to attack my country conjointly with the English and French." The second message was much to the same effect, only adding that as Mr. Rassam must have seen the railway in construction, he ought to have informed his Majesty of it. The third question was, "Is it not true that the Egyptian railway was built by the English?" Fourthly, "Did he not give a letter to Consul Cameron for him to deliver to the Queen of England, and did not the Consul return without an answer? Did not Mr. Rosenthal say that the English Government had laughed at his letter?" Altogether; there were some seven or eight questions, but the others were insignificant, and I do not remember them. A few days before a Greek priest had arrived from the coast with a letter for his Majesty: Whether these statements were contained in the missive; or were merely a pretext invented by Theodore himself, to give a reason for the ill treatment he intended to inflict upon his innocent guests, it is impossible to say. The concluding message was, "You must remain here; your arms his Majesty no longer trusts in your hands, but your property will be sent to you."

Mr. Rosenthal obtained permission to return to Gaffat to see his wife, and I was granted leave to accompany Samuel, as Mrs. Waldmeier was that day in a very critical state. Mr. Rassam and the other Europeans remained in the tent. Mr. Waldmeier, on account of his wife's serious illness, had remained at Gaffat, and he was much startled and grieved when he heard of our new misfortune; especially as it would deprive his wife of medical attendance at a time her life was despaired of. He begged me to remain near her for an hour, whilst he would gallop to Debra Tabor to entreat his Majesty to let me remain with him until his wife should be out of danger. Mrs. Waldmeier is a daughter of the late Mr. Bell, who was held in great esteem and affection by the Emperor. Not only did Theodore at once grant Waldmeier's request, but added, that if Mr. Rassam had no objection, he would allow me to remain at Gaffat, as sickness was prevailing there, during the expedition he intended to make. As I was much reduced by chronic diarrhoea and overexertion, I was much pleased at the prospect of remaining at Gaffat, instead of campaigning during the rains. Mr. Rassam himself on the following day requested his Majesty to allow me and some of our companions to remain for the rainy season at Gaffat. In my case and in Mr. Rosenthal's, permission was granted, but was refused to all the others.

Every day we heard that orders had been issued for the camp to be struck, but his Majesty did not leave. He daily inquired after Mrs. Waldmeier, and sent me his compliments. He visited Gaffat twice during the few days I was there, and on each occasion sent for me and received me courteously. Mr. Rassam and the other Europeans were allowed to come to Gaffat and spend the day with us; and although now and then the word "Magdala" was whispered, still it seemed as if the storm had blown over, and we hoped before long to be all again united at Gaffat, and there in peace spend the rainy season. On the 3rd of July an officer brought me the Imperial compliments, and stated that his Majesty was coming to inspect the works, and that I might present myself before him. I went at once to the foundry, and on the road I met two of the Gaffat workmen also proceeding there. A little incident then occurred, which was followed by serious consequences. We met the Emperor near the foundry, riding ahead of his escort; he asked us how we were, and we all lowed and took off our hats. As he passed, along, the two Europeans with whom I walked, covered themselves; but aware how touchy his Majesty, was on all points of etiquette, I kept my head uncovered, though the sun was hot and fierce. Arrived at the foundry, the Emperor again greeted me cordially; examined for a few minutes the drawing of a gun his workmen proposed to cast for him, and then left, all of us following. In the courtyard he passed close to Mr. Rosenthal, who did not bow, as Theodore took no notice of him.

As the Emperor issued from the foundry fence a poor old beggar asked for alms, saying, "My lords (gaitotsh) the Europeans have always been kind to me. Oh! my king, do you also relieve my distress!" On hearing the expression "lord" applied to his workmen, he got into a fearful passion. "How dare you call any one 'lord' but myself. Beat him, beat him, by my death!" Two of the executioners at once rushed upon the beggar, and began beating him with their long sticks, Theodore all the while exclaiming, "Beat him, beat him, by my death!" The poor old cripple, at first in heartrending terms, implored for mercy; but his voice grew fainter and fainter, and in a few minutes more there lay his corpse, that none dare remove or pray for. The laughing hyenas that night caroused undisturbed on his abandoned remains.

Theodore's rage was by no means abated by this act of cruelty; he advanced a few steps, then stopped, turned, his lance in rest, looking around, the very image of ungovernable fury. His eyes fell upon Mr. Rosenthal. "Seize him!" cried he; Immediately several soldiers rushed forward to obey the imperial command. "Seize the man they call a Hakeem." Instantly a dozen ruffians pounced upon me, and I was held fast by the arms, coat, trousers—by every place that afforded a grip. He then addressed himself to Mr. Rosenthal. "You donkey, why did you call me the son of a poor woman? Why did you abase me?" Mr. Rosenthal said, "If I have offended your Majesty, I beg for pardon." All the while the Emperor was shaking his lance in a threatening manner, and every minute I expected that he would throw it; I feared that, blind with rage, he would not be able to control himself; and I well knew that if once he began to give vent to his passions, my fate was also sealed.

Fortunately for us both, Theodore turned towards his European workmen and abused them in no measured terms. "You slaves! Have I not bought you with money? Who are you that you dare call yourselves 'lords?' Take care!" Then addressing the two I had met on the road, he said, "You are proud, are you? Slaves! Women! Rotten donkeys! you cover your heads, in my presence! Did you not see me? Did not the Hakeem keep his head uncovered? Poor men that I have made rich!" He then turned towards me, and seeing me held by a dozen soldiers, he cried out, "Let him go; bring him before me." All drew back except one, who conducted me to within a few feet from the Emperor. He then asked me, "Do you know Arabic?" Though I understand a little of that language, I thought it more prudent, under the circumstances, to reply in the negative. He then told Mr. Schimper to translate what he was going to say. "You, Hakeem, are my friend. I have nothing against you; but others have abused me, and you must come up with me to witness their trial." Then ordering Cantiba Hailo to give me his mule, he mounted, I and Mr. Rosenthal following; the latter on foot, dragged the whole way by the soldiers who had first seized him.

As soon as we reached Debra Tabor, the Emperor sent word to Mr. Rassam to come out with the other Europeans, as he had something to tell him. Theodore sat upon a rock, about twenty yards in front of us; between him and ourselves stood a few of his high officers, and behind us a deep line of soldiers. He was still angry, breaking the edges of the rock with the butt-end of his lance, and spitting constantly between his words. He at once addressed himself to the Rev. Mr. Stern, and asked him, "Was it as a Christian, a heathen, or a Jew, that you abused me? Tell me where you find in the Bible that a Christian ought to abuse? When you wrote your book, by whose authority did you do it? Those who abused me to you, were they my enemies or yours? Who was it told you evil things against me?" &c. He afterwards said to Mr. Rassam, "You, also, have, abused me." "I?" replied Mr. Rassam. "Yes, you; in four instances. First, you read Mr. Stern's book, wherein I am abused; secondly, you did not reconcile me with the prisoners, but wanted to send them out of the country; thirdly, your Government allows the Turks to keep Jerusalem—it is my inheritance. The fourth I have forgotten." He then asked Mr. Rassam whether he knew or not that Jerusalem belonged to him, and that the Abyssinian convent there had been seized by the Turks? As the descendant of Constantine and Alexander the Great, India and Arabia belonged to him. He put many foolish questions of the same kind. At last he said to Samuel, who was interpreting, "What have you to say if I chain your friends?" "Nothing," replied Samuel; "are you not the master?" Chains had been brought, but the answer somewhat pacified him. He then addressed one of his chiefs, saying, "Can you watch these people in the tent?" The other, who knew his answer, replied, "Your Majesty, the house would be better." On that he gave orders for our baggage to be conveyed from the black tent to a house contiguous to his own, and we were told to go.

The house assigned to us was formerly used as a godown: it was built of stone, with a large verandah all around, and closed by a single small door, with no window or other aperture. It was only when several lighted candles had been brought that we could find our way into the dark central room, and it only required numbers to react the fearful drama of the Calcutta Black Hole. Some soldiers carried in our bedding, and a dozen guards sat near us, holding lighted candles in their hands. The Emperor sent us several messages. Mr. Rassam took advantage of this circumstance to complain bitterly of the unfair treatment inflicted upon us. He said, "Tell his Majesty that I have done my best to bring on a good understanding between my country and him; but when to-day's work is known, whatever the consequences may be, let him not throw the blame upon me." Theodore sent back word, "If I treat you well or not; it is the same; my enemies will always say that I have ill-treated you, so it does not matter."

A little later we were rather startled by a message from his Majesty, informing us that he could not rest before comforting his friend, and that he would come and see us. Though we did our best to dissuade him from such a step, he soon afterwards came; accompanied by some slaves carrying arrack and tej. He said, "Even my wife told me not to go out, but I could not leave you in grief, so I have come to drink with you." On that he had arrack and tej presented to all of us, himself setting the example.

He was calm, and rather serious, though he made great efforts to appear gay. He must have remained at least an hour; conversing on different topics, the Pope of Rome being the principal one discussed. Amongst other things: he said, "My father was mad, and though people often say that I am mad also; I never would believe it; but now I know it is true." Mr. Rassam answered, "Pray do not say such a thing." His Majesty replied, "Yes, yes, I am mad," Shortly before leaving, he said, "Do not look at my face or take heed of my words when I speak to you before my people, but look at my heart: I have an object." As he returned, he gave orders to the guards to withdraw outside, and not to inconvenience us. Though we have seen him since then once or twice, at a distance, it is the last time we conversed with him.

The two days we spent in the black hole at Debra Tabor, all huddled up together, obliged to have lighted candles day and night, and in anxious uncertainty about our future fate, were really days of mental torture and physical discomfort. We hailed with joy the announcement that we were going to move; any alternative was preferable to our position—be it rain in a worn-out tent, be it chains in one of the ambas—anything was better than close confinement, deprived of all comforts, even of the cheering light of day.

At noon on the 5th of July, we were informed that his Majesty had already left, and that our escort was in attendance. All were delighted at the prospect of seeing fresh air and green fields and bright sun. We did not require a second command, and did not even give a second thought to the journey, rain, mud, and such like inconveniences. On that day we made but a short stage, and encamped on a large plain called Janmêda, a few miles south of Gaffat. Early morning the following day the army moved off, but we waited in the rear at least three hours before the order came for us to start. Theodore, seated on a rock, had allowed the whole force, camp-followers included, to go on in advance, and like us, unprotected from the pouring rain, and seemingly in deep thought, examined the different corps as they passed before him. We were now strictly watched; several chiefs with their men guarded us day and night, a detachment marched ahead of us, another in the rear, and a strong party never lost sight of us.

We halted that afternoon on a large plain near a small eminence called Kulgualiko, on which the Imperial tents were pitched. The following day, the same mode of departure was adopted, and after travelling all night we halted at a place called Aibankab, at the foot of Mount Guna, the highest peak in Begemder, often covered during the rainy season with frozen hail.

We remained the 8th at Aibankab. In the afternoon his Majesty told us to ascend the hill on which his tents were pitched, to see the snow-covered summit of the Guna, as from our position below we could not obtain a good view of it. A few polite messages passed between us, but we did not see him.

Early on the 9th, Samuel, our balderaba, was sent for. He stayed away a long time, and on his return informed us that we were to go on in advance, that our heavy baggage would be sent after us, and that we must keep with us a few light articles which the soldiers of our escort and our mules could carry. Several of the officers of the Imperial household, to whom we had shown some kindness, came to bid us good-by, all looking very sad — one with tears in his eyes. Though no one informed us of our destination, we all surmised that Magdala and chains were our lot.

Bitwaddad Tadla, with the men under his command, now took charge of us. We soon perceived that we were more strictly guarded than ever; one or two mounted soldiers had special charge of each separate individual of our party, flogging the mules if they did not go fast enough, or causing those in front to wait until the less well mounted could come up. We made a very long march on that day, from 9 A.M. to 4 P.M., without a halt. The soldiers, who carried a few parcels, came on shortly after us, but the baggage mules only arrived at sunset, and dead tired. As the small rowties we had brought with us had not arrived, the head of the guard had a house in the village of Argabea cleared out for our reception. No food being forthcoming, we killed a sheep and broiled it over the fire, Abyssinian fashion; hungry and tired, we thought it the most exquisite meal we had ever made.

At sunrise, the following morning, our guards told us to get ready, and soon after we were in the saddle. Our route lay E.S.E. Any slight doubts we might still have had about our destination now vanished; the former prisoners knew too well the road to Magdala to have any misgivings on the subject. On the previous day the road was a gradual ascent over a well-cultivated and populous district; but on the 10th, the country bore a wild aspect, few villages were to be seen, and but few dark tufts of cedars graced the summit of the distant hills, proclaiming the presence of a church. The scenery was grand, and for the artist no doubt full of attractions; but for Europeans, driven like cattle by semi-barbarians, the precipitous descents and steep acclivities had certainly no charms. After a few hours' march, we arrived at an almost perpendicular precipice (almost 1,500 feet in height, and not more than a quarter of a mile in breadth), that we had both to descend and ascend in order to reach the next plateau. Another couple of hours' march brought us to the gate's of Begemder. In front of us arose the plateau of Dahonte, only about a couple of miles distant, but we had to ascend a more abrupt precipice than the one we had just passed and climb again a steeper ascent before we could reach it. The valley of the Jiddah, a tributary of the Nile, was between us and our halting-place—a stiff march, as the silver thread we viewed from the narrow passage between the basaltic columns of the Eastern Begemder ridge was 3,000 feet below us. Tired and worn out, at last; we accomplished our task.

We halted for the night at a place called Magat, on the first terrace of the Dahonte plateau, about 500 feet from the summit. Our small tent arrived in time, our servants had carried with them a few provisions, and we managed to make a frugal meal; but only one or two of the best baggage mules made their appearance, so that we had to lie on the bare ground—those best off on leathern skins. It was five days after our arrival at Magdala before a small portion of our luggage arrived, and until then we could not even change our clothes, and had nothing to protect ourselves against the cold nights of the rainy season. Early on the morning of the 11th we continued our ascent, and soon reached the splendid plateau of Dahonte. This small province is but a large circular plain about twelve miles in diameter, covered at the time of our journey, with fields in all stages of cultivation, and with beautiful green meadows, where grazed thousands of heads of cattle, and where mules, horses, and innumerable flocks everywhere meet the eye. The whole circumference of this plain is dotted with small rounded hillocks, and from their base to the summit numerous well-built villages arise. Dahonte is certainly the most fertile and picturesque district I have seen in Abyssinia.

By noon we reached the eastern extremity of the plateau, and there before us again appeared one of those awful chasms we had encountered twice on our road since leaving Debra Tabor. We did not at all rejoice at the idea of having to descend, then wade through the wide and rapid Bechelo, and again climb the opposite precipice—a perfect wall—to complete our day's work. Fortunately, our mules were so tired that the chief of our guard halted, for the night half way down the descent, at one of the villages that are perched on the several terraces of this basaltic mountain. At dawn on the 12th we continued our descent, crossed the Bechelo, and ascended to the opposite plateau of Watat, where we arrived at eleven A.M. There we made a slight halt and partook of a frugal breakfast, sent by the chief of Magdala to Bitwaddad Tadla, who kindly shared it with us.

From Watat to Magdala the road is an inclined plain, constantly but gradually shelving upwards towards the high plateau of the Wallo country—the end of our journey, as Magdala is on its border. The amba, with a few isolated mountains, all perpendicular and crowned with walls of basalt, seem like miniatures of the large expanses of Dahonte and Wallo—small particles detached from the neighbouring gigantic masses.

The road on nearing Magdala is more abrupt; one or two conical hills have to be crossed before the amba itself is reached. Magdala is formed of two cones, separated by a small plateau named Islamgee, a few hundred feet lower than the two peaks it divides. The northern peak is the higher of the two, but on account of the absence of water and the small space it affords, it is not inhabited; and to Magdala alone belonged the privilege of being Theodore's most famous fortress, his treasury, and his gaol.

From Islamgee the ascent is steeper, but we were able to ride on our mules up to the second door; a feat we could not perform whilst ascending from the Bechelo and Jiddah, as we had not only to descend almost all the way on foot, but had frequently to dismount at the ascent, and climb on all-fours, leaving the mules to find their way as best they could. The distance from Watat to Magdala is generally accomplished in five hours, but we were nearly seven, as we had to make frequent halts, and messengers came to and fro from the Amba. Many of the chiefs of the mountain came out to meet Bitwaddad Tadla.

At Islamgee another long halt was made, I suppose while our *lettre de cachet* was examined by the chiefs in council. At last, one by one, counted like sheep, we passed the doors, and were taken to a large open space in front of the King's house. There we were met by the Ras (Head of the mountain) and the six superior chiefs, who join with him in council on every important occasion. As soon as they had greeted Bitwaddad Tadla they retired a few yards, and consulted with him and Samuel. After a few minutes, Samuel told us to come on; and, accompanied by the chiefs, escorted by their followers, we were taken to a house near the Imperial fence. A fire was lighted. To fatigued and dejected men the prospect of a roof, after so many days passed in the rain, cheered us even in our misery, and when the chiefs had retired, leaving a guard at the door, we soon forgot—talking, smoking, or sleeping near the fire—that we were the innocent victims of base treachery. Two houses had been allowed to our party. At first we all slept in one of them, the other being made over to the servants, and used as a kitchen.

CHAPTER XI

It was already dark when we had arrived the evening before. Our first thought in the morning was to examine our new abode. It consisted of two circular huts, surrounded by a strong thorny fence, adjoining the Emperor's Enclosure. The largest hut was in a bad state of repair; and as the roof, instead of being supported by a central pole, had about a dozen of lateral ones forming as many separate divisions, we made it over to our servants and to our balderaba Samuel. The one we kept for ourselves had been built by Ras Hailo, at one time a great favourite of Theodore, but who had unfortunately fallen under his displeasure. Ras Hailo was not chained during the time he remained in that house: for a time he was even "pardoned," and made chief of the mountain. But Theodore, after a while, again deprived him of his command and confidence, and sent him to the common gaol, chained like the other prisoners. For an Abyssinian house it was well built; the roof was almost the best I saw in the country, being made with small bamboos closely arranged and bound with rings of the same material. After Ras Hailo had been sent to the gaol, his house had been made over to the favourite of the day, Ras Engeddah; but, according to custom, Theodore took it away from him to lodge his English guests.

For us it was small: we were eight, and the place could not contain easily more than four. The evenings and nights were bitterly cold, and the fire occupying the centre of the room, some of us had to lay half the body in a recess that leaked, and half in the room. At first we felt our position bitterly. The rainy season had set in, and hailstorms occurred almost every day. Many of us (Prideaux and myself amongst them) had not even a change of clothes, no bedding, nor anything to cover ourselves with during the long cold damp nights; and I always shall remember with feelings of gratitude the Samaritan act of Samuel, who, pitying me, kindly lent me one of his shamas.

We had hardly any money, and we had not the remotest idea from whence we could obtain any. Though there was some talk of rations being supplied from the Imperial stores, the former captives only laughed at the idea; they knew, from bitter experience, that prisoners on Amba Magdala "were expected to give, but never to receive." The event proved that their surmises were right: we never received anything from the man who on all occasions loudly proclaimed himself our friend but a small jar of tej, that for some months was daily sent to Samuel: (I believe all the time it was intended for him; at all events, he and his friends drank it;) and on great feast days a couple of lean, hungry-looking cows, of which, I am delighted to say, I declined a share.

To the European, accustomed to find at his door every necessary of life, the fact that not a shop exists throughout the breadth and width of Abyssinia may appear strange; but still it is so. We had, therefore, to be our own butchers and bakers, and as for what is called grocery stores, we had simply to dispense with them. Our food was abominably bad; the sheep we purchased were little better than London cats; and as no flour-mill is to be found in Abyssinia, far less any bakers, we were obliged to purchase the grain, beat it to remove the chaff, and grind it between two stones—not the flat grinding-stones of Egypt or India, but on a small curved piece of rock, where the grain is reduced to flour by means of a large hard kind of pebble held in the hand. It was brown bread with a vengeance. On the mountain we might buy eggs and fowls; but as the first were generally bad when sold to us, we soon got disgusted with them; and though we put up with the fowls as a change of diet, their toughness and leanness would have made them rejected everywhere else. Being the rainy reason, we had great difficulty in purchasing a little honey. Wild coffee was now and then obtainable; but it made, in the absence of sugar, and with or without smoky milk, such a bitter, nauseous compound, that, after a while, I and others preferred doing without it. Such was then the amount of "luxuries" we had to depend on during our long captivity,—coarse, vitreous-looking, badly-baked bread; the ever-returning dish of skinny, tough mutton, the veteran cock, smoked butter, and bitter coffee. Tea, sugar, wine, fish, vegetables, &c., were not, either for love or money, to be obtained anywhere. The coarseness and uniformity of our food, however, was as nothing compared with our dread of being starved to death; for even the few and inferior articles I have mentioned would fail us when our money was expended.

I was very badly off for clothes. Before leaving Debra Tabor, I was told to leave everything behind in the charge of the Gaffat people, and only take with me the few things I required for the road. My only pair of shoes, what from rain, sun, and climbing, had become so thoroughly worn-out, and so hard, as to bring on a wound that took months to heal, so that until the arrival of one of my servants from the coast, many months afterwards, I had to walk, or rather crawl, about on naked feet.

Life in common among men of different tastes and habits is, indeed, dreadful. There we were, eight Europeans, all huddled up in the same small place, a waiting-room, a dining-room, a dormitory; most of us entire strangers before, and only united by one bond—common misfortune. Adversity is but little fitted to improve the temper: on the contrary, it breaks down all social habits; the more so if education and birth do not enable the sufferer to contend against the greatest difficulties. We feared above all things that familiarity which creeps on so naturally between men of totally different social positions, and leads to harsh words and contempt. We had to live on terms of equality with one of the former servants of Captain Cameron; we had to be quiet if some remained talking part of the night, and put up silently with the defects of others in the hope that our own might meet with the same leniency.

A party of soldiers, varying from fifteen to twenty, came every evening a little before dusk, and pitched a small black tent almost opposite our door. As it frequently rained at night, the greater number of the soldiers remained in the tent; only two or three, supposed to be watching, went to sleep under the shelter of a projecting part of the roof. They did not disturb us, and, if we went out after dark, they merely watched where we went, but did not follow. In the daytime we had four guards, two taking it in turn to watch the gate of our inclosure. These men were never changed during all the time of our stay; but we had not much reason to be satisfied with the selection made, as, with one exception, our day guards were fearful rascals and dangerous spies.

We had already spent three days at Magdala, and were beginning to hope that our punishment would be limited to "simple imprisonment," when about noon on the 16th we perceived the chief, accompanied by a large escort, coming in the direction of our prison. Samuel was sent for, and a long consultation took place between him and the chief outside the gate. We were yet in ignorance of what was going on, and felt rather uncomfortable when Samuel returned to us with a serious countenance, and told us that we must all go into the room, as the chief had a "little business" with us. We obeyed, and shortly afterwards the Ras (Head of the mountain), the five members of council, and about eight or ten more presented themselves. The Ras and the principal chiefs, all armed to the teeth, squeezed themselves into the room, the others remaining outside. The ordinary Abyssinian conversation—that is to say, a great deal of talking about religion, looking pious, taking God's and the King's name in vain every minute—opened the proceedings. I was sitting near the door, and as the conversation did not interest me much, I was looking at the motley crowd outside, when all at once I perceived that two or three men were carrying large bundles of chains. I pointed them out to Mr. Rassam, and asked him if he believed they intended them for us; he spoke to Samuel in Arabic on the subject, and the affirmative answer he received revealed to us the subject of the long consultation that had taken place outside.

The Ras now dropped the desultory conversation he had been holding since his arrival, and in quiet terms informed us that it was the custom of the mountain to chain every prisoner sent there; that he had received no instructions from the Emperor, and would at once despatch a messenger to inform him that he had put us in irons, and he had no doubt that before long his master would send orders for our fetters to be removed, but that in the meanwhile we must submit to the rules of the amba; he added that in our case it was with regret that he felt himself obliged to enforce them. The poor fellow really meant well; he was kind-hearted and, for an Abyssinian, had gentlemanly manners; he had some hope that Theodore might have by that time regretted the unnecessary and cruel order, and would perhaps seize the opportunity he thus offered him and cancel it. I may as well add here that, not many months afterwards, the Ras was accused of being in correspondence with the king of Shoa; he was taken in irons to the camp, where he shortly afterwards died from the consequences of the many tortures inflicted upon him.

The chains were brought, and the real business of the day began; one after another we had to submit to the operation, the former captives being first served and favoured with the heaviest chains. At last my turn came. I was made to sit down on the ground, tuck up my trousers, and place my right leg on a large stone that had been brought for the purpose. One of the rings was then placed on my leg a couple of inches above the right ankle, and down came, upon the thick cold iron, a huge sledge-hammer: every stroke vibrated through the whole limb, and when the hammer fell not quite straight it pressed the iron ring against the bone, causing most acute pain. It took about ten minutes to fix on properly the first ring; it was beaten down until a finger could just be introduced between the ring and the flesh, and then the two pieces, where they overlapped one another, were hammered down until they perfectly joined. The operation was then performed on the left leg. I was always afraid of the blacksmith missing the iron and smashing my leg to pieces. All at once I felt as if the limb was being torn asunder; the ring had broken just when the operation was nearly completed. For the second time I had to submit to the hammering process, and this time the fetter was rivetted to the entire satisfaction of the smith and chief.

I was now told that I might rise and go to my seat; but that was no easy matter, and, having no practice in this, for me, quite new way of locomotion, I could hardly take the necessary three or four steps. Although I was in great bodily pain, and felt deeply the degradation we were subjected to, I would not give the officers of the man who was thus ill-treating us cause to believe that I cared in the least about it. On rising to my legs I lifted up my cap and shouted, to their great astonishment, "God save the Queen," and went on laughing and chatting as if I felt perfectly happy. As every detail of our life was reported to Theodore, and my contempt for his chains was public, he was at once informed of it: but he only mentioned the fact twenty-one months afterwards, when he alluded to it in conversation with Mr. Waldmeier, to whom he said that every one allowed themselves to be chained without saying a word; that even Mr. Rassam had smiled upon them; but that the doctor and Mr. Prideaux had looked at them with anger.

After the operation was over, and the witnesses of the scene had each favoured us with a "May God open thee," the messenger the chiefs were sending to Theodore (a fellow named Lib, a great spy, and confidant of the Emperor; the same who had brought our *lettres de cachet,*) was introduced to receive any message Mr. Rassam desired to convey to his Majesty. That gentleman, in quiet and courteous words, reproached his Majesty for his treachery, and cast upon him the onus of the consequences such unfair treatment would most likely bring upon him. Unfortunately Samuel, always timid, and at this time almost dead with fright, as he did not know whether chains were not in reserve for him also, declined to interpret, and simply sent the ordinary compliments instead.

When our gaolers had withdrawn, we looked at one another, and the sight was so ridiculous, so absurd, that for all our sorrow we could not help laughing heartily. The chains consisted of two heavy rings connected together by three small thick links, leaving just a span between one ring and the other; and these we wore for nearly twenty-one months! At first we could not walk at all; our legs were bruised and sore from the hammering on, and the iron pressing on the ankles was so painful that we were obliged to tie bandages under the chains during the daytime. At night I always took off the bandages, as the constant impediment to the circulation they occasioned, caused the feet to swell; yet at night we felt the weight and pressure even more than during the day: our legs seemed for a long time never to get rest; we could not move them about, and when in our sleep we turned from one side to the other, the links, by striking the bone of the leg, caused such acute pain as to awake us at once. Though after a time we got more accustomed to them, and could walk about our small inclosure with more ease, still every now and then we had to remain quiet for some days, as the legs got sore, and small ulcers appeared on the parts where the greatest pressure bore. Even since they have been removed, for months my legs were weaker than before, the ankles smaller, and the feet somewhat enlarged.

The evening we were put in chains we had to cut open our trousers as the only way of getting them off. During their former captivity at Magdala, Messrs. Cameron, Stern and others, either wore petticoats or native drawers, which they had been taught to pass between the leg and the chain. But we had no material at hand to make the first, and as for passing even the thinnest cambric through the rings in the swollen condition of the limb, that was quite out of the question. Necessity, it is said, is the mother of invention: at all events I invented the "Magdala trousers." On taking off mine that evening, I cut them near the outward seam, and collecting all the buttons I could obtain, had them sewed on, and button-holes made along the Beam as near to one another as my limited supply allowed. Some weeks afterwards I was able, with the assistance of a native, to pass through the rings calico drawers; and as my legs grew thinner, in time, I was able to put on trousers made of thin Abyssinian cotton cloth; and such is the force of habit and practice, that at last I could take off or put on my trousers as quickly almost as if my legs were free.

We had gone to bed early that evening, not knowing what to do, when we heard a discussion going on outside our hut between Samuel and the chief of the guard that night, named Mara, a descendant of some Armenian and a great worshipper of his Imperial master. Samuel at last came in and told us that he had endeavoured to persuade the officer not to disturb us, but that he insisted on examining our chains to see if they were all right. We declined at first to submit to the inspection, and only consented, in order to get rid of the fellow, to shake our chains under the shama with which we were covered, as he passed from one to another.

As we expected to be at least six months in Magdala—giving time for the news to reach England, and the troops to arrive that we felt certain would immediately be despatched to set us free and punish the despot— Mr. Rassam endeavoured, through Samuel, to obtain a few more huts for our accommodation. Samuel spoke to the Ras and to the other chiefs, and they agreed to give us a small hut and two godjos, (small huts, the roof formed by the ends of the twigs being tied together at the free extremity, and the whole covered with straw,) when they would have collected wood enough to make a new fence. In the meanwhile two of us, Pietro and Mr. Kerans, were induced to live in the kitchen, where they would have more room and leave more space for ourselves.

Our first thought on reaching Magdala was to communicate the intelligence to our friends and to Government; since we had been chained we knew that every hour lost was a day added to our discomfort and misery, and that we ought to lose no time in sending a trusty messenger to Massowah. It was always very difficult for us to write, but more so in the beginning, as we were afraid even of Samuel, afterwards so useful in all that concerned our messengers. All the country up to Lasta still recognized Theodore, and we were obliged to be very guarded in our expressions, in case the letter should fall into the hands of some of his chiefs and be forwarded to him. On the 18th, our packet was ready; but, strange to say, it was the only time our letter came to grief. We could only trust servants that had been some time with us,—at least, so we thought at the time,—and therefore selected an old servant of Cameron who had been formerly, on several occasions, employed as messenger. He was a good man, a first-rate walker, but very quarrelsome; and to spite his adversary was capable of anything. To accompany him through the rebel country we obtained a servant from a political prisoner, Dejatch Maret: they were to travel together and return with an answer from Mr. Munzinger. Soon after, leaving Magdala, the two began to quarrel, and on reaching the rebels' outposts, a question of precedence between them led to the discovery of our packet; both messengers were seized, tied with ropes for a few days, and when released, our man was told to go back, and the letters were burnt. Afterwards we made better arrangements: the messengers carried in their belts the letters which were of a dangerous nature; otherwise we sewed them up in leather, in the shape of the amulets and charms worn by the natives, or had them stitched between patches on old trousers, or near the seams. Those writing from the coast used the same precautions; and though we must have sent about forty messengers with letters during our captivity, without mentioning those employed elsewhere, they all, with the one exception I have mentioned, reached in safety.

Next came the question so vital to us, how to get money. It so happened that Theodore, about that time, gave a thousand dollars to each of his workmen. Many of them, judging from the political condition of the country that the Emperor's power would soon fall entirely, were desirous of sending their money out of the country, and as we were only too anxious to get some, the matter was easily arranged to our mutual satisfaction. We sent servants to Debra Tabor; and as the road was still safe, and we had, by suitable presents, made friends of the chiefs of the districts that lay in the way, the servants were not molested or plundered. They carried the dollars either in bags, on mules, laden at the same time with grain or flour which the Gaffat people now and then sent us, or tied in the long cotton sash that Abyssinians wear as a belt. Directions were also given to Mr. Munzinger to forward money to Metemma, from whence we could draw it by sending servants. It was only during the second year of our captivity that we experienced any serious difficulty on that score. The Emperor's power became more and more limited; rebels and thieves infested the roads; the route between Metemma and Magdala was closed; the Gaffat people had none to spare; and at one time it seemed as if it was perfectly impossible for messengers to reach us. Though for months we were rather hard up, what by employing servants of political prisoners, friends or relatives of the rebels, by using the influence of the Bishop, or through the protection of Wagshum Gobazé, money again found its way to Magdala, and relieved us from our apprehensions. Theodore knew indirectly that we sent servants to the coast, but as it is the custom to allow prisoners' servants to go to their masters' families to beg for them, he could not well forbid us; the more so as he never gave us anything. If messengers had fallen into his hands he would probably have plundered the money, but not injured them. As for letters it was quite a different affair: if those we wrote had by accident come into his possession, he would have made short work of the messenger, and most certainly of us also.

It might appear strange that the Abyssinians—a race of thieves—should have proved themselves so honest on these occasions, and not absconded with the couple of hundred dollars entrusted to them: a fortune for a poor servant. Though it would be ungrateful to run down these men, who exposed themselves to great perils, often travelled the whole distance from Massowah to Magdala at night, and who, I may say, saved us from starvation; still I believe that they acted more on the old adage that honesty is the best policy, than from any innate virtue. First, they were handsomely rewarded, well treated, and expected a further reward (which they very properly received) should fortune once more smile upon us; Secondly, all the great rebel chiefs befriended us, and we should have had but to communicate with them directly, or, better still, through the Bishop; for them to have at once seized the delinquent, deprived him of his ill-gotten wealth, and punished him severely. This they knew perfectly well.

Looking back, I cannot imagine how I got through the long, dreary days of idleness, always the same, for twenty-one months. Chains were nothing compared to the fearful want of occupation. Suppose we had kept a daily diary, the entries would have been generally as follows:—"Took a bath (a painful operation, as the chains, unsupported by the bandages, hurt fearfully); small boy helps to pass my trousers between the chains. To-day, being dry, we crawled up and down our fifteen yards' walk. Breakfast; felt happier that task over. Sick came for medicine. As I am doctor and apothecary, prescribed and made the medicine myself. Samuel, or some trusty native friend who knows that my tej is ripe, came for a glass or two. Go now and smoke a pipe with Cameron. Lay down and read McCulloch's *Commercial Dictionary*; very interesting book, but sends me to sleep. Afternoon, lay down and got up again; tried once more the *Commercial Dictionary*. Dinner (I wonder what age the cock we ate had reached); crawled about for, an hour between the huts; lay down, took Gadby's *Appendix*; but as I knew it by heart, even his curious descriptions have no more attraction. Small boy lighted the fire; the wood was green, the smoke fearful. Had a game of whist with Rassam and Prideaux. I do not suppose they would play with our dirty cards in a guard-room. Lost twenty points. Small boy took off the trousers. The guards were cursing us because they had to sleep outside in the rain. Bravo, Samuel, you are a friend indeed!"

This imaginary page I might repeat *ad infinitum*. As a change, sometimes we wrote to our friends, or received letters and some scraps of newspapers—delightful days; few and far between. On Sundays we had divine service; Mr. Stern, though sick and weary, always did his utmost to comfort and encourage us. Such was, as a rule, our daily life: it is true we had our exciting times, perhaps too much of it at the end; we had also, now and then, a few other occupations, such as building a new hut, making a small garden, settling a quarrel amongst the servants: details that will come in our narrative as we proceed. I mentioned that the chiefs had promised to enlarge our fence; they kept to their word. Four or five days after we had undergone the chaining operation, they made us another visit, consulted, discussed for a long time, and at last agreed to make a small break in the fence and inclose the three huts they had promised us. Samuel, who had the distribution of the new premises, gave the small house to Rassam, took one of the godjos for himself, and gave the third one to Prideaux and myself. Kerans and Pietro were still to remain in the kitchen, so that our first house was left to Messrs. Cameron, Stern, and Rosenthal.

On the 23rd July, 1866, Prideaux and myself entered our new abode: and, without exaggeration, if a dog were tied up in a similar shed in England I may say that the owner would be prosecuted by the Society for the Protection of Animals. As it was, we were only too happy to get it, and at once went to work—not to make it comfortable, that was quite out of the question, but—to try to keep out the rain.

CHAPTER XII

Amba Magdala, distant about 320 [Footnote: According to Mr. C. Markham.] miles from Zulla, and about 180 from Gondar, arises in the province of Worahaimanoo, on the border of the Wallo Galla country. The approach is difficult on account of the steep ascent and narrow precipitous ravines that separate it from the rivers Bechelo and Jiddah and from the table-land of Wallo. It stands almost isolated—amongst gigantic surrounding masses, and viewed from the western side possesses the appearance of a crescent. On the extreme left of this curve appears a small flat plateau called Fahla, connected by a strip of land with a peak higher than the amba itself, and called Selassié (trinity), on account of the church erected upon it, and designated by that name. From Selassié to Amba Magdala itself there is a large plain called Islamgee, several hundred feet lower than the two peaks it separates. At Islamgee several small villages had been erected by the peasants who cultivate the land for the Emperor, the chiefs, and soldiers of the amba. The servants of the prisoners had also there a spot given to them where they were allowed to build huts for themselves and cattle. On Saturday a weekly market, formerly well supplied, was held at the foot of Selassié. Numerous wells were generally sunk during the dry season close to the springs of Islamgee, which wells afforded a small but constant supply of water. From Islamgee the road up to Magdala is very steep and difficult. To the first gate it follows, at times very abruptly, the flank of the mountain. To the right, the sides of the amba rise like a huge wall; below is a giddy abyss. From the first to the second gate the road is exceedingly narrow and steep, turning to the right at a sharp angle with the first part of the road. Small earthworks had been erected on the flanks near the gates, protecting every weak point; The summit of the ridge was strongly fenced and loopholed. Two other gates led from the amba to the foot of the mountain; one had some time before been closed, but the other, called Kafir Ber, opened in the direction of the Galla country. The amba is well fortified by nature, and Theodore, to increase its strength, added some rude fortifications.

The Magdala plateau is oblong and somewhat irregular, about a mile and a half in length, and on the average about a mile broad. It was one of the strongest fortresses in Abyssinia, and by its position between the rich and fertile plateau of Dahonte, Dalanta, and Worahaimanoo, easily provisioned. Magdala is more than 9,000 feet above the level of the sea; and enjoys a splendid climate. In the evenings, almost all the year round, a fire is welcome, and, though a month or two before the rains the temperature rises somewhat, in the huts we never found it too hot to be uncomfortable. The high land that surrounds the amba in the distance is barren and bleak, due to the great altitude, and many of the peaks in the Galla country are, for several months in the year, covered with snow or frozen hail. Water, during and for some months after the rainy season, is abundant, but from March to the first week in July it gets scarcer and scarcer, until it is obtained only with difficulty. In order to remedy this disadvantage, Theodore, with his usual forethought, had several large tanks constructed on the mountain, and also sunk wells in promising places. The effort was pretty successful; the wells gave only a small supply of water, it is true, but it was a constant one all the year round. The water collected in the tanks was of very little use. Those reservoirs were not covered after the rains, and the water, impregnated with all kinds of vegetable and animal matter, soon became quite unfit to drink. The principal springs are at Islamgee; there are a few on the amba itself, and numerous less important ones issue from the sides, not many feet from the summit, at the base of the ridge itself.

Magdala was not only used by Theodore as a fortress, but also as a gaol, a magazine, a granary, and as a place of protection for his wives and family. The King's house and the granary stood almost in the centre of the amba; in front towards the west a large space had been left open and clear; behind stood the houses of the officers of his household; to the left, huts of chiefs and soldiers; to the right, on a small eminence, the godowns and magazines, soldiers' quarters, the church, the prison; and behind again another large open space looking towards the Galla plateau of Tanta.

Theodore's houses had nothing regal about them. They were built on the same pattern as the ordinary huts of the country, but only on a larger scale. He himself, I believe, never, or at least very rarely, lived in them; he preferred his tent at Islamgee, or on some neighbouring height, to the larger and more commodious abode on the amba. To his dislike to houses in general, I believe was added a particular objection to shutting himself up in the fort. The majority of these houses were occupied by Theodore's wives and concubines, the eunuchs, and female slaves. The granary and tej houses were in the same inclosure, but separated from the ladies' department by a strong fence; the granary consisted of half a dozen huge huts, protected from the rain by a double roof. They contained barley, tef, beans, peas, and a little wheat. All the grain was kept in leather bags piled up until they reached almost to the roof. It is said that, at the time of the capture of Magdala by our troops, there was grain in sufficient quantity stored in these granaries to last the garrison and other inhabitants of the amba for at least six months. The dwellings of the chiefs and soldiers were built on the model of the Amhara houses—circular, with a pointed thatched roof. The huts of the common soldiers were built without order, in some places in such close proximity that if, as it happened on one or two occasions, a fire broke out, in a few seconds twenty or thirty houses were at once burnt to the ground: nothing could possibly stop the conflagration but rapidly pulling down to leeward the huts not as yet on fire. The principal chiefs had several houses for themselves, all in one inclosure, surrounded and separated from the soldiers' huts by a high and strong fence. Since about a year before his death Theodore had been gradually accumulating at Magdala the few remnants of his former wealth. Some sheds contained muskets, pistols, &c.; others books and paper; others carpets, shamas, silks, some powder, lead, shot, caps; and the best the little money he still possessed, the gold he had seized at Gondar, and the property of his workmen sent over to Magdala for safe custody. All the store-huts were during the rainy season covered with black woollen cloth, called màk, woven in the country. Once or twice a week the chiefs would meet in consultation in a small house erected for that purpose in the magazine inclosure to discuss public affairs, but, above all, to assure themselves by personal inspection that the "treasures" entrusted to their care were in perfect order and in safe keeping.

The Magdala church, consecrated to the Saviour of the World (Medani Alum), was not in any respect worthy of such an important place. It was of recent date, small, unadorned with the customary representations of saints, of the life of the Apostles, of the Trinity, of God the Father, and the devil. No St. George was seen on his white charger, piercing the dragon with his Amhara lance; no martyr smiled benignly at his fiend-like tormentors. The mud walls had not even been whitewashed; and every pious soul longed for the accomplishment of Theodore's promise—the building of a church worthy of his great name. The inclosure was as bare as the holy place itself; no graceful juniper, tall sycamore, or dark green guicho solemnized its precincts, or offered cool shade where the hundred priests, defteras, and deacons who daily performed service, could repose after the fatiguing ceremony—the howling and the dancing to David's psalms. On the same line, but below the hillock on which stood the church, the Abouna possessed a few houses and a garden; but, alas for him, his *pied-à-terre* had for several years become his prison.

The prison-house, a common gaol for the political offenders, thieves, and murderers, consisted of five or six huts inclosed by a strong fence, and surrounded by the private dwellings of the more wealthy prisoners and guards, extending from the eastern slope of the hillock to the edge of the precipice and to the open space towards the south. At the time of our captivity these houses cannot have contained less than 660 prisoners. Of these, about 80 died of remittent fever, 175 were released by his Majesty, 307 executed, and 91 owed their liberty to the stormers of Magdala. The prison rules were in some respects very severe, in others mild and foreign to our civilized ideas. At sunset every prisoner was ordered into the central inclosure. As they passed the gate they were counted and their fetters examined. The women had a hut for themselves; only a late arrangement, however, as before they had to sleep in the same houses as the men. The space was very limited and the prisoners were packed in like herrings in a barrel. Abyssinians themselves, hard-hearted as they are, described the scene at night as something fearful. The huts, crowded to excess, were close, the atmosphere fetid, the stench unbearable. There lay, side by side, the poor, starved vagabond, chained hands and feet, and often with a large forked piece of wood several yards long fixed round his neck, and the warrior who had bled in many a hard-won fight, the governor of provinces—nay, the sons of kings and conquered rulers themselves. In the centre the guards, keeping candles lighted all night, laughed or played some noisy game, indifferent to the sufferings of the unfortunates they watched. At day-dawn, always about 6 A.M. in that latitude, the prison-door was opened, and those who were lucky enough to possess any, repaired to the huts they had erected in the vicinity of the sleeping-houses, while the poorer crawled about the prison inclosure, awaiting their pancake loaf with all the impatience of hungry men, just kept from immediate starvation by the *bounty* of the Emperor. Others strolled about in couples, begging from their more favoured companions, or, when leave was granted, went from house to house imploring alms in the name of the "Saviour of the World."

The prison guards were the greatest ruffians I have ever seen. They had been for so many years in contact with misery in its worst shape that the last spark of human feeling had died out in their callous hearts. Instead of showing compassion or pity for their prisoners, many of them innocent victims of a low treachery, they added to their misery by the harshness and cruelty of their conduct. Had a chief received at last a small sum of money from his distant province, he was soon made aware that he must satisfy the greed of his rapacious gaolers. But that was nothing compared to the moral tortures they inflicted on their prisoners. Many of them had been for years confined on the amba, and had brought their families to reside near them. Woe to the woman who would not listen to the solicitations of these infamous wretches; threatened and even beaten, few indeed of the sorrowful wives and daughters held out; others willingly met advances; and when the chief, the man of rank, or the wealthy merchant, left his day house, he knew that his wife would immediately receive her chosen lover, or, what was still more heartrending, a man she despised but feared.

Such was the daily life of those whose fault was to have given ear to the fair words of Theodore, an error that weighed heavier upon them than a crime. But when the Emperor, on his way, stopped a few days at Magdala, what anxiety, what anguish, reigned in that accursed place! No day house, no hours spent with the family or the friend, no food hardly; the prisoners must remain in the night houses, as the Emperor at any moment might send for some one of them to set him at liberty, or, more likely, to put an end to his miserable existence. Let us take, for example, his visit to Magdala in the first days of July, 1865, on his return from his unsuccessful campaign in Shoa. No doubt long-continued misfortunes crush the better qualities of men, and induce them to perform acts at the mere thought of which in better days they would have blushed. Such was the case with Beru Goscho, formerly the independent ruler of Godjam. Since years he had lingered in chains. In the hope of improving his position, he had the baseness to report to his Majesty that when a rumour was started that he had been killed in Shoa, a great many of the prisoners had rejoiced. Theodore, on receiving this message, gave orders for all the political prisoners who were only chained by the leg to have hand chains put on—exempting only from this order his informer Beru Goscho. However, some days later, this chief having sent a servant to Theodore to ask as a reward to be allowed to have his wife near him, the Emperor, who did not approve of treachery in others, pretended to be annoyed at his request, and gave orders that he should also be put in hand chains. But this was trifling compared with the massacre of the Gallas, which happened during that same visit of Theodore. After subduing the Galla country he required hostages. Accordingly, the Queen Workite sent him her son, the heir to the throne; and many chiefs, believing in the high character of Theodore, willingly accompanied him. The Galla prince had at first been kindly treated; even made governor of the mountain; but soon, on some pretext or other, he was disgraced: first made a prisoner at large, and then sent to the common gaol, to endure chains and misery for years.

Menilek, the grandson of Sehala Selassié, had been since his youth brought up near the Emperor; he was entrusted with an independent command, and in order to strengthen his adherence to his cause, Theodore gave him his daughter in marriage. Under these circumstances, I can easily fancy the rage and passion of Theodore when, one morning, he was informed that Menilek had deserted with his followers, and was already on his way to claim the dominions of his fathers. The Emperor with a telescope saw on the distant Wallo plain Menilek received, with honour by the Galla Queen Workite. Blind, with rage, he had no thought but revenge. He dared not venture to pursue Menilek and encounter the two allies; at hand he had easy victims—the Galla prince and his chiefs. Theodore mounted his horse, called his body-guard, and sent for those men, who had already lingered long in captivity through trusting to his word, and then followed a scene so horrible that I dare not write the details. All were killed some—thirty-two, I believe—and their still breathing bodies hurled over the precipice. It is probable that shortly afterwards Theodore regretted having allowed himself to be guided by passion. With Menilek he had lost Shoa; by the murder of the Galla prince he had made those tribes his deadly foes. He sent word to the Bishop, "Why, if I was acting wrongly, did you not come out with the 'Fitta Negust' (Abyssinian code of law) in your hands, and tell me I was wrong?" The Bishop's reply was simple and to the point:—"Because I saw blood written in your face." However, Theodore soon consoled himself. The rains were late, and water scarce on the amba: the next day it rained. Theodore, full of smiles, addressed his soldiers, saying, "See the rain; God is pleased with me because I have killed the infidels."

Such is Magdala, the sun-burnt barren rock, the arid lonely spot where we had to undergo nearly two years of captivity in chains.

We furnished our house without much expense; two tanned cows' hides were all we required. These, together with a few old carpets Theodore had presented us with at Zagé, was about the extent of our worldly goods. I had a small folding table and a camp-stool (some of our kit had arrived a few days before); but our hovel was too small to admit them and us. The rainy season had fairly set in, and the broken roof of our godjo was rapidly giving way under the weight of the wet grass; we propped it up as best we could by means of a long stick, still it looked very shaky, and leaked worse and worse. The ground, always damp now, had quite the appearance of an Irish bog; and if the straw that was placed underneath the skins to make our bed a little softer was not removed every other day, the steam rose even through the old carpets that adorned our abode. At last I could stand it no longer: I was afraid of falling ill. It was bad enough to be in chains and in a hovel, but sickness into the bargain would have driven me to despair. I sent my Abyssinian servants to cut some wood, and made a small raised platform; it was rather irregular and hard, but I preferred it to sleeping for so long on the wet ground.

Well do I still remember that long, dreary, rainy season, and with what impatience we looked for the Feast of the Cross, about the 25th of September; as the natives told us that the rains always ceased about that time! I had brought with me from Gaffat an Amharic grammar. "Faute de mieux," I struggled hard to study it, but the mind was not fitted for such work; and, book in hand, I was in spirit, thousands of miles away, thinking of home, dreaming awake of beloved friends, of freedom and liberty. Towards the end of August, shortly after the return of our ill-fated messenger, we wrote again and sent another man: by this time we had abundant proof that Samuel,—formerly our introducer, now our gaoler,—was completely in our interests; and by his good arrangements the messenger started without any one knowing of it, and managed to reach Massowah with his letter.

I have spoken often of Samuel, and shall again and again have to mention his name in my narrative. He was, from the beginning, mixed up with the affairs of the Europeans, and I believe at one time he was rather unfriendly towards them; but since our arrival and during our captivity, he behaved exceedingly well. He was a shrewd, cunning man, and one of the first who perceived that Theodore was losing ground. Outwardly he swore by his name, and kept his confidence; but all the while he was serving us, and helping us in our communications with the coast, the rebels, &c. In his youth his left leg had been broken and badly set; and though Theodore liked him, he did not give him a military command, but always employed him in a civil capacity. He did not like to speak of the accident that occasioned his deformity, and would, if asked, always give an evasive answer. Pietro, the Italian, was a great gossip, and his stories could not always be relied upon. His account of the broken leg was that when Samuel went to Shoa, some Englishman there gave him a kick which sent him rolling down some small ravine, and in the fall the leg was broken. It was on account of that blow from an Englishman, Pietro said, that Samuel hated them all so much, and was so bitter against them at first. It may be so; but I believe that he had not been understood.

Samuel fancied that he was a very great man in his own country. His father had been a small sheik; and Theodore, after Samuel's native country had rebelled, made him governor of it. With all the appearance of great humility, Samuel was proud; and by treating him as if he was in reality a great man, he was as easily managed as a child. He had suffered from a severe attack of dysentery during our stay at Kourata. I attended him carefully, and he always felt grateful for my attentions towards him. When we separated and lived in different houses, he did not allow the guards to sleep inside our hut. It is true it would have been difficult; but Abyssinian soldiers are not particular: they sleep anywhere,—on their prisoner's bed, if there is no other place, making use of him as a pillow. Of course Mr. Rassam had none; but he was the great man, the dispenser of favours. Stern, Cameron, and Rosenthal, being neither rich nor favourites, had the advantage of the presence of two or three of those ruffians as their companions every night; nor were those in the kitchen better off, as some soldiers were always sent in at night not to watch Kerans and Pietro, but the King's property (our own kit).

Samuel soon made friends with some of the chiefs. After a while, two of them were constantly in our inclosure, and, under the pretext of coming to see Samuel, would spend hours with us. Kerans, a good Amharic scholar, was the interpreter on those occasions: one of them, Deftera Zenab, the King's chief scribe, (now tutor to Alamayou,) is an intelligent; honest man; but he was quite mad on astronomy, and would listen for hours to anything concerning the solar system. Unfortunately, either the explanations were faulty or his comprehension dull as each time he came he wanted the whole dissertation over again until at last our patience was fairly exhausted, and we gave him up as a bad job. His other intimate was a good-natured young man called Afa Negus Meshisha, son of a former governor of the Amba; Theodore, on the death of the father, had given Meshisha the title, but nothing more. His forte was playing the lute, or a rude instrument something like it. Samuel could listen to him for hours; but two minutes was quite enough to make us run off. He was, however, useful in his way, as he gave us good information about what was going on in Theodore's camp,—intelligence which his position as an occasional member of the council enabled him to obtain.

Such, apart from ourselves, was our only society. It is true that the Ras and the great men would occasionally call on Mr. Rassam, much more frequently since he give them arrack and toj, instead of the coffee he used to offer them at first; but, unless one of them wanted some medicine, it was very rare that they honoured us with a visit; they thought that they had done quite enough—indeed bestowed a great favour, for which we ought to be grateful—if, as they passed near our hut, they shouted "May God open thee!"

But our enemy was one of the day guards, named Abu Falek, an old rascal who delighted in making mischief; he was hated by every one on the mountain, and on that account outwardly respected. The day he was on guard it was very difficult to write, as he was always putting his ugly grey head in at the door to see what we were doing. He did his best to do us harm, but could reach no higher than our servants: our dollars were too much for him.

Everything has an end. With Maskal (the Feast of the Cross) came sunshine and pleasant cool weather. We had already been two months and a half in chains, and we expected that soon some comforting news would reach us, telling us "Be of good cheer; we are coming."

Since our arrival at Magdala we had not received a single letter: and more than six months had elapsed without news from our friends, or any intelligence whatsoever from Europe.

Immediately after the rains, Mr. Rassam had his house repaired and improved, and a new hut built, as Mrs. Rosenthal was expected to join our party; Samuel obtained a piece of ground adjoining our inclosure, which was afterwards included in it, and on which he built a hut for himself and family. Samuel had several times spoken to me about pulling down our wretched godjo, and building a larger hut instead; but I thought it was hardly worth the while, as before many months some change or the other would take place: another reason was, that part of the old fence stood in front of my godjo, and I should hardly have gained more than a foot of ground. Samuel promised to do his best to have the fence removed if I would build; I agreed to do so, and he endeavoured to fulfil his part of the contract, but failed. However, a few weeks later, one of the chiefs, whom I had attended almost since our arrival, in his first burst of gratitude at being cured, took upon himself to break down the fence, and promised to send me his men to help me.

All the materials—wood, bamboos, cow-hides, straw—could be purchased below the mountain, and in a few days all was ready. I sent word to my patient, who came at once, with about fifty soldiers, who, by his orders, broke down the fence, and pulled down my godjo. The ground was afterwards levelled, the circumference of the hut traced with a stick, fixed to the centre by a piece of string, and a trench a foot and a half deep dug. Two strong sticks were placed at the spot where the door would be, and each soldier, carrying several of the branches with which the walls are built, placed them in the ditch, filling up the vacant space with the earth that had been taken out; they had only to tie, with strips of cow-hide, flexible branches transversely in order to keep the vertical ones together, and the first part of the structure was complete. A few days afterwards they returned, made the framework of the roof, and lifted it up on the walls; it then only required the thatcher to render our new abode inhabitable. The servants brought water and made mud, with which the walls were coated inside, and a week from the day the godjo had been pulled down, Prideaux and myself were able to give our house-warming. The soldiers were delighted with their job, and always came in large numbers when we required their assistance, as we treated them very liberally: for instance, the materials for our new hut cost eight dollars, but we spent fourteen dollars in feasting those who had assisted us. We had now seven feet of ground each, the table could be placed in the centre, and the folding chair offered to a visitor. Mr. Rassam had tried, with success, to whitewash the interior of his hut with a kind of soft white yellowish sandstone, that could be obtained in the vicinity of the Amba; we, therefore, also put our servants to work, but first had the mud walls several times besmeared with cow-dung, in order to make the whitewash adhere. We enjoyed very much the neat clean appearance of our hut. Unfortunately, being situate between two high fences and surrounded by other huts, it was rather dark. To obviate this defect, we cut out of the walls some of the framework, and made four windows; this was certainly a great improvement, but at night we felt the cold bitterly. Luckily, our friend Zenab gave us some parchment; out of an old box we made some rude frames, and the parchment, previously well soaked in oil served instead of glass.

We were obliged to keep a large staff of servants, as we had to prepare everything for ourselves. Some women were engaged to grind flour for us and the Abyssinian servants; others to bring water or wood. Men-servants went to the market or to the neighbouring districts to purchase grain, sheep, honey, &c.; many were employed as messengers to the coast or to Gaffat. I had with me two Portuguese, who were the torment of my life, as they were always quarrelling, often drunk, impertinent, and unwilling to work. The Portuguese lived in the kitchen, but as they were always fighting with the other servants, and we were perfectly helpless, and could not possibly enforce our commands, I had a small hut erected for them. The inclosure had been enlarged again by the chief, and Cameron had built a log-house for himself, and Mr. Rosenthal had had one made for his servants; mine for the Portuguese was built on the same spot, and before the rainy season I had another one made for the Abyssinians, as they grumbled and threatened to leave, if they had to spend the rains in a tent.

All these arrangements took us some time; we had been glad to have something to do, as the days passed much quicker, and time did not weigh so heavily upon us. Our Christmas was not very merry, nor did we on New Year's Day wish one another many returns of a similar one; but we were on the whole more accustomed to our captivity, and certainly in many respects more comfortable.

CHAPTER XIII

About this time a servant of Mr. Rassam, whom he had sent to his Majesty some months previously, returned on the 28th of December with a letter from Theodore, in which was inclosed one from our Queen. Theodore informed Mr. Rassam that Mr. Flad had arrived at Massowah, and had sent him the letter which he had forwarded us for perusal; he told Mr. Rassam to await his arrival, as he would be coming before long, and they would consult together about an answer. We were greatly rejoiced at the tenor of the Queen's letter: it was plain that at last a higher tone had been adopted, that the character of Theodore was better known, and all his futile plans would be frustrated by the attitude our Government had taken.

On the 7th of January, 1867, Ras Engeddah arrived on the Amba, having accompanied thither a batch of prisoners. He sent us his compliments and a letter from Theodore. Theodore's letter was rather a boastful and imperious one: he, first gave a summary of Flad's letter to himself, in which he had been informed by that gentleman that everything he had required had been consented to, but that in the meanwhile he had changed his behaviour towards us. Theodore also gave us his intended reply: he said Ethiopia and England had formerly been on a footing of friendship; and for that reason he had loved the English exceedingly. But since then (to use his own words), "having heard that they have calumniated and hated me with the Turks, I said to myself, Can this be true? and I felt some misgiving in my heart." He evidently wanted to ignore the ill treatment he had inflicted upon us, as he said: "Mr. Rassam and his party you sent to me I have placed in my house in my capital at Magdala, and I will treat them well until I obtain a token of friendship." He concluded his letter by ordering Mr. Rassam to write to the proper authorities, so that the things should be sent a to him; he desired Mr. Rassam's letter to be forwarded to him, and quickly, so that Mr. Flad might come without delay.

This letter must probably have been a post-prandial one; it was not the line of conduct he wanted to adopt: he knew too well that his only chance was to natter, appear humble, meek and ignorant; he might, he knew, enlist England's sympathy by appearing in that light, and that an overbearing tone would not suit his purpose, nor secure him the object he longed for. Early the following day a messenger arrived from the Imperial camp with a letter from General Merewether, and another from Theodore. How different this letter from the one brought by Ras Engeddah! It was insinuating, courteous; he orders no more, he humbly requests; he meekly entreats and begs: he begins by saying:—"Now in order to prove the good relationship between me and yourself, let it be shown by your writing, and by getting the skilful artisans and Mr. Flad to come *viâ* Metemma; This will be the sign of our friendship." He quotes the story of Solomon and Hiram on the occasion of the building of the temple; then adds, "And now when I used to fall girded at the feet of the great Queen, her nobles, people; hosts, etc., could it be possible to be more humble?" He then describes his reception of Mr. Rassam, and the way he treated him; how he released the former captives the very day of his arrival, in order to comply with the request of the Queen; he explains the cause of our imprisonment by reproaching Mr. Rassam with having taken away the prisoners without first bringing them to him; and concludes by saying, "As Solomon fell at the feet of Hiram, so I, beneath God, fall at the feet of the Queen, and her Government, and her friends. I wish you to get them (the artisans) *viâ* Metemma, in order that they may teach me wisdom, and show me clever arts. When this is done I will make you glad and send you away, by the power of God."

Mr. Rassam replied to his Majesty at once, informing him that he had complied with his request. The messenger, on his arrival at the Emperor's camp, was well received, presented with a mule, and quickly despatched on his errand. For several months we heard nothing more upon the subject.

General Merewether, in his letter to Theodore, informed him that he had arrived at Massowah with the workmen and presents, and that on the captives being made over to him he would allow the workmen to proceed to his Majesty's camp. We were quite overjoyed when we heard that General Merewether was entrusted with the negotiation: we knew his ability, and had full confidence in his tact and discretion. Indeed, he deserves our sincere gratitude; for he was the captives' friend: from the moment he landed at Massowah to the day of our release, he spared himself neither trouble nor pains to effect our deliverance.

Messengers now were despatched more regularly; by them we wrote long accounts of Theodore's proceedings, and urged that force should be employed to obtain our release. We knew the great risk we ran, but we preferred death to a continuance of such a miserable existence. We informed our friends that we had quite made up our minds, and that our safety was not to weigh for one instant in the balance. It was a chance: the only one left to us, and we implored that we might have the advantage of it. We gave all the information in our power as to the resources of the country, the movements of his Majesty, the strength of his army, the course he would probably follow should troops land, how to deal with him, and the means to adopt in order to insure success. We knew that should any of such letters fall into Theodore's hands, we had no mercy, no pity to expect; but we considered it our duty to submit our opinion, and to the best of our ability assist those who were labouring for our release.

At this time we frequently received news from our friends, as well as newspapers, or a few articles cut out of them, and inclosed in an envelope. War was still but little talked of; the press, with but few exceptions, seemed to look upon it as a rash undertaking that would only lead to failure. Correspondents, to our despair and disgust, expatiated on guinea-worms, poisonous flies, absence of water, and such like rubbish. For another two months and a half we led the same monotonous life. My medicines were getting low, and as the number of my patients was great, I was very anxious to receive some more.

On the 19th of March Ras Engeddah arrived on the Amba with a few thousand soldiers. He had brought with him some money, powder, and various stores which Theodore thought would be safer at Magdala. At the same time he sent us some stores, medicines, &c., which Captain Goodfellow had forwarded to Metemma soon after Mr. Flad's arrival. I will give credit to Theodore for having behaved well on that occasion. As soon as we were informed that the stores had arrived at Metemma, Mr. Rassam wrote to the Emperor, asking his permission to send servants and mules, in order to have them conveyed to Magdala. Theodore said that he would have them carried himself, and moreover kept his word. He sent one of his officers to Wochnee, with instructions to the various chiefs of districts to have our things carried to Debra Tabor. I had long ago given everything up, and was agreeably surprised when those few comforts reached us. For some days, we treated ourselves to green peas, potted meats, cigars, &c., and felt in better spirits; not so much on account of the stores themselves, as for the attention our dangerous host had shown us.

I remember that during the following months we felt more than at any time the burden of such an existence. We had expected great things, and nothing was effected: we could not have believed, on our first arrival at Magdala, that another rainy season was in reserve for us; we never would have credited the assertion that long before that date all would not have been over, some way or the other. What we disliked above all things was the uncertainty in which we were now placed: we trembled at the idea of the cruelties and tortures Theodore inflicted upon his victims; and each time a royal messenger arrived, we could be seen going from one hut to the other, exchanging anxious looks, and repeatedly asking our fellow-sufferers, "In there any news? Is there anything concerning us?"

General Merewether, with kind forethought, had sent us some seeds, and we obtained more from Gaffat. Rassam's inclosure had been considerably enlarged by the chiefs, and he was able to arrange a nice garden. He had before sown some tomato seeds; these plants sprang up wonderfully well, and Mr. Rassam, with great taste, made with bamboos a very pretty trellis-work, soon entirely covered by this novel creeper. Between our hut, the fence, and the hut opposite ours, we had a small piece of ground, about eight feet broad on the average, and about ten feet long. Prideaux and myself laboured hard, delighted at the idea of having something to do; with slit-up bamboos we made a small trellis-work, dividing our garden into squares, triangles, &c., and on the 24th of May, in honour of our Queen's birthday, we sowed the seed. Some things came out very quickly; peas, in six weeks, were seven or eight feet high, mustard, cress, radishes, and salads prospered. But our central flower-bed remained for a long time barren; and when at last a few plants came out, they belonged to some biennial species, as they only flowered in the following spring. A few peas, just to taste (our garden was too small to enable us to get from it more than a scanty dish or two), raw lettuces (we had no oil, and only inferior vinegar made out of tej), with now and then a radish, were luxuries we immensely enjoyed after our long meat diet. When a second parcel of seeds reached us, we transformed into "gardens" every available spot, and had the pleasure of eating a few turnips, more lettuces, and a cabbage or two. Soon after the rainy season everything withered away; the sun burnt up our treasures, and left us again to our mutton and fowls.

A month or so before the rainy season of 1867, fever of a malignant type broke out in the common gaol. The place was dirty enough before, and the horrors of that abode were indescribable even when sickness did not prevail; but when about 150 men of all ranks lay prostrate on the ground, contaminating still more the already impure atmosphere, the scene was horrible in the extreme, giving a better idea of the place of torments than even Dante's vivid description. The epidemic lasted until the first rains set in. About eighty died; and many more would have succumbed, had not, fortunately, some of the guards contracted the disease. As long as it was only the prisoners, they turned a deaf ear to all my suggestions; now they had become willing listeners, and quickly adopted the advice they had spurned but a short time before. To all who claimed my services I willingly sent medicine; and, when some of the guards also came to me for treatment, I gave them some also: but on condition that they would treat with more kindness the unfortunate men in their charge.

General Merewether, always thoughtful and kind, aware that much of our comfort depended on our being on friendly terms with the garrison, sent me some vaccine lymph in small tubes. I explained to some of the more intelligent natives the wonderful properties of that prophylactic, and induced them to bring me their children to be inoculated. Amongst semi-civilized races it is often difficult to introduce the blessings of vaccination; but on this occasion they were universally and gratefully accepted. For about six weeks an immense crowd collected outside the gates on vaccinating days; so much so that it was with some difficulty that they were kept back, so anxious were they to avail themselves of the famous medicine that protected from the dreaded "koufing" (small-pox). It so happened that, amongst the children I operated upon, was the child of old Abu Falek (or rather his wife's), the day guard I have already mentioned. He was naturally ill-natured and disobliging, and to save himself the trouble of bringing his child to have others inoculated from it, and at the same time so as not to be accused of selfishness, he spread the rumour that the children from whom the lymph was taken would shortly afterwards die. This was the death-blow to my endeavours to introduce vaccine amongst the natives; numbers still collected to be vaccinated, but none came to give the lymph, and as I had no more tubes, I was obliged to discontinue an experiment which had so wonderfully succeeded.

The rainy season of 1867 set in about the end of the first week in July. We had better shelter, and had time to make arrangements for provision for our followers and ourselves before the rains fairly commenced, and in that respect were better off than the year before; but, for other reasons, such as the political condition of the country, the daily increasing difficulty of communicating with the coast, it was perhaps, on the whole, more trying and disagreeable.

The chiefs of the mountain had not been long in finding out that the English captives had money. They all had frequently been presented with *douceurs*, in the shape of dollars for themselves, shamas or ornaments for their wives; also tej and arrack, which was brewed by Samuel under Mr. Rassam's direction, of which they partook frequently and freely. They tried to cut one another out; each one in his private visits pretending to be "the best friend;" but they could not openly leave the council-room, and start off for a glass, without being accompanied by the whole batch, so they forbade every one but themselves from visiting us. Poor Zenab for months took no more lessons in astronomy, and Meshisha played the lute to his wives and followers. They even went so far as to forbid the petty chiefs and soldiers coming to me for medicine. But this was too much; though a despotism, the constitution of the country only acknowledged one master. The soldiers therefore sent their petty chiefs in a body to the Ras and members of the council; they talked even of representing the matter to Theodore; and, as the chiefs were far from being immaculate, and dreaded nothing so much as reports to their master, they were obliged to give in, and cancel the order.

Theodore had, after his capture of Magdala, appointed a chief as governor of the Amba, giving him a kind of unlimited power over the garrison; but some years later he adjoined to him a few chiefs as his councillors, still allowing the Head of the mountain to retain a great deal of his former power. Always suspicious, but less able to satisfy his soldiers than before, he took every precaution to avoid treachery, and to make certain that, when engaged on distant expeditions, he might depend on his fortress of Magdala. With that object he ordered a council to assemble on all important occasions, and to consult on all matters concerning the internal economy of the mountain. Every head of department, and every chief of a corps, had a voice; the officers in command of the troops were to send separate and private messengers; the Ras was still considered as the Head of the mountain, but his authority was limited, and his responsibility great, should he think proper to overrule his companions. Under these circumstances, it is not astonishing that, as a rule, he would follow the advice of those chiefs whom he knew to be the greatest worshippers of his master, his most faithful spies and beloved tale-bearers.

The Head of the mountain on our arrival, Ras Kidana Mariam, was, on account of his family connections and his position in the country, considered "dangerous" by Theodore, and, as I have already mentioned, was on a false charge taken to the camp. Shortly before depriving Ras Kidana Mariam of his command he had promoted him from a Dedjazmatch to the rank of Ras. Every umbel (colonel) was promoted by the same order to be a Bitwaddad (something like a Brigadier-General), or a Dedjazmatch, a title only applied in former days to governors of one large or of several small provinces; bachas (captains) were made colonels, and so on throughout the whole garrison; which after this consisted only of officers and non-commissioned officers, the lowest in rank being at least a sergeant. Theodore wrote to them at the time to inform them that they would draw the pay and rations according to their rank, and when, as he expected before long, he should see them, he would treat them so generously that even the "unborn babe would rejoice in his mother's womb." Theodore, on three or four occasions, out of his few remaining dollars, gave them a small advance of pay. About forty dollars was the amount a general touched during the time we were there; a sergeant, during the same period, about eight, I believe. With that they were supposed to feed and clothe themselves, families, and followers; for no rations were distributed at the same time as the money. At first they were all dazzled by their new ranks—the only thing Theodore could distribute with a liberal hand; but they soon found out what these were worth, and, ragged, hungry, and cold, they were the first to joke about their high-sounding but empty titles.

A distant relation of Theodore by his mother's side, named Ras Bisawar, was, on the dismissal of Kidana Mariam, selected for the vacant post. He had in his youth been brought up for the church, had even been made a deftera, when the brilliant example of his relative took him from the peaceful and quiet life he had first chosen to cast him amidst the turmoil of camp life. He was a great big hulking fellow, bald-headed, and rather good-natured; but for all his sword and pistols could not conceal his first pursuit in life: he was still the deftera in borrowed plumage. His great fault was to be too weak; he had no decision of character, no firmness, and was always guided in his actions by the last talker.

Next in importance came Bitwaddad Damash, the ugliest and most pompous puppy and the biggest-boasting villain on the whole mountain. He was very sick when we first arrived, but though he could not come himself he was far too much interested in our affairs not to be at all hours of the day informed of our doings; for that purpose he sent his eldest son, a lad of about twelve, several times in the day with compliments and inquiries after our welfare. As soon as he could walk about a little he came now and then himself, to see me for advice, and when restored to health, in the thankfulness of the first moment, he helped to build our house. But gratitude is not a lasting quality—in Abyssinia it hardly exists—and not long afterwards Damash gave strong hints that if we wanted him to be our friend we must not "forget him." Prideaux and myself had not much money to spare, but as he was known to be a great scoundrel, we thought it would not be prudent to make an enemy of him, and therefore sent him, as a token of friendship, Prideaux's small folding looking-glass, the only presentable thing we had between us. For some time the looking-glass consolidated our friendship, but when, on a second application for "tokens," we turned a deaf ear to his soft words, he would have nothing more to do with as; he called us bad men, sneered at us, made us take off our caps before him, and even went so far as to insult Cameron and Stern, shaking his head at them in a threatening manner as, more or less intoxicated, he left in the afternoon the room of his beloved and generous friend, Mr. Rassam. Damash had command of half the gunmen, some 270, the Ras of the rest, about 200.

The third member of council was Bitwaddad Hailo, the best of the lot; he was in charge of the gaol, but was never known to abuse his position. His two brothers had commanded our escort from the frontier to the Emperor's camp in Damot; his mother, a fine old lady, also accompanied us part of the way: the brothers and the mother had been well treated by us, so that even before we came to the Amba we were known to him, and he always conducted himself very civilly, and proved useful on many occasions. When he heard of Theodore's approach, as he knew that charges were going, to be brought against him, he ran, away and joined the English camp.

He managed his escape, in a very clever manner indeed. According to the, rules of the mountain, not even a Bitwaddad could pass the gate without permission from the Ras, and since desertions had taken place the permission was no more granted. His wife and child were also on the Amba, and since he was suspected, if they had left he would have been strictly watched. His mother had accompanied Theodore's camp, being desirous of seeing her son. When his Majesty encamped in the valley of the Bechelo, she asked his permission to be allowed to go to Magdala, and on her arrival at Islamgee she sent word to her son to give orders at the gate to let her in; but he declined, stating publicly, as the motive of his refusal, that, not having received intimation from his Majesty that he had granted her request, he could not take upon himself to admit her into the fort. The mother had been made a party to the plot beforehand, and played her part well; it was market-day, and therefore the place was crowded with soldiers and petty chiefs. On hearing of her son's refusal to admit her, she pretended to be driven to despair, tore her hair and cried aloud, quite overcome by the ingratitude of the son she had made such a long journey to embrace. The spectators took her part, and, in her name, sent to him again; but he was firm. "To-morrow," he said, "I will send word to the Emperor; if he allows you to come I will be only too happy to admit you; to-day, all I can do is to send you my wife and child to remain with you until the evening." The old lady, with the wife and child, retired to a quiet corner for a friendly chat, and when no more noticed, quietly walked away. At about ten at night, accompanied by one of his men, and assisted by some friends, Hailo made his escape and rejoined his family.

Another member of council was called Bitwaddad Wassié: he also was in charge of the prison alternatively with Hailo. He was a good-tempered man, always laughing, but, it appears, not beloved by the prisoners, for, after the taking of Magdala, the women flew at him, and gave him a sound thrashing. He was remarkable in one respect: he would never accept anything, and though money was repeatedly offered to him he always declined it. Dedjazmatch Goji, in command of 500 spearmen, a tall old man, was as big a fool as he was bulky; he loved but one thing, tej, and worshipped but one being, Theodore. Bitwaddad Bakal, a good soldier, a simple-minded man, in charge of the Imperial household, and a few insignificant old men, completed the quorum.

Let us suppose a wet day during the rainy season of 1867. Our money was getting very scarce, and all communication with Metemma, Massowah, or Debra Tabor was completely interrupted. War had been talked of more seriously at home, and, in the absence of news, we were in anxious expectation of what would be decided. The weather did not permit us to do much gardening; and other occupations were few. We wrote home, (an easier task during the rains, as the guards kept to their huts,) studied Amharic, read the famous *Commercial Dictionary*, or visited one another, and smoked bad tobacco, simply to kill time. Mr. Rosenthal, a very clever linguist, managed, with an Italian Bible, to master that language, and, to drive away dull care, spent his evenings studying French with only the help of a portion of Guizot's *Histoire de la Civilisation*. If it cleared up a little, we puddled about in the small road between the now increased huts; but probably, before long, would be scared away by some one shouting out,— "The Ras and the chiefs are coming!" If we could directly run away we did so; but if perceived, we had to put on our blandest smile, bow to the rude inquiry, "How art thou? good afternoon to thee" (the second person singular is only employed as a sign of disrespect, towards an inferior), and, O gods! pull off our ragged caps and keep our heads uncovered. To see them waddling along, ready to burst with self-conceit; whilst we knew that the clothes they were clad with, and the food they had partaken of that day, were all purchased with British money, was very annoying. As they accepted bribes the least they could do was to be civil; on the contrary, they looked down upon us as if we were semi-idiots, or a species between them and monkeys,—"white donkeys," as they called us when they spoke of us among themselves. Preceded by Samuel, they would make straight for Mr. Rassam's house; they were hardly swore civil to him than to us, though they always swore to him eternal friendship. I often admired Mr. Rassam's' patience on these occasions: he could sit, talk, and laugh with them for hours, gorging them with bumpers of tej until they reeled out of his place, the laughing-stocks, yet envied objects, of the soldiers who helped them to regain their homes. On the whole they were a vile set: to please their master they would have shuddered at no crime, and stopped at no infamy. When they thought that any cruel act of theirs might please Theodore, their god, no consideration of friendship or family ties would arrest their hands or soften their hearts. They came to Mr. Rassam, though he was kind to them, out of no regard, only because it was part of their instructions, and they could indulge their appetite for spirituous drinks; but had we been, by want of money, reduced to appeal to them, I doubt whether they would have sanctioned for us, to whom they owed so much, even the small pittance daily doled out to the poor Abyssinian prisoners.

About that time these wretches had a good opportunity of showing their zeal for their beloved master. One Saturday two prisoners took advantage of the bustle always attending market-days, to attempt their escape. One of them, Lij Barié, was the son of a chief in Tigré; some years before he had been imprisoned on "suspicion," or, more likely, because he might prove dangerous, as he was much liked in his province. His companion was a young lad, a semi-Galla, from the Shoa frontier, who had been kept for years in chains on the Amba awaiting his trial. One day, as he was cutting wood, a large splinter flew off, and, striking his mother in the chest, caused her death. Theodore was, at the time, on an expedition, and to conciliate the Bishop, he made over the case to him; who, however, declined to investigate it as it did not fall under his jurisdiction. Theodore, vexed at the Bishop's refusal, sent the lad to Magdala, where he was chained, awaiting the good pleasure of his judges. Lij Barié had only been able to open one of the rings, the other being too strong; so he fastened the chain and ring on one leg by means of a large bandage as well as he could, and put on the shirt and cloth of one of the servant-girls, who was in his confidence, and, carrying on his shoulder the gombo (earthen jar for water), left the prison inclosure without being seen. The boy had fortunately been able to get rid of his fetters altogether, and he slipped out also without being noticed; not being encumbered with much clothing, and quite free in his limbs, he soon reached the gate, passed out with the followers of some chief, and was already far away and in safety before his disappearance was noticed.

Lij Barié failed in his attempt. What with the chain fastened on one leg, the woman's dress, and the gombo, he could not advance quickly. He was, however, already half way between the prison and the gate, somewhere not far from our inclosure, when a young man, perceiving a good-looking girl coming in his direction, advanced to speak to her; but as he came closer, his eyes fell upon the bandage, and to his astonishment he saw a piece of chain peeping through the interstices of the cloth. He guessed at once that this was a prisoner endeavouring to escape, and followed the individual until he met some soldiers; he told them his suspicions, and they fell upon Lij Barié and made him a prisoner. A crowd soon collected around the unfortunate young man, and the alarm being given that a prisoner had been seized as he was endeavouring to escape, several of the guards rushed to the spot, and at once recognizing their old inmate, claimed him as their property. In an instant all his clothes were torn off his back, and the cowardly ruffians struck him with the butt-ends of their lances, and with the back of their swords, until his whole body was a mass of wounds and sores, and he lay senseless, nearly dead, on the ground. But even this was not enough to satisfy their savage revenge; they carried him off to the prison, hammered on hand and foot chains, placed a long heavy log of wood round his neck, put his feet in the stocks, and left him there for days, more dead than alive, until the good pleasure of the Emperor should be known.

An immediate search was made for his companion and for the servant-girl, his accomplice. The first was already beyond their reach, but they succeeded in capturing the unfortunate young woman. The Ras and council immediately assembled, and condemned her to receive, in front of the Emperor's house, one hundred blows from the heavy girâf. The next morning the Ras, accompanied by a large number of chiefs and soldiers, came to the spot to witness the execution of the sentence. The girl was thrown down on the ground, stripped of her skirt, and leather ropes tied to her feet and hands to keep her at full stretch. A strong, powerful ruffian was entrusted with the execution of the punishment. Each fall of the whip could be heard from our inclosure, resounding like a pistol-shot; every blow tore off a strip of flesh; and after every ten strokes the girâf became so heavy with blood that, it had to be wiped before the operation could be continued. She never said a word, nor even groaned. When she was removed, after the hundredth stroke, the naked ribs and the back-bone were visible through the flowing blood: the whole of the flesh of the back having been torn to pieces.

Some time afterwards a messenger brought back Theodore's answer. Lij Barié was first to have his hands and feet cut off, before all the Abyssinian prisoners, and afterwards to be thrown over the precipice. The chiefs made quite a holiday of that execution; and even sent a polite message to Samuel requesting him to "come and see the fun." Lij Barié was brought out, a dozen of the bravest fell upon him at once; and, with their ungainly blunt swords, hacked away at his hands and feet with all the delight an Abyssinian has for spilling blood. Whilst submitting to this agonizing torture, Lij Barié never lost his courage or presence of mind, and it is very remarkable that whilst they were so unmercifully murdering him, he prophesied, almost to a letter, the fate that before long awaited them. "You cowards," he shouted out, "fit servants of the robber your master! He can seize no man but by treachery; and you can kill them only when they are unarmed and in your power. But before long the English will come to release their people; they will avenge in your blood the ill treatment you have inflicted upon their countrymen, and punish, you and your master for all your cowardice, cruelties, and murders." The wretches took little notice of the dying words of the brave lad; they hurled him over the precipice, and, in a body, walked over to our place to finish the day, so well begun, by partaking of Mr. Rassam's generous hospitality.

CHAPTER XIV

Another Maskal (Feast of the Cross) had gone by and September ushered in fine, pleasant weather. No important change had taken place in our daily life: it was the same routine over again; only we were beginning to be very anxious about the long delay of our messengers from the coast, as our money was running short: indeed, we had hardly any left, and every necessary of life had risen to fabulous prices. Five oblong pieces of salt were now given in exchange for a Maria Theresa dollar, whilst formerly, at Magdala, during their first captivity, our companions had often got as much as thirty, never less than fifteen or eighteen. Though the value of the salt had so greatly increased, the articles purchased with it had not followed the same proportion, they were, on the contrary, lowered in amount and quality. When the salts were abundant we could buy four old fowls for a salt; now that they were scarce, we could only buy two; and everything in the same ratio; consequently all our expenses had risen 200 per cent. Supplies. in the market were also getting very scarce; and often we could not purchase grain for our Abyssinian servants. The soldiers on the mountain suffered greatly from this scarcity and high prices; they were continually begging, and many, no doubt, were saved from starvation by the generosity of those they kept prisoners. Very fortunately, I had put aside a small sum of money in case of accident, otherwise I believe the Abyssinian difficulty would have been at an end, so far as we were concerned. I kept a little for myself, and handed the rest over to Mr. Rassam, as he usually supplied us with money from the sums forwarded to him by the agent at Massowah. We dismissed as many servants as we possibly could, reduced our expenses to a minimum, and sent messengers after messengers to the coast to bring us up as much money as they could. At that time, if we had fortunately been provided with a large sum of ready cash, I do really believe that we might have bought the mountain; so discouraged and mutinous were the soldiers of the garrison at the long privations and semi-starvation they were enduring for a master of whom they had no reliable information. The agent at the coast did his best. Hosts of messengers had been despatched, but the condition of the country was such that they had to bury the money they were carrying in the house of a friend at Adowa, and abide there for several months, until they could, with great prudence and by travelling only at night, venture to pass through districts infested with thieves, and a prey to the greatest anarchy.

On the morning of the 5th of September, whilst at breakfast, one of our interpreters rushed into the hut, and told us that our friend Afa Negus Meshisha (the lute-player), and Bedjerand Comfou, one of the officers in charge of the godowns, had run away. Theirs was a long-preconcerted and ably managed plan. At the beginning of the rainy season, ground had been allotted to the various, chiefs and soldiers, at Islamgee and at the foot of the mountain. Some of the chiefs made arrangements with the peasants living below for them to till the soil on their account, they supplying the seed grain, and the harvest to be divided between the two; others, who had many servants, did the work themselves. Afa Negus Meshisha's and Bedjerand Comfou's lots happened to be at the foot of the mountain; they themselves undertook the cultivation, occasionally visited their fields, and sent once or twice a week all their male and female servants to pull out the weeds under the superintendence of their wives. The whole of the land they had received had not been put under cultivation, and, a few days before, Comfou spoke to the Ras about it, who advised him to sow some tef, as, with the prevailing scarcity, he would be happy to reap a second harvest. Comfou approved of the idea, and asked the Ras to send him a servant on the morning of the 5th, to allow him to pass the gates. The Ras agreed. On that very morning Meshisha went to the Ras, and told him that he also wanted to sow some tef, and asked him to allow him to go down. The Ras, who had not the slightest suspicion, granted his request. Both had that morning sent down several of their servants to weed the fields, and, not to excite suspicion, had sent their wives by another gate, also under the same pretence. As the Gallas often attacked the soldiers of the garrison at the foot of the mountain, the door-keepers were not surprised to see the two officers well armed and preceded by their mules; nor did they take much notice of the bags their followers carried, when they were told that it was tef they were going to sow, a statement moreover corroborated by the Ras's servant himself. Off they started in open daylight, meeting many of the soldiers of the mountain on the way down. Arrived, at the fields, they told their servants to follow them, and made straight for the Galla plain. Some of the soldiers who were at the time working at their fields suspected that all was not right, and at once returned to the Amba and communicated their suspicions to the Ras. He had but to take a telescope to perceive the two friends winding their way in the distance along the road that led to the Galla plain. All the garrison was at once called out, and an immediate pursuit ordered; but during the interval the fugitives had gained ground, and were at last perceived quietly resting on the plain above, in company with such a respectable-looking body of Galla horsemen that prudence dictated to the braves of Magdala the advisability of not following any further. On their way back they found, hiding herself in the bushes, the wife of Comfou, carrying her infant babe in her arms. It appears that, flurried and excited, that young woman failed to find the place of rendezvous, and was concealing herself until the soldiers had passed by, when the cries of her child attracted their attention. She was triumphantly brought back, chained hand and feet, and cast into the common gaol, "awaiting orders."

Whilst the garrison had been sent on their unsuccessful errand, the chiefs had met together, and as one of the runaways was superintendent of the storehouses and magazines, an immediate search was made, in order to ascertain whether he had helped himself to some of the "treasures" before taking his unceremonious leave. To their horror they soon found out that silks, caps, powder, even the Emperor's gala dress, his favourite pistol and rifle, together with a large sum of money, were missing: in fact, the *bags of tef* were full of spoils. The Ras felt the gravity of his position; he had not only allowed himself to be grossly duped, but, moreover, some of the most valuable of the Emperor's property intrusted to his care had been carried off by his former friend. He utterly lost his head; he painted to himself Theodore's rage on hearing the news; he saw himself an inmate of the gaol, loaded with fetters, or perhaps condemned to a speedy and cruel death. He assembled the council, and laid the case before the chiefs; the wisest and most experienced were for trusting to his relationship with the Emperor, and to his well-known friendship for him; others proposed an expedition in the Galla country, a night attack on the village where it was supposed the fugitive would spend the nights: a few hundred would start in the evening, they said, surprise the fugitives, bring them back, recover the lost property, and, at the same time, murder a few Gallas, and plunder as much as they could—exploits that would immensely gratify their royal master, and make him forget the easy way the Ras had been imposed upon.

This last advice was carried out; and, though some still dissented, the Ras overruled their objections: he was already so deeply compromised that he clutched at every chance that offered itself of retrieving his position. Bitwaddad Damash, the friend and countryman of Theodore, the brave warrior, was intrusted with the command; under him were, placed Bitwaddad Hailo, Bitwaddad Wassié, and Dedjazmatch Goji, all of them "old friends of ours," and of whom I have given a short description. Two hundred of Damash's gunmen, and two hundred of Goji's spearmen, all picked soldiers, well armed and well mounted, formed the attacking party. Towards sunset they all assembled. Before leaving, Damash, clad in a silk shirt, wearing gallantly over his shoulders a splendid tiger's skin, armed with a pair of pistols and a double-barrelled gun; came to our prison to bid us good-by; or rather to gratify his vanity by our compelled admiration, and to obtain a parting blessing from his friend Mr. Rassam, who courteously performed the ceremony.

Twice before, Damash had, during our stay at Magdala, started for Watat, a village some twelve miles distant from Magdala, not far from where the Bechelo separates the province of Worahaimanoo from the plateau of Dahonte. There the Emperor's cattle were kept, and messengers had been sent to the Amba by the peasants requesting immediate assistance, as a Galla force had made its appearance, and they felt themselves unable to protect Theodore's cows. On these occasions the very sight of Damash and his gunmen had driven the Gallas away: at least so they said on their return; but *mauvaises langues* asserted that it was only a trick of the country people themselves, who desired to be reported to the Emperor as faithful subjects of his and anxious to protect the cattle they had in charge. Many of the younger and inexperienced soldiers felt confident that on this occasion the result would be the same; the fugitives would be surprised, and the Gallas run away in all directions at the sight of Damash and his valiant companions, leaving their homesteads and property at the mercy of the invaders.

The Ras passed an anxious, sleepless night; at day-dawn he and his friends went upon the small hillock near the prison, and telescope in hand anxiously watched the Galla plain. Hours passed away, and they saw nothing. What had occurred? why had not Damash and his men come back? such were the questions every, one asked: the old men shook their heads; they had fought in their days in the Galla country, and knew the valour of these savage horsemen. Even our old spy, Abu Falek, probably to see what we would say exclaimed, "That fool Damash had the impudence to make a raid in the Galla country, when even Theodore himself could not go there now." At last the welcome intelligence that Damash and his men were coming back, spread like wild-fire all over the mountain: they had been seen descending a steep ravine, not the road they had taken on going, but a shorter one. Soon afterwards horses and men were perceived on the plain; and something like confusion, and cattle being hurried down could be made out by the glasses. The party from the garrison were seen to halt at a short distance from the ravine they had descended, and march on very slowly. Something was wrong evidently; horsemen were at once despatched by the Ras to ascertain the result of the expedition. They returned with a doleful tale, and the Amba soon rang with the wailing of widows and orphans; eleven dead, thirty wounded, scores of fire-arms lost, the fugitives at large, was in sum the intelligence they brought back to the desponding Ras.

A Galla renegade had the night before led Damash and his men straight to the village of the chief in whose company they had been seen in the morning, and under whose hospitable roof he justly surmised that they would spend the night. At first all succeeded as they had expected. They reached the doomed village an hour before day-dawn, and surrounded at once the house of the chief, whilst a small body was sent to search and plunder the village itself. A fearful massacre took place; surprised in their sleep, the men were murdered before they were aware of the presence of the enemy; only a few were spared, together with some women and children, by the less blood-thirsty of these midnight assassins. Before retiring to rest, Meshisha and Comfou, thinking that perhaps an attempt might be made to capture them, advised the chief to be on his guard, and proposed to sleep with him in a small broken-down hut at some distance from his house. Fortunately for them and the chief, they adopted that prudent course; awoke by the cries and shouts in the village, they bridled their ready-saddled steeds, and were off before even their presence had been suspected.

Damash collected his men, and with his prisoners and plunder at once retraced his steps, glorying in his great deed and rejoicing in his success; it is true he had not caught the fugitives, but after all that was the Ras's business. He had planned the expedition, carried fire and sword into the Galla country; and without the loss of a single man was returning to the Amba with prisoners, horses, cows, mules, and other spoils of war. He knew how pleased Theodore would be, and he fancied himself already the fortunate successor of the disgraced Ras. He was within a few hundred yards of the short road he intended to take on his way back, leading from the Tanta plateau to the valley below Magdala, when he saw on the distant horizon a few horsemen riding towards him at full speed. The cattle and prisoners under charge of Goji and a few men were already engaged in the narrow road, and retreat was impossible. He placed his gunmen so as to face the horsemen, only a dozen, hoping to scare that handful off by the very sight of his large force; but he was mistaken. Brave Mahomed Hamza had the blood of his relations to avenge, and, though at the head of only twelve men, he bravely charged the 400 Amhara soldiers. A shot struck him in the forehead, and he fell dead from his horse. His companions, however, before the Amharas could reload, made a second brilliant charge, avenged their chief, and carried away the body all were anxious to mutilate. More horsemen came pouring in from all directions; the war-cry was echoed far and wide; men, women, and children assailed the Amharas with lances and stones. Mahomed's brothers, now supported by fifty lances, charged again and again the affrighted enemy, and drove them like sheep to the very brink of the precipice.

Damash, however, had not come to fight but to slay; he was only brave when he had prisoners to bully, defenceless men to murder, and children to reduce to slavery: the cattle had reached the valley below and the road was clear, so throwing away his tiger's skin, his shield, his pistols, his gun, and abandoning his horses, he gave the example of the *sauve qui peut*, and rolled rather than ran down the steep descent. His example was followed by all the Amharas. A complete rout followed; the ground was strewed with matchlocks, spears, and shields; wounded and dead were alike abandoned on the battlefield. The Gallas did not follow them down the ravine as they could not charge on the broken ground below; they, however, killed several with sharp stones—a dreadful weapon in a Galla's hand—as their terrified foe hurried down the narrow pass and tumbled one over the other in their eagerness to reach the valley, where these cowards knew well that they would be safe.

Almost all the wounded came to me; and for twelve hours I was busy bandaging and dressing their wounds. In several cases, where I knew that recovery was impossible, I informed the relations of the fact; as otherwise their death would have been laid to me, a rather serious matter in our critical position. Those thus warned always sought native advice, but they found out very soon that charms and amulets were of no avail, and that my prognostic had been but too true. I remember one case: a chief who had often been on guard at night over our prison had his left leg completely smashed by a stone; without entering into professional details, suffice it to say that I at once pronounced amputation as the only possible remedy; but to please the chiefs, who took a great interest in him, I agreed to dress his wound for a week, and after that time, should I be still of the same opinion to inform them of it. He had a small godjo built in our inclosure, and remained there until I gave for the second time as my opinion that nothing could save his life but immediate amputation. He was on that taken to his house and made over to a Shoa doctor, who promised not only to save his life but also the limb. The poor man was tortured by that ignorant quack for a week or ten days, until death put an end to his misery.

Two days after, on a female spy reporting that in the ravine where the Amharas had been slaughtered, she had seen two wounded men hidden among the bushes, and still alive; an old chief, also a Galla renegade, with a few hundred men, was ordered to proceed to the spot, and endeavour to bring them back and bury the dead; they were on no account to engage in any action with the Gallas, but to retreat at once should he meet with resistance. He saw no enemy except his old comrade Comfou, who, from a rock above, fired at them with his rifle, without wounding or killing any one; they returned his fire, but to no purpose, and, having fulfilled their instructions, brought in the two wounded men: both, however, died shortly afterwards. One of them had his right arm and left leg broken; moreover, a spear had cut open the abdominal integuments, and the bowels protruded: he said that he had suffered greatly from thirst, but that his greatest trouble was, with his left hand, to keep off the vultures from tearing his intestines.

The Ras, it is true, was now in a worse plight than before; but this time not alone. Damash had abandoned his men, run away, and lost the gun, pistols, and horse the Emperor had given, or rather lent, him. Many of the petty chiefs and soldiers had followed Damash's example, and some twenty-five matchlocks could not he accounted for, and of spears and shields the number missing was still greater. By-the-by, Damash pretended to be wounded, and for a long time we saw nothing of him, a circumstance at which we rejoiced extremely, but *his friends* told us that he was only suffering from a few excoriations due to his rather too rapid retreat.

If force had failed, perhaps negotiations might succeed. It was known that the two fugitives were still living in some of the villages belonging to the relations of Mahomed, awaiting the return of a messenger they had sent to the Galla Queen Mastiate, whose camp was a few days distant. The Magdala chiefs, therefore, proposed to the Gallas in their power that if they could induce their relations to give up the two fugitives, with the things they had taken away with them, they would set them all—men, women, and children—free, and restore the cattle that had been plundered. A woman, the wife of one of the principal men captured, volunteered to go. To the honour of the Gallas, they proudly and with scorn refused to give up their guests: they preferred to allow their relatives to linger in chains at Magdala, and abandon them to tortures and death, rather than obtain their release by a dishonourable action.

The Magdala magnates had now to give up all hope of redeeming their conduct in the eyes of Theodore; the good understanding between them was much shaken: they taxed one another, when in their cups, with cowardice, sent messengers separately to the Emperor, accusing one another, and lived in as much dread of the arrival of an Imperial messenger as we did ourselves. But Theodore, surrounded by difficulties, almost cut off from his amba, was far too cunning to show his displeasure: his letter on the subject was perfect. What if two of his servants had run away? they were unfaithful, and he was only too glad that they had left his amba; as for the arms lost, what did it matter? he had more to give them; and when he came they should take their revenge. A few, not many, were taken in, but all pretended to be so, and several only awaited a favourable opportunity to follow the example of those they had endeavoured to capture.

Every one suspected that Mastiate, the Galla Queen, would resent the foray made in her country, and avenge the death of her subjects so treacherously murdered. She would probably, they feared, destroy their crops at the foot of the Amba, stop the market, and starve out the place. She had, they knew, faithful allies in Comfou and Meshisha, and as the latter had been almost brought up on the mountain, and knew the many paths by which to lead; at night, the Galla host, much anxiety, therefore, prevailed, and great precautions were taken to protect the Amba against a sudden attack.

I believe that it was indeed Mastiate's plan, and that she was on the point of executing it when a serious danger from, another side required her presence. Wakshum Gobazé, at the head of a powerful army, had invaded her dominions.

Our days of calm repose were at an end; if it was not one rebel chief or the other that threatened the Amba, it was the good news from home that at last an expedition for our deliverance had been decided upon, or the less welcome information that the King was about to move in our direction; and one excitement had hardly subsided before we were again a prey to another—one day full of hope, the next, perhaps, desponding and cast down.

Watshum Gobazé's career, had been full of adventure. As a young man he accompanied his father, Wakshum Gabra Medhin, the hereditary chief of Lasta, to the Imperial camp. On Theodore's first campaign in Shoa, which ended in the submission of that country, Gobazé's father fell under Theodore's displeasure, and was on the point of being executed when the Bishop interfered, and, as he was of great use to Theodore at the time, his request was granted. However, not long afterwards, Gobazé and his father seized their opportunity, deserted from Theodore's army, and retired into Lasta. They had not much difficulty in inducing the mountaineers to espouse their cause, and declare themselves independent. Theodore deputed to suppress that insurrection the rebel's own cousin, called Wakshum Teferi, a brave soldier and splendid horseman. He pursued his relative, totally defeated his army, and brought him a chained prisoner to the foot of the throne. Theodore was at the time in Wadela, a high plateau situate between Lasta and Begemder. He condemned the rebel chief to death; and as but few trees are to be found on that elevated plateau, he had him hung on the one near which his tent was pitched, so that the body of his enemy might be seen far and wide. Gobazé had managed to escape; and some time afterwards, Theodore, who was afraid of Wakshum Teferi, as he was beloved and admired by the soldiers, put him in chains,—forgetting that the man had served him so faithfully as even to bring to the scaffold his blood relation, —on the pretext that he had willingly allowed Gobazé to escape.

Gobazé for a while remained hidden in the fastnesses of the high mountains of Lasta, but no sooner did he perceive that the Emperor's power was weakened and that the peasants were discontented with his tyrannical rule, than he came forth from his retreat, and having collected around him some of the former followers of his father, hoisted the standard of rebellion, and loudly proclaimed himself the avenger of his race. All Lasta soon acknowledged him. His rule was mild; and before long Gobazé found himself at the head of a considerable force. He advanced in the direction of Tigré, subdued the provinces of Enderta and Wajjerat, marched into Tigré proper, conquered Theodore's lieutenant, and left there his deputy, Dejatch Kassa. He himself returned to Lasta, having in view the extension of his power towards Yedjow and the Galla country, so as to protect Lasta from being invaded by these tribes during his proposed conquest of the Amhara country. Circumstances were greatly in his favour, and for a while he was the man to whom all Abyssinia looked to as their future ruler. On his return to Lasta he was at once acknowledged by Wadela, and at the same time some runaway chiefs of Yedjow having come to him, he availed himself of their assistance to make himself master of that province. He had some trouble, however, in settling it, as part of it was strongly in favour of an alliance with the Wallo Gallas: he deemed it the wisest course, therefore, to invade the Wallo country after the rainy season, and dictate his terms. He detached a small force, and sent with it one of his relations to receive the submission of Dalanta; and not long afterwards Dahonte was evacuated by the Gallas, and occupied by his troops. In the beginning of September he entered the Wallo Galla country by its north-eastern frontier, not far from Lake Haïk. On the intelligence reaching Queen Mastiate she hastened to oppose his march, and encamped a few miles in advance of his army, on a large plain, where her splendid cavalry would have all advantage. For at least a fortnight or three weeks the two armies remained in front of each other; Gobazé awaiting his enemy on the broken ground he had encamped upon, and where the Galla horse could not charge, but where his gunmen would be all-powerful; while the Queen, on her side, would not leave the ground she had chosen, and where she was almost certain of victory.

Gobazé had been long before in communication with the Bishop and with Mr. Rassam. Before the rainy season of 1867, he had sent word to the Bishop that he was coming to Magdala, presented him a few hundred dollars, and asked him to afford all the assistance in his power should he advance towards the place. The Bishop said he would do his utmost, and that as soon as the Amba was invested he would leave no stone, unturned to facilitate his plans. Gobazé sent back word that if the Bishop would secure him the services of Damash, Goji, and the Ras (the three who had all the garrison under their joint command), that he would come at once. This request was simply absurd; if we had been able to gain over these men to our cause, we could have dispensed with the presence of Gobazé altogether. What the Bishop proposed was, that Gobazé should encamp at Islamgee; the moment he appeared below the mountain, the Bishop would supply us and some men upon whom he could depend with fire-arms and ammunition. We should in the meanwhile open our chains with the assistance of our servants, and arm all those amongst them who could be trusted; and on the Bishop being informed, that we were ready, he would come out in full canonicals, carrying the holy cross, and excommunicate Theodore and every one who adhered to him, placing under an irrevocable curse all who attempted to arrest him or us. Our party, including Portuguese, natives of Massowah, and messengers, would have amounted to at least twenty-five; the Bishop could bring fifty men, and surround himself with about 200 priests and defteras, so as to form a mixed sortie; all, however, ready to fight in case of need. Should persuasion or threats fail to force the way to the gate, they were to shoot down any one attempting to molest us in our advance. Arrived at the gate, the Bishop and the priests would stand before the inner door, whilst the armed party would seize upon the outer gate and hold it until the Wakshum and his men, ready at hand, would march in and take possession of the fort.

The plan was a very good one, and no doubt would have succeeded. We knew well, that no pity would have been shown to us had we been recaptured, and we would have fallen one after the other, rather than allow ourselves to be made prisoners again. In presence of even a handful of men, determined to sell their lives dearly, few of the soldiers would have ventured on an open attack; the affair would have been sudden, and the garrison taken by surprise: moreover, we had to deal with bigoted people, and many who might have rushed upon us, would have been kept back by the presence of the Bishop, and would kiss the ground before his feet rather than encounter his dreaded excommunication. The Bishop informed Gobazé of this plan, and for days we lived in a fearful state of excitement, always hoping that the messenger would return with the grateful intelligence that Gobazé had accepted it. However, we were doomed to disappointment: Gobazé did not approve the suggestion; he sent word to the Bishop, "It is better for me to go to Begemder and attack there my blood enemy: only give me your blessing. On the fall of Theodore, the Amba belongs to me; it is far preferable that I should fight him instead of attacking Magdala, as you know well that we cannot take forts." The blessing was duly given; but Gobazé thought better of it: he did not venture to attack the murderer of his father, and a few days afterwards we heard that he had marched into Yedjow. Gobazé behaved always very well towards us; he assisted, as much as lay in his power, our messengers on their way to the coast, and was anxious to effect our deliverance; unfortunately he had not sufficient courage to fight when Theodore was his opponent.

Gobazé and Mastiate after a time got tired of staring at one another. The latter was aware that before long she would have to deal with even a more serious enemy, in the person of her rival Workite, and she would willingly have come to terms. She sent a horse to Gobazé as a peace-offering, but he returned the present, accompanied with a parcel of cotton and a spindle, with a message to the effect that she had nothing to do with horses, and as her occupation was to spin cotton, he had sent her the necessary articles. Gobazé, however, shortly afterwards heard that in Tigré, Dejatch Kassa, who for some months had abandoned his cause, had made himself very powerful, and marched upon Adowa. Supplies also began to run short in his camp, whilst Mastiate being in her own country, could draw them with all facility; he therefore retraced his steps towards Yedjow. Mastiate followed him in the rear, only biding her time to fall upon him when a favourable opportunity presented itself. Gobazé found his position difficult, and made advances. Mastiate saw her advantage and made her own terms. She promised not to interfere in the affairs of Yedjow, on condition that he made over to her the provinces of Dahonte and Dalanta, which he had shortly before occupied. He agreed, and peace was made between the two parties; it was even reported that an offensive and defensive alliance had been concluded between them; but this could hardly have been the case, as soon afterwards, when Mastiate was hard pressed by Menilek, her new ally did not afford her any assistance.

To us these constant changes of rulers was most annoying, more so as we had no money, and were constantly obliged to make presents to the new chiefs appointed by the conqueror of the day. We had hardly made "friends" with the shums (governors) Theodore had left in those provinces, than we had to open communications with the deputies of the Galla Queen, and again with those of Gobazé on the evacuation of those districts by the Gallas, and a fourth time on their reoccupation by the Gallas: we had to ensure their neutrality, at least,—for they had already plundered several of our messengers—by suitable offerings and promises of more, should they favour our cause. In one respect we were very fortunate: on our arrival we were saved from much discomfort, if not from something worse, by the money the Emperor gave to his workmen; who made it over to us. During the rainy season we were again saved from starvation by a few dollars I had kept in reserve; for the third time, everything appeared desperate, and we were so reduced that some sold and others were talking of selling their mules and anything available, when a messenger at last reached us with a few hundred dollars.

Whilst Mastiate was negotiating with Gobaz, her son wrote to Mr. Rassam and to the Bishop. He asked Mr. Rassam to use his influence and give him the mountain, promising in return to treat us honourably if we liked to remain in his country, or enable us to reach the coast if we desired to return to our own native land. To the Bishop he promised all protection; he would allow him to take away his property, and would not injure what he called "his idols."

So long as we could get out of the clutches of Theodore, it did not matter much into whose hands we fell: not that we ever expected,—such, at least, was the opinion of the majority amongst us,—that we should be allowed to leave the country: but, at all events, we should not be in daily fear of our lives, of tortures, and of starvation, as we were then. We should not have liked to fall into the hands of the peasants or of some petty chief: the first would have at once put us to death out of hatred to the white men; the second, most probably would have ill-treated us or have sold us to the highest bidder. The great rebels would have acted differently: we should have been, for a time, at least, comparatively free, and allowed to depart on a suitable ransom being given. Therefore, to Ali, to Gobaz, to Ahmed the son of Mastiate, or to Menilek the King of Shoa, Mr. Rassam's answer was always the same, "Come; invest this place, and then we will see what we can do for you."

It amused us sometimes to watch all these different rivals of Theodore, each of them endeavouring to seize upon Magdala even before Theodore was quite out of the way. Gobazé and Menilek, had both in view to make themselves rulers of Abyssinia, by the possession of Magdala: (indeed the latter had also written before the rainy season, informing the Bishop of his coming to take possession of *his* amba, and requesting the bishop to take care of *his* property.) Apart from the great prestige it would confer upon them, they would obtain the three things they rightly judged would most likely insure the fulfilment of their ambitious views: viz., the throne, the Bishop, and the English prisoners. All wanted Mr. Bassam, not merely to help them, but to *give* them the mountain: they were aware that the chiefs were on friendly terms with us, and supposed that we were in possession of fabulous sums of money, so that, by means of friendship and bribery, we might open the gates to the candidate we selected.

Magdala could only become theirs by treachery: in their immense armies, they could not have found twenty men with sufficient courage to venture on an assault. Magdala had the reputation of being impregnable; and, indeed, against natives badly armed, it was very nearly so. Even Theodore only took possession of it because the Galla garrison, through fear, evacuated the place during the night. He had pitched his camp at the foot of the Amba, and attempted an assault; but soon retired from his hopeless task before the shower of missiles thrown from above. It was not until several days after the Gallas had retired, that one of the chiefs, suspecting the place to be empty, cautiously ventured to ascertain the fact, and returned to inform Theodore that he might quietly walk in as the enemy had disappeared.

CHAPTER XV

On the 25th of October, Abouna Salama (the Bishop of Abyssinia) died after a long and painful illness.

Abouna Salama was in many respects a remarkable man. Two such characters as Theodore and himself are seldom met with at the same time in those distant lands. Both ambitious, both proud, both passionate, it was inevitable that sooner or later they must come into collision, and the stronger crush the weaker.

Abyssinia had been for years without a bishop. Priests could no more be consecrated, nor new churches dedicated to Christian worship, as the ark could not contain the tabot blessed by the bishop of the land. Ras Ali, although outwardly a Christian and belonging to a converted family, had still too many connections amongst the Mussulman Gallas, his true friends and supporters, to care for more than an apparent profession of the State religion, and troubled himself very little about the inconvenience to which the priesthood was subjected by the long-continued vacancy of the bishopric.

Dejatch Oubié was at that time the semi-independent ruler of Tigré. From the position of a simple governor he had gradually risen to power, and now at the head of a large army strove for the title of Ras. Though still on apparent terms of friendship with Ras Ali, even to a certain degree acknowledging him as his superior, he was all the while secretly exerting his influence to overthrow the Ras's power in order to reign in his stead. For these reasons he despatched some of his chiefs, with Monsignor de Jacobis, an Italian nobleman and Roman Catholic bishop at Massowah, to Egypt, to obtain a bishop for the Abyssinian see; [Footnote: According to the rules of the Abyssinian Church, the bishop must be a Coptic priest ordained at Cairo. The expenses required for the consecration of a bishop amount to about 10,000 dollars] and in order to secure for himself such a powerful weapon as the support of the priesthood, he incurred the heavy expense required for the consecration of an Abouna. De Jacobis made strenuous efforts to have a bishop anointed who would favour the Roman Catholics; but he failed, as the Patriarch chose for that dignity a young man who had received part of his education at an English school at Cairo, and whose views were more in favour of Protestantism than of the Copt's long-standing adversary, the Church of Rome.

Andraos, this young priest, was only in his twentieth year. When informed that he must leave his monastery and the companionship of the monks his friends to proceed to the distant and semi-civilized land of Habesch, he firmly declined the honour proposed for him. He requested his superiors to fix their choice on a worthier man, declaring himself unfit for the dignity so suddenly thrust upon him. His objections were not admitted, and as he still persisted in his refusal, the superior of the convent put him in irons; wherein he should remain, he was told, until he agreed to obey the head of the Coptic Church. Andraos gave in; and having been duly anointed and consecrated Bishop of Abyssinia, under the title of Abouna Salama, with all the pomps and ceremonies proper to the occasion, started shortly afterwards in an English man-of-war, reaching Massowah in the beginning of 1841.

Dejatch Oubié received him with great honours; added numerous villages and large districts to those the hereditary possession of the bishops, and made every endeavour to attach him to his cause. He succeeded even beyond his expectations. Abouna Salama, instead of needing the persuasions of Oubié to join him in the overthrow of Ras Ali, proposed the attempt. Through his influence Oubié concluded an alliance with Goscho Beru, the ruler of Godjam. The two chiefs agreed to march on Debra Tabor, attack Ras Ali, wrest from him the power he had usurped, and divide the government of Abyssinia, confirming the Bishop's alleged rights to a third of the revenue of the land.

Oubié and Goscho Beru kept to their engagements, offered battle to Ras Ali near Debra Tabor, and utterly routed his army; Ras Ali with difficulty escaping from the field with a small body of well-mounted followers. It so happened, however, that Oubié celebrated his success in potations too many and deep. Some of the fugitive soldiers of Ras Ali accidentally entered Oubié's tent, found their master's conqueror in the condition known as dead drunk, and availed themselves of his helpless condition to make him their prisoner. This sudden contretemps changed the aspect of affairs. Certain well-mounted horsemen galloped after Ras Ali and succeeded in overtaking him towards evening. He would not at first believe in his good fortune; but others of his soldiers arriving and confirming the glad tidings, he returned to Debra Tabor, reunited his scattered followers, and was able to dictate terms to his captive conqueror. Oubié was pardoned and allowed to return to Tigré, the Bishop being answerable for his fidelity. Ras Ali treated the Bishop with all respect, fell at his feet and implored him not to listen to the calumnies of his enemies, assuring him that the Church had no more faithful son than himself, nor any more willing to comply with the holy father's wishes. The Bishop, now on friendly terms with all parties, and all but worshipped by them, soon made his authority felt; and had not Theodore risen from obscurity, Abouna Salama would, no doubt, have been the Hildebrand of Abyssinia.

During the campaigns of Lij Kassa against the ruler of Godjam, and during that period of revolution ending in the overthrow of Ras Ali, Abouna Salama retired to his property in Tigré, residing there in peace under the protection of his friend Oubié. Ever since his arrival in Abyssinia Abouna Salama had shown the bitterest opposition to the Roman Catholics: an enmity not so much engendered by conviction, perhaps, as inflamed by the fact that some of his property had been seized at Jiddah at the instigation of some Roman Catholic priests, who had through his influence been plundered, ill-treated, and expelled from Abyssinia. When the intelligence reached the Abouna that Lij Kassa was marching against Tigré, he publicly excommunicated him, on the ground that Kassa was the friend of the Roman Catholics, protected their Bishop, De Jacobis, and wanted to subvert in favour of the creed of Rome the religion of the land. But Kassa was a match for the Abouna; he denied the charge, and at the same time stated "that if Abouna Salama could excommunicate, Abouna de Jacobis could remove it." The Bishop, alarmed at the influence his enemies might possibly obtain, offered to recall his anathema, on condition that Kassa would expel De Jacobis. These terms having been agreed upon, Abouna Salama shortly afterwards consented to place the crown of Abyssinia on the usurper's head, and did so in the very church Oubié had erected for his own coronation, under the name of Theodore II.

Pleased with the Bishop's compliance, Theodore showed him the utmost respect. He carried his chair, or walked behind him with a lance and shield as if he was nothing but a follower of his, and on all fit occasions fell down to the ground in his presence and respectfully kissed his hand. Abouna Salama for a time believed that his influence over Theodore was unbounded, as it had been over Ras Ali and Oubié; mistook Theodore's show of humility for sincere admiration and devotion; and the more humble Theodore seemed disposed to be, the more arrogant did the Bishop, publicly show himself. But he had not quite understood the character of the Emperor he had anointed; and overrating his own importance, at last he made of Theodore an open and relentless enemy. The crisis came when Abouna Salama least expected it. One day Theodore went in state to pay him his respects. Arrived at the Abouna's tent, he informed him of his visit; the Bishop sent word that he would receive him when convenient, and meanwhile bade him wait without. Theodore complied; but as time passed and the Bishop made no appearance, Theodore walked away, the enemy of his prelate, and burning for revenge.

For years afterwards they lived in open enmity, or enmity slightly masked: each worked hard at the destruction of the other. If Theodore's reign had been a peaceful one, the Abouna would have gained the day; but the Emperor, surrounded as he was by a large army of devoted followers, found ready listeners to his descriptions of the Bishop's character. Abouna Salama was never very popular; he was, without being a miser, far from liberal. Friendship in Abyssinia means presents: it is accepted as such by all; and every chief, every man of note, who courts popularity, lavishes with an unsparing hand. The Emperor naturally took advantage of this want of liberality in the Bishop's character, to contrast it with his own generosity. He insinuated that the Abouna was only a merchant at heart; that instead of selling the tribute he received in kind to the people of the country, as was formerly the custom, he sent it by caravans to Massowah, trafficked with the Turks, and hoarded all his money in Egypt. Little by little Theodore worked on the minds of his people, impressing them with the idea that, after all, the Bishop was only a man like themselves; and, at least in Theodore's camp, he had already lost much of his prestige when the Emperor spread the report that his honour had been assailed by the Bishop whom they all worshipped.

Theodore, when detailing to us his grievances one day on our way to Agau Medar, introduced the subject of his quarrel with the Abouna. He then stated as the reason of his enmity against him that, one day when he was entertaining his officers at a public breakfast, the Bishop, taking advantage of his absence, and under pretence of confessing the Queen, went into her tent. When Theodore returned after the breakfast was over, he presented himself at the door of his wife's apartment, but on being informed that she was engaged in her religious duties with the Abouna he walked away. In the evening he returned again to his wife's tent. When he entered, she flew to him, and sobbing on his neck told him that she had been that day unwillingly unfaithful to him, having been unable to resist the violence of the Bishop. He forgave her, he said, because she was innocent; and as for the suborner of his honour he could not punish him: nothing but death could avenge such a crime, and how could he lay violent hands on a dignitary of the Church?—There is no doubt that the whole was an abominable invention; but Theodore had evidently told the same story over and over again until at last he had come to believe it himself.

Abouna Salama lost reputation, though, perhaps, few people believed the Emperor's assertion. But on the principle that if you throw mud some will stick, the Abouna's character was amongst a certain class fairly gone; and henceforward his friends were only to be found amongst the King's enemies, while his foes were Theodore's bosom friends. In public Theodore still always treated him with respect, though not with such a great show of humility as before; but he evidently, for the sake of his people, made a distinction between the official character of the Abouna, respecting it on account of his Christian faith, and his private one, for which he expressed the greatest scorn.

For a long while the question of the Church lands was a great deal discussed between them. Theodore could not tolerate any power in the State but his own. He had fought hard to be the supreme ruler of Abyssinia; he had done his utmost to bring the Abouna into contempt, and when he thought the occasion favourable to do away entirely with his power and influence, he confiscated all the Church lands and revenues—some of the Bishop's hereditary property by the same stroke—and placed himself virtually at the head of the Church. The Abouna's anger knew no bounds. Naturally of a violent temper, he grossly abused Theodore on every occasion. Some of their quarrels were most unbecoming; the intense hatred burning in the prelate's heart showing itself in expressions that ought never to have fallen from his lips. The Bishop of Abyssinia was never tolerant. I have mentioned that towards Roman Catholics he was most intolerant. He persecuted them at every opportunity, and even when himself a prisoner at Magdala he never sought to obtain the release of an unfortunate Abyssinian who had been years before cast into chains at his instigation, for the sole reason that the man had visited Rome and become a convert there. Towards Protestants he was better inclined; still, he would not hear of "conversions." Missionaries might instruct, but they had to stop there; and when, as it happened, some Jews were led by the teachings of the missionaries to accept Christianity, they had to be baptized and received as members of the Abyssinian Church. He showed himself on all occasions friendly towards Europeans, not Roman Catholics, and in time of trouble proved of good service to the European captives; even helping them with small sums of money at a time of great scarcity and want. But his friendship was dangerous. Theodore distrusted, nay, disliked any one who was on friendly terms with his great enemy; the horrid torture the Europeans suffered at Azzazoo was due entirely to that cause; and the quarrels or reconciliations between Church and State always influenced their and our fate. The Abouna left Azzazoo with the King's camp after the rainy season of 1864.

A serious rebellion had broken out in Shoa, and Theodore, leaving his prisoners, wives and camp-followers at Magdala, made a quick march through the Wallo Galla country; but he found the rebels so strong that he could do nothing against them. He was greatly annoyed at the Bishop's refusal to accompany him. The Shoa people are of all Abyssinians the most bigoted, and have the greatest regard for their Abouna; with him in his camp many of the opposing chiefs would at once have laid down their arms and returned to their allegiance. But the Bishop, who had in view his fertile districts in Tigré, proposed accompanying Theodore first to that province; and after the rebellion had been put down in that part of the kingdom, to proceed with him to Shoa. Their interview on that occasion was very stormy; and Theodore must have had great command over himself to have refrained from extremities. Abouna Salama remained at Magdala, according to his desire; but a prisoner. He was never put in chains; though it is said that Theodore had several times resolve it should be done, and even had the fetters prepared; but he was always restrained by dread of the effect that such a measure might have on his people. The Bishop was allowed to go as far as the church, should he desire it; but at night a small guards always watched outside his house; sometimes even a few of the soldiers passed the night in the Abouna's apartment. Almost all his servants were spies of the King. He could trust no one, except a few of his slaves—young Gallas given to him in former days by Theodore—and a Copt, who, with some priests, had accompanied the Patriarch David on his visit to Abyssinia: some of them had accepted the King's service, whilst others, like the Copt servant I have mentioned, devoted themselves to their compatriot and bishop.

During the former imprisonment of the captives at Magdala, the intercourse between the Bishop and them had been very limited. They never saw each other; but occasionally a young slave of the Bishop's would carry a verbal message, or a short Arabic note containing some piece of news, generally some exaggerated rumours of the rebels' doings (always believed by the too credulous Abouna), or simple inquiries about medicine, &c.

The day of our arrival, and whilst the chiefs were reading Theodore's instructions concerning us, the young slave above mentioned came up to Mr. Rosenthal with kind compliments from the Abouna, to inform us that as far as his master then knew there was nothing bad for the present, but great fears for the future. The Bishop, we knew, had frequent communications with the great rebel chiefs (Theodore was also well aware of the fact, and hated him all the more for it); he had shown himself at all times well disposed towards us, and as he was as anxious as ourselves to escape from the power of Theodore, we deemed it of the highest importance to open communication with him. But the difficulties in the way were enormous. Nothing would have injured our prospects more than the betrayal of our intercourse with the Bishop to the Emperor. Samuel in that respect could not for a long time be trusted; as a deadly enmity existed between himself and the Bishop. It required all the persuasive powers of Mr. Rassam to bring on a good understanding between the two; he, however, managed the affair so skilfully that he not only succeeded, but after mutual explanations, they became affectionate friends. But, until this difficulty had been overcome, great precautions were necessary.

The small slave was soon suspected by our vigilant guards. It would have been dangerous to confide to him anything of importance, for he might at any time be seized and searched. We therefore employed servant-girls, who were known to the Bishop, as they had resided on the mountain with the former captives. The Bishop accepted with eagerness our proposal to escape from the Amba, and, sanguine as he was hasty, at first gave us great hopes; but when we came to the details of his plot, as far as we were concerned, we found it was perfectly ridiculous. He wanted some nitrate of silver in order to blacken his face, so as to pass unperceived through the gates. Once free, he was to join either Menilek or the Wakshum, excommunicate and depose Theodore, and proclaim the rebel emperor in his place. He had evidently forgotten that the days of Oubié and Ras Ali were gone long ago, that the man who held Magdala cared but little for excommunication, and that, deposed or not, Theodore still would virtually be king. The Bishop might have succeeded, perhaps; but had he been caught, or had it ever been known that we were parties to his escape, no power in the world would have saved us from the rage of the infuriated monarch.

After the Bishop's reconciliation with Samuel our relations with him were more frequent and intimate. He was at all times willing to help us to the best of his ability, lent as a few dollars when we were hard pressed for money, wrote to the rebels to protect our messengers, invited them to come to our release, promising to the successful one his support, and, I believe, would even have accepted a reconciliation with the man from whom he had received so many injuries, solely for our sake.

Disappointed in his ambition, deprived of his property, insulted, degraded, without power, without liberty, Abouna Salama succumbed to the too common temptation of men who suffer much. Almost without society, leading a dull misanthropic life, he did not remember that sobriety in all respects was essential to his health and that over-indulgence at table was not consistent with his forced seclusion. Constant annoyances, added to intemperate habits, could but bring on sickness. During our first winter I attended him, through Alaka Zenab, our friend and his, and under my care he recovered. Unfortunately, he only listened to my advice and obeyed my injunctions for a short time; soon missing the stimulants he had for years been accustomed to, he gradually felt the want of their cheering influence, and again resorted to them. During the rainy season of 1867 he had a more serious attack. This time Samuel, being able to visit him at night, was our medium, and being a very intelligent man could give us a correct account of his condition. For a while his health improved; but he was even more unreasonable than formerly: hardly was he convalescent than several times a day he sent to inquire if he could drink some arrack, take a little opium, or indulge in some of his more favourite dishes. It is not astonishing that relapse quickly followed: though I showed him the danger of the course he was pursuing, he persisted in it.

In the beginning of October the Bishop's condition became so critical that he applied to the Ras and chiefs to allow me to visit him. They met in consultation, and in a body repaired to Mr. Rassam, when I was called and asked if I would attend him. I replied that as far as I was concerned I was perfectly willing. The chiefs then retired to consider the matter; and on one of them insinuating that Theodore would not be sorry if his enemy the Abouna died, and that he would be angry if he knew that the Bishop had been brought in contact with the Europeans, they decided on refusing his request; though they consented to the attendance of the *cow-doctor*. With the Abouna we lost a staunch ally, a good friend; nay, the only one we had in the country. Had a rebel succeeded in making himself master of the Amba his protection would have been invaluable: not that I believe his influence would have been sufficient to ensure our release; but still, with him, we should have met at the hands of any of the great rebel chiefs nothing but good treatment and courteous demeanour.

The messenger sent to convey the tidings of the Abouna's death to the Emperor, was rather puzzled how to express himself, not knowing in what light his Majesty would receive the news. He adopted a middle course as the safest, and tried to appear neither sorry nor rejoiced. Theodore listened to his tale and exclaimed, "Thank God, my enemy is dead!" Then, addressing the messenger, he added, "You fool! why did you not on reaching me shout out 'Miserach' (good tidings)? I would have given you my best mule."

With the death of the Bishop, our hopes, though always of the faintest kind, when natives were expected to be the deliverers, seemed for ever crushed. Wakshum Gobazé had, for a time at least, by his treaty with Mastiate, given up his pretensions to the possession of Magdala; and Menilek, even if he kept to his word and attempted the siege of our amba, would, no doubt, fall back on Shoa as soon as he should be apprised of the death of his friend whom he was so anxious to release. We had no precise information as to the steps that were taken at home for our rescue; and, until certain that troops had landed, we felt very anxious lest some *contretemps* should, at the last instant, occur, and the expedition be abandoned, or some more or less chimerical plan adopted in its stead. We had received a little money of late, but as everything was scarce and dear, we had to be very careful, and refuse many a "friend's" request—rather a dangerous proceeding in those days.

We believed—but events proved we were wrong—that if any great rebel, any rising man of influence, should present himself before the Amba, the discontented, half-starved wretches would be only too glad to open the gates and receive him as a saviour. The garrison, we knew, would not on any account surrender to the Gallas. For years they had been at enmity, and the marauding expeditions which the soldiers of the mountain had lately made into their territory, had increased that bad feeling, and quite destroyed any hope of reconciliation. This was the more vexatious, as now that Mastiate had, by her treaty with Gobazé, obtained possession and garrisoned all the districts around Magdala, it was but natural to expect that she would make some efforts at least to seize upon a fortress that lay within her dominions. Not many days after the departure of Gobazé for Yedjow, she issued orders to the people of the neighbourhood to cease supplying the Amba, and forbade any of her subjects from attending the weekly market; she even fixed a day for the troops she had detached to Dalanta and Dahonte to rendezvous at a short distance from Magdala, as she intended to destroy the whole of the country for miles around, and reduce the garrison by famine.

The Wallo Gallas are a fine race, far superior to the Abyssinian in elegance, manliness, and courage. Originally from the interior of Africa, they made their first appearance in Abyssinia towards the middle of the sixteenth century. These hordes invaded the fairest provinces in such numbers, they excelled so greatly the Amharas in horsemanship and in courage, that not only did they overrun the land, but lived for years on the resources of the country in imprudent security. After a while they settled down on the beautiful plateau extending from the river Bechelo to the highlands of Shoa, and from the Nile to the lowland inhabited by the Adails. Though retaining most of the characteristics of their race, they adopted many of the customs of the people they conquered. They lost in great measure their predatory and pastoral habits, tilled the soil, built permanent dwellings, and to a certain, extent adopted in their dress, food, and mode of life the usages of the former inhabitants.

In appearance the Galla is tall, well made, rather slender, but wiry; the hair of both men and women is long, thick, waving, rather than curly, and is altogether more like coarse European hair than the semi-woolly texture that covers Abyssinian skulls. Their dress is in many respects identical; both wear trousers, only those of the Gallas are shorter and tighter, somewhat resembling those worn by the people of Tigré. They both wear a large cotton cloth, a robe by day and a covering by night; the only difference being that the Galla seldom weaves in the side the broad red stripe, the pride of the Amhara. The food of both races is nearly the same; both enjoy the raw meat of the cow, the shiro or hot spiced dish of peas, the wât, and the teps (toasted meat); they only differ in the grain they use for bread, the Amhara delighting in pancakes made of the small seed of the tef, whilst the Galla's bread is more loaf-like, and is prepared with the flour of wheat or barley, the only grain that prospers on their elevated land. The Galla women are generally fair; and when not exposed to the sun, their large, black, brilliant, shining eyes, their rosy lips, their long, black, and neatly-braided hair, their little feet and hands, their graceful and well-rounded forms, make them comparable to the fairest daughters of Spain or Italy. The long shirt falling from the neck to the ankle, and fastened round the waist by the ample folds of a white cotton belt; the silver anklets, from which hang tiny bells, the long necklace of beads and silver, the white and black rings covering the taper fingers, are all very much the same articles as those that are thought necessary for the toilette of the Galla amazon and the more sedentary Amhara lady.

The most apparent difference is in their religion. At the time of their first appearance, the Wallo Gallas, like many of the divisions of the same family who, having settled further inland and having less intercourse with foreigners, are still plunged in the grossest idolatry, worshipped trees and stones; or rather under these natural objects rendered adoration to a being called the Unknown, who was to be propitiated by human sacrifices. It is impossible to obtain any correct information as to the exact date of their conversion to Islamism; but it has been accepted by the Wallo tribe almost universally. None at the present day are given to heathen practices, and only a few families belong to the Christian faith.

If we compare the races still further, and examine the morality and social habits of the two, at a first glance it would seem that both are licentious, both dissolute. But, on closer inspection, the degradation of the one is seen to be so thorough, that the other may claim, by contrast, something like primitive simplicity. The Amhara's life is one round of sensual debauchery; his conversation seldom deviates to pure or innocent subjects: no title is so envied by the men as that of libertine, and the women, also, are all ambitious of a like distinction: an "unfortunate" is not regarded as unfortunate there. The richest, the noblest, the highest in the land are profligates in love, or mercenary: more frequently both. Nothing is so disagreeable to an Abyssinian lady's ear as an insinuation that she is virtuous; for that would be taken to mean that she is either ill-looking or for some other reason is not favoured with many lovers.

In some parts of the Galla country the family exists in the old patriarchal form. The father is in his humble hut as absolute as the chief is over the tribe. If a man marries and is afterwards obliged to leave his village on a distant foray, his wife is immediately taken under the close protection of his brother, who is her husband until the elder's return. This custom was for many years very prevalent; now it is more limited: it is most common in the plateau arising from the Bechelo to Dalanta or Dahonte, where Galla families, almost isolated from the general tribe, have preserved many of the institutions of their forefathers. The stranger invited under the roof of a Galla chief will find in the same large smoky hut individuals of several generations. The heavy straw roof rests on some ten or twelve wooden pillars, having in the centre an open space, where the matrons, sitting near the fire, prepare the evening meal, while a swarm of children play around them. Opposite the rude door of small twigs, held together by nothing but a few branches cut from the nearest tree, stands the simple alga of the "lord of the manor." Near his bed neighs his favourite horse, the pet of young and old. In other partitioned places are his stores of barley or wheat. When the evening meal is over, and the children sleep where they last fell in their romping games, the chief first sees that the companion of his forays is well littered; he then conducts his guest to the spot where some sweet-smelling straw has been spread under a dried cow-hide. Nor is that the end of his hospitality, which at this point becomes rather embarrassing to the married traveller. But the strange way in which the guest is honoured must not be set down to licentiousness; it really is simplicity.

Every Galla is a horseman, every horseman a soldier; and thus is formed a perfect militia, an always ready army, where no discipline is required, no drill but to follow the chief. As soon as the war-cry is heard, or the signal fire is seen on the summit of the distant peak, the ever-ready steed is saddled, the young son jumps up behind his father to hold his second lance, and from every hamlet, from every apparently peaceful homestead, brave soldiers rush to the rendezvous. When Theodore himself, at the head of his thousands, invaded their land, then farewell to their homes. His revengeful hand burnt forms and villages far and wide wherever he was opposed, and the defenceless peasants fled in order to save their lives, knowing well how futile were their hopes of safety, should they fall into his power.

The Wallos are divided into seven tribes. Presenting no differences amongst themselves, they were simply separated by civil wars. Could these brave horsemen only understand the motto "Union is strength," they could make as easy a conquest of the whole of Abyssinia as their fathers did of the plains they now dwell upon. When united, they have always carried their arms successfully into an enemy's country. Children of their race, the Gooksas, the Mariés, the Alis, have held the Emperor in their sway, and governed the land for years. Unfortunately during the days of our captivity, as had been but too frequently the case before, petty jealousies, unworthy rivalries, weakened to such an extent their power that, far from being able to impose their laws on others, they in turn became but tools in the hands of the Christian kings and rulers. With Abusheer died the last vestige of union. If not at actual war, one party was always working against another; and no distant campaign could be thought of when their enemies in their own country dwelt.

Abusheer, the last Imam of the Wallo Gallas, left two sons by different wives, Workite [Footnote: Fine gold.] and Mastiate. [Footnote: Looking-glass.] The son of the former, as we mentioned in a previous chapter, was killed by Theodore on the escape of Menilek to Shoa, and Workite had no option left but to seek the hospitality of the young king for whom she had sacrificed so much.

Thus for more than two years Mastiate was left in undisturbed possession of the supremacy vested in her by the unanimous consent of the chiefs, a regent for her son until he attained his majority.

Menilek, after his escape, had no easy task before him: the chief who had headed the rebellion in the name of his king, after the gallant repulse and the check he inflicted upon Theodore, declared himself independent— became the Cromwell instead of the Monk of Abyssinia. Menilek was, however, well received by a small party of faithful adherents; Workite had also been accompanied by a small force of trusty followers; and on a large number of the chiefs abandoning the usurper and joining the standard of Menilek, he marched against the powerful rebel, who still held the capital and many strong places, utterly defeated his army and made him a prisoner.

This victory was shortly afterwards followed by the complete submission of Shoa to his rule; chief after chief made their obedience, and all acknowledged as their king the grandson of Sahela Selassi. Once his rights admitted by his people, he led his army against the numerous Galla tribes who inhabit the beautiful country extending from the south-eastern frontier of Shoa to the picturesque lake of Guaragu. But, instead of plundering these agricultural races, as his father had done, he promised them honourable treatment, a kind of mild vassalage, on the payment of a small annual tribute. The Gallas, surprised at his unexpected generosity and clemency, willingly accepted his terms, and, from former foes, enrolled themselves as his followers, and accompanied him on his expeditions. Theodore had left a strong garrison on an almost impregnable amba, situated at the northern frontier of Shoa, commanding the entrance into the pass leading from the Galla country to the highlands of Shoa. Menilek, before his campaign in the Galla country, had invested that last stronghold of Theodore in his own dominions, and, after a six months' siege, the garrison, who had repeatedly applied to their master for relief, at last gave in and opened their gates to the young king. Menilek treated them exceedingly well, many were honoured with appointments in his household, others received titles and commands, or were placed in positions of trust and confidence.

Menilek owed much to Workite; without her timely protection he would have been pursued, and as Shoa had shut its gates upon him, his position would have become one of great difficulty and danger. He could not forget, either, that to save his life she had sacrificed her only son and lost her kingdom: his debt of gratitude towards her was immense, and nothing he could do could adequately repay her for her devotion. But if he could not give her back her murdered son, he would, at all events, march against her rival, and restore by force of arms the disgraced queen to the throne she had lost on his account. At the end of October, 1867, Menilek, at the head of a considerable army, computed at 40,000 to 50,000 men, composed of 30,000 cavalry, some 2,000 or 3,000 musketeers, and the rest spearmen, entered the Wallo Galla plain: he proclaimed that he came not as an enemy, but as a friend; not to destroy nor to plunder, but to re-establish in her rule the deposed and lawful queen Workite. She was accompanied by a young lad who, she asserted, was her grandson, the child of the prince who had been killed more than two years before at Magdala. She stated that he had been born in the Wallo country, before her departure for Shoa, the result of one of those frequent casual unions so common in the country, and that she had taken him away when she sought refuge in the land of the man whom she had saved. To avoid any attempt being made by her rival to secure the person of her grandchild, she had until then kept the matter secret. However, her story was but little credited: I know on the Amba the soldiers laughed at it; still it offered an excuse to many of her former adherents for again joining her cause, and if they did not credit her tale they pretended at least to do go.

The Galla chiefs for some time remained undecided. Menilek kept to his word; he neither plundered nor molested any one, and, before long, he reaped the reward of his wise policy. Five of the tribes sent in their adhesion, and recognized Workite as regent for her grandson. Mastiate, in presence of such defection, adopted the most prudent course of retiring with her reduced army before the overwhelming forces of her adversaries; they followed her for some days, but without overtaking her. Menilek, believing that they had nothing more to fear on that side, settled as he best could the claims of Workite, and, accompanied by a large force of his new allies, marched against Magdala.

Menilek had evidently placed much confidence in the well-known disaffection of the garrison, and he expected that, through the influence of the Bishop (of whose death he was not aware), of his uncle Aito Dargie, and of Mr. Kassam, he would find on his arrival a party in his favour, who would materially assist him, if not make over the Amba to him at once. No doubt, had the Bishop been still alive he would either have succeeded by promises, threats, or force in opening the gates to his beloved friend. Aito Dargie, I believe, contrived to secure a promise of assistance from a few chiefs; but they were not powerful enough, and at the last moment lacked courage.

As for Mr. Rassam, he adopted the most prudent course of suiting his policy to the movements of Menilek; too much caution could not be used, as there was much reason to fear that the great deeds about to be achieved would end in empty boasting. To Menilek he gave great encouragement, offered him the friendship of England, and even went so far as assuring him that he would be acknowledged by our Government as king, should we be indebted to him for our deliverance; he requested him to encamp at Selassié, fire his two guns against the gate, and should the garrison not give in, to encamp between Arogié and the Bechelo, and keep Theodore from reaching the Amba until the arrival of our troops.

We had been greatly disappointed by Wakshum Gobazé: for six weeks he was always coming, but never came. Next we had Mastiate as our great excitement: she, we thought, would strive to gain possession of her amba; but she also never made her appearance; and now for nearly a month we were in daily expectation of the arrival of Menilek. We had already given him up when, to our great surprise, on the morning of the 30th of November, we perceived a large camp pitched on the northern slope of Tanta; and on the top of a small eminence commanding the plateau, and opposite to Magdala, stood the red, white, and black tents of the King of Shoa, the ambitious young prince who styled himself already "King of kings." Our astonishment was complete when, towards noon, we heard the report of a steady musketry-fire mingled with the occasional discharge of small cannon. We at once gave credit to Menilek for greater pluck than we ever believed him capable of; expecting that under cover of his fire the elite of his troops would assault the place; and aware of the little resistance he would meet with, we already rejoiced at the prospect of liberty, or at least of an advantageous change of masters. We had not finished our mutual congratulations when the firing ceased: as everything was calm and quiet on the Amba, we could not make out what was going on, until some of our guards came into our huts and asked us if we had heard Menilek's "faker." Alas, it was indeed nothing but a mere boast: he had fired from the verge of the Galla plateau, far out of range, to terrify into submission the wavering garrison; then, satisfied with his day's work, he and his men had retired to their tents, awaiting the result of their warlike demonstration.

The fact of Menilek being encamped on the Galla plain was full of peril for ourselves without being of any avail to him. The next morning he sent a message to us through Aito Dargie, asking what he should do. We again strongly urged upon him the necessity of his attacking the Amba by the Islamgee side; and in case he deemed it impossible to assault the place, to stop all communication between the fortress and the Imperial camp. Our great fear was that Theodore, on hearing that Menilek was besieging his amba, would send orders for the immediate execution of all prisoners of note, ourselves included. No doubt great disaffection existed on the Amba, and if Menilek had gone the proper way to work, before many days the place would have been his. But he never did anything; he remained encamped on the spot he had first chosen, and made no other attempt to rescue us.

Waizero Terunish, Theodore's queen, acted well on that occasion: she gave an adderash (public breakfast), presided over by her son Alamayou, to all the chiefs of the mountain. It being a fast-day, the feast was limited to tef bread, and a peppery sauce; and as the supply of tej in the royal cellars was scanty, the enthusiasm was not very considerable. Still it had the desired effect—chiefs and soldiers had publicly to proclaim their loyalty to Theodore; as with the party, still strong, that would give ear to no treachery, she was prepared to seize the malcontents individually, before they had time to declare themselves in open rebellion as the adherents of Menilek. Every one who thought that he was in any way suspected, and many who had no doubt made promises to Menilek and accepted his bribes, felt very nervous. Samuel was sent for; he did not like the prospect at all, and we were very much afraid for him ourselves, and glad when we saw him come back. On its being perceived that some of the chiefs had not made their appearance, inquiries were made as to the cause of their absence; they, seeing that there was very little hope of securing a strong party in favour of Menilek, gave explanations that were accepted, conditionally that on the following day they would repair to the King's inclosure, and there, in presence of the assembled garrison, proclaim their loyalty. They went as they had been ordered, and were the loudest in their praise of Theodore, in their expressions of devotion to his cause, and in their abuse of the "fat boy" who had ventured near a fortress entrusted to their care.

The Queen had done her duty well and honourably. The Ras and chiefs consulted together, and considered it advisable, in order to show their affection and devotion for their master, to do something themselves also. But what should be done? They had already placed extra guards at night on the gates, and protected every weak point on the Amba; nothing remained but to bully the prisoners. The second evening after the arrival of Menilek before the mountain, Samuel received orders from the chiefs to make us all sleep at night in one hut; the only exception being made in favour of the king's friend, Mr. Rassam. But poor Samuel, though sick, went to the Ras and insisted on having the order cancelled: I believe his influence was backed on that occasion by a douceur he quietly slipped into the Ras's hand. The chiefs in their wisdom had also decreed, and the next morning enforced the order that all the servants, Mr. Rassam's excepted; should be sent down from the mountain. The messengers and other public servants employed by Mr. Rassam were also obliged to leave. To Prideaux and myself they allowed, apart from our Portuguese, a water-girl and a small boy each. I had no house down at Islamgee; Samuel could not think of allowing me to pitch a tent, so the poor fellows would have been very badly off if Captain Cameron had not very kindly allowed them to share his servants' quarters. We were put to great inconvenience by this absurd and vexatious order, and I had some trouble, when everything was again quiet, in getting the servants up again; it required all the influence of Samuel and a douceur to the Ras, out of my pocket, to gain my object.

As may well be expected, the Abyssinian prisoners were not spared; all their servants were counted, and sent down the mountain, one only being allowed to three or four during the daytime to carry wood, water, and prepare their food. They were not suffered to leave the night-houses, but had to remain day and night in those filthy places. Every one on the mountain was exceedingly anxious that Menilek should decide on something, and put an end to that painful state of anxiety.

Early on the morning of the 3rd of December we were apprised by our servants that Menilek had struck his camp and was on the move. Where he was going to no one knew; but, as we were to some extent in his confidence, we flattered ourselves that he had accepted our advice, and would before long be seen on Selassié, or on the plateau of Islamgee. We spent a very anxious morning; the chiefs seemed perplexed, evidently expecting an assault from that direction, and we were confidentially informed that we should be called upon to man the guns should the Amba be attacked. However, our suspense was shortly at an end. The smoke rising in the distance, and in the direction of the road to Shoa, showed us but too clearly that the would-be conqueror had, without striking a blow, returned to his own country, and, with great gallantry, was burning a few miserable villages, whose chiefs were adherents of Mastiate.

The excuse Menilek gave for his hasty retreat was, that his supplies had run short, and that, having no camp-followers with him he could not have flour prepared; that his troops being hungry and dissatisfied, he had decided on returning at once to Shoa, collect his camp-followers, and advance again better provisioned, and remain in the neighbourhood of

Magdala until it fell. The truth was, that to his great disappointment he had heard from his camp the muskets fired during the "fakering;" he knew that, as far as treachery was concerned, his chance was gone for a while, and that he must await the effects of want and privation induced by a long siege. Supplies he might have obtained in abundance, as he was the ally of Workite and in a friendly country. Should he even have required more, the undefended districts of Worahaimanoo, Dalanta, etc., would have been quite willing to send abundant provisions into his camp on the assurance that they would not be molested. But if this "fakering" somewhat deranged his plans, something he saw on the evening of the second day, a mere speck of smoke, made him fairly run away. That smoke was kindled by the terrible Theodore. He was, it is true, still far away; but who could say? His father-in-law, Menilek knew well, was a man of long marches and sudden attacks. How his large army would be scattered like chaff before the wind at the cry, "Theodore is coming," he was well aware, and he came to the conclusion that the sooner he was off the better.

Our disappointment was something beyond description. Our rage, our indignation and scorn for such cowardice, I cannot express. The "fat boy," as we also now called him, we hated and despised. Had we been imprudent enough openly to take his part, what would have become of us? Menilek, doubtless, meant well, and probably would have succeeded had the Bishop lived a few weeks longer. As it is, he did us a great deal of harm. Had he and Workite never left Shoa, Mastiate would have laid siege to the mountain. Sooner or later it must have surrendered, and neither Theodore nor his messengers would ever have ventured south of the Bechelo if Mastiate had been there with her 20,000 horsemen.

With Menilek's departure, I, for one, made up my mind never again to credit any of the promises of the native chiefs, which always ended in mere moon-shine. Since then, I heard with the utmost indifference that so-and-so was marching in such a direction, that he or she would attack Theodore, or invest the Amba and stop all communication between the rascals on the top and "our friend" Theodore. We had been a long time without messengers, and the last had not brought us the intelligence so anxiously looked for. Our impatience was greater since we knew that we could expect nothing from the natives, and believed the expedition from England to be on its way: we felt that something was going on and we longed for the certainty.

How well I remember the 13th of December, a glorious day for us! No lover ever read, with more joy and happiness the long-expected note from the beloved one, than I did that day the kind and cheering letter of our gallant friend, General Merewether. Troops had landed! Since the 6th of October, our countrymen were in the same land that saw us captives. Roads, piers, were being made; regiment after regiment were leaving the shores of India, some already marching across the Abyssinian Alps to rescue or avenge. It seemed too delightful to be true: we could hardly credit it. Ere long all must be over! Liberty or death! Anything was better than continued slavery. Theodore was coming—*qu'importe?* Was not Merewether there? the brave leader of many a hard fight; the gallant officer and accomplished politician. With such men as a Napier, a Staveley at the head of British troops, who could feel but contempt for petty vexations? We were prepared even for a worse fate, if it was to be our lot. At least, England's prestige would be restored, her children's blood not left unrevenged. It was one of those exciting moments in a man's life that few can realize who have not passed through months of mental agony, and then been suddenly overcome with joy. We laughed more than ever at the idea of giving even a thought to such poltroons as Gobaz and Menilek. The hope of meeting our brave countrymen cheered us. In the mind's eye we beheld them, and in our hearts we thanked them for the toils and privations they would have to undergo before they could set *the captives free.* For the second time, Christmas and New Year's Day found us in fetters at Magdala; but we were happy: they would be the last, at all events, and, full of trust in our deliverance, we now looked forward to spending the next *at home.*

CHAPTER XVI

Theodore remained at Aibankab for only a few days after our departure, and returned to Debra Tabor. He had told us once, "You will see what great things I will achieve during the rainy season," and we expected that he would march into Lasta or Tigré before the roads were closed by the rains, to subdue the rebellion that for years he had allowed to pass unnoticed. It is very probable that if he had adopted that course he would have regained his prestige, and easily reduced to obedience those provinces. No one was so much Theodore's enemy as himself; he seems to have been possessed with an evil spirit urging him to his own destruction. Many a time he would have regained the ground he had lost, and put down to a certain extent rebellion; but all his actions, from the day we left him until he arrived at Islamgee, were only calculated to accelerate his fall.

Begemder is a large, powerful, fertile province, the "land of sheep" (as its name indicates), a fine plateau, some 7,000 or 8,000 feet above the sea, well watered, well cultivated, and thickly populated. The inhabitants are warlike, brave for Abyssinians, and often have repulsed the rebels venturing to invade their province, so firm in its allegiance to Theodore. Not many months before Tesemma Engeddah, a young man, hereditary chief Of Gahinte, a district of Begemder near its eastern frostier, with the aid of the peasants, attacked a force sent into Begemder by Gobazé, utterly routed it and put every man to death; except a few chiefs who were kept for the Emperor to deal with as he thought fit.

Begemder paid an annual tribute of 300,000 dols., and supplied at all times the Queen's camp with grain, cows, &c., and during the stay of the Emperor in the province liberally provided his camp. Moreover, it furnished 10,000 men to the army, all good spearmen, but bad shots. Theodore, therefore, preferred for his musketeers the men of Dembea, who showed more skill in the use of fire-arms.

Begemder, the proverb says, "is the maker and destroyer of kings;" certainly it was so in the case of Theodore. After the flight of Ras Ali, Begemder at once acknowledged him, and caused him to be looked upon as the future ruler of the land. Theodore was well aware of the difficult game he had to play, but believed his precautions were such that he would inevitably succeed. At first he was all smiles; chiefs were rewarded, peasants flattered; his stay would be short; every day he expected he would leave. The annual tribute was paid; Theodore gave handsome presents to the chiefs, honoured many with silk shirts, and swore that as soon as the cannons his Europeans were casting should be completed, he would start for Godjam, and with his new mortars destroy the nest of the arch-rebel Tadla Gwalu. He invited, all the chiefs to reside in his camp during his stay, to rejoice his heart. They were his friends, when so many rose against him. Would they advance him a year's tribute? could they not provide more liberally for the wants of his army? He was going away for a long time, and would not for years trouble them for tribute or supplies. The chiefs did their best; every available dollar, all the corn and cattle the peasants could spare, found its way into Theodore's treasury and camp. But the peasants at last got tired, and would not listen any longer to the entreaties of their chiefs. Good words Theodore perceived would be of no avail any more, so he adopted an imperious, menacing tone. One after the other, on some *good* ground, he imprisoned the chiefs; but it was only to test their fidelity: they would, he knew get for him what he wanted, and then he would not only release them, but treat them with the greatest honour. The poor men did their best, and the peasants, in order to obtain the deliverance of their chiefs, brought all they had as a ransom. At last, both chiefs and peasants found that all their efforts failed to satisfy their insatiable master.

This state of things lasted for more than eight months, and during that period, first by plausible and honeyed words, afterwards by intimidation, he kept himself and army without difficulty and without trouble. He made no expeditions during that time, except one against Gondar. He hated Gondar—a city of merchants and priests, always ready to receive with open arms any rebel: any robber chief might sit undisturbed in the halls of the old Abyssinian kings and receive the homage and tribute of its peaceful inhabitants. Several times before Theodore had vented his rage on the unfortunate city; he had already more than once sent his soldiers to plunder it, and the rich Mussulman merchants had only saved their houses from destruction by the payment of a large sum. It was no more the famous city of Fasiladas, nor the rich commercial town that former travellers had described; confidence could no longer dwell under the repeated extortions of king and rebel, nor could the metropolis of Abyssinia afford to answer the repeated calls made upon its wealth. But still the forty-four churches stood intact, surrounded by the noble trees that gave to the capital such a picturesque appearance; no one had dared extend a sacrilegious hand to those sanctuaries, and until then Theodore himself had shrunk from such a deed. But now he had made up his mind: the gold of Kooskuam, the silver of Bata, the treasures of Selassié should refill his empty coffers; her churches should perish with the doomed city: nothing would he leave standing as a record of the past, not a dwelling to shelter the people he despised.

On the afternoon of the 1st of December, Theodore started on his merciless errand, taking with him only the elite of his army, the best mounted and the best walkers amongst his men. He never halted until he came, the next morning, to the foot of the hill on which Gondar is built—a march of more than eighty miles in less than sixteen hours. But though he suddenly pounced upon his enemy, it was too late; the news of his approach had spread faster. The joyous *elelta* resounded from house to house; the anxious and terrified inhabitants desired to appear happy in presence of the dire calamity such a visit presaged. The rebel's deputy had left the palace in time, and accompanied by a few hundred horsemen, awaited, at some distance from the town, the result of Theodore's coming. He had not long to wait. The invaders searched every house, plundered every building, from the churches to the poorest hut, and drove away before them like cattle the 10,000 remaining inhabitants of that large city. Then, the work of destruction began: fire spread from house to house, the churches and palace, the only remarkable buildings the country possessed, became a heap of blackened ruins. But the priests looked sullen; some entreated, others murmured, a few were bold enough to curse; at an order given by Theodore, hundreds of aged priests were hurled into the flames. But his insatiate fury demanded fresh victims. Where were the young girls who had welcomed his entrance. Was it not their joyous shouts that had scared away the rebel? "Let them be brought!" cried the fiend, and these young girls were thrown alive into the fire!

The expedition had been successful; Gondar was utterly destroyed. Four inferior churches only had escaped destruction. Gold, silks, dollars were now abundant in the royal camp. Theodore was received on his return to Debra Tabor with all the triumphal honours bestowed on a victor; the Gaffat people went to meet him with lighted torches; and compared him to the pious Hozekiah. If Theodore's star had been dim before this wanton barbarity, it disappeared altogether from that day: all went against him—success never attended him more.

The burning of Gondar increased immensely the power of the rebels. They advanced steadily and cautiously, seizing district after district, until whole provinces acknowledged their sway, and all joined in anathematizing the sacrilegious monarch who had not hesitated to destroy churches that even the Mussulman Gallas had respected. As long as the soldiers had money the peasants willingly sold them their goods; but this could not last long: soon scarcity prevailed in the camp. Theodore applied to the chiefs; they must use their influence and force the "bad peasant" to bring in more supplies. The peasants would listen no longer; they told the chiefs, "Let the king set you free and then we will do anything you tell us, but now we know that you are only acting under compulsion." Theodore ordered the chiefs to be tortured: "If they cannot bring grain they must give money." Some who had a few savings sent them—for torture was worse than poverty; but this did not improve their condition. Theodore believed that they had more, and as they had nothing to give, many died under the daily repetition of the tortures Theodore now inflicted on his prisoners; amongst whom were his bravest soldiers, his staunchest supporters, nay, his bosom friends.

Desertions were now more frequent than ever; chiefs left in the open day with their followers; the gunman threw away his weapon, and joined his oppressed brother the peasant; great numbers of the Begemder soldiery daily abandoned his cause and returned to their villages. Theodore, in this plight, resorted to a former practice of his. He must plunder, and feed his army by plunder. But the Begemder men would not plunder their own countrymen, and he did not place much confidence in the bravery of his Dembea men: therefore he pitted the man of Gahinte against the peasant of Ifag, the sons of Mahdera Mariam against those of Esté—all districts of the same province, but far distant from one another, and with long feuds existing between some of them. At first he succeeded, and returned from his expeditions with ample supplies; but his fearful cruelties at last aroused the peasants. Joined by the deserters they fought in their own way, cut·off stragglers, sent their families to distant provinces, and for miles around Debra Tabor ceased cultivating the soil.

In March, 1867, Theodore started for Kourata, the third town in importance in Abyssinia, and the greatest commercial centre after Gondar and Adowa. But this time he failed completely; ever since his expedition to Gondar, the peasants of all the surrounding districts were always on the alert: beacon-fires were ready, the people telegraphed to each other in their rude way, and the victims evaded the tyrant.

At Kourata he found no one, and hardly any plunder; the rich merchants, priests, every one had embarked with all their goods in the small native boats, and, out of range of Theodore's rifles, quietly awaited his departure to return to their homes. Theodore was greatly disappointed; he expected to reap a rich harvest and found nothing. He must revenge himself; but here, again, he was frustrated. The soldiers deserted *en masse*; few, very few would remain with him, he was told, if he destroyed Kourata. The sacred town, houses, streets, trees, had all been dedicated to God's service; such a sacrilege was beyond the rascality of even the Abyssinian soldier. Theodore had to return to Debra Tabor. Sometimes once or twice a week he would go forth and plunder; but with little success: each time his difficulties increased; the peasants had lost their first great dread of him; they fought well at places, and defied the gaily-dressed chiefs: none as yet stood before him, but the day was not far off when his prestige had fallen so low that a man was found who challenged his anointed king.

The position of the Europeans near Theodore was, indeed, most painful. Always to please a ferocious, mad, enraged tiger, would have been trifling compared to what they had to undergo during the last year they served him. Theodore was quite changed; no one who had known him in former days would have now recognized the elegant and chivalrous young prince, or the proud, but just Emperor, in the homicidal monomaniac of Debra Tabor.

A few days before we left for Magdala (after the political trial), Messrs. Staiger, Brandeis, and the two hunters, foreseeing that captivity, and probably chains, would be our lot before long, availed themselves of a former permission they had obtained to remain near Mrs. Flad during her husband's absence, in order to keep clear of the coming storm. McKelvie (a former captive, and servant of Capt. Cameron,) pretended sickness, also remained behind, and shortly afterwards took service with his Majesty. Mackerer (also a former captive, and servant of Capt. Cameron,) had previously been in Theodore's service, and preferred to return to him rather than go through a second captivity at Magdala. Little were they aware at the time how much they would have to go through themselves.

Mrs. Rosenthal, on account of her health, could not accompany us then; afterwards she several times applied for leave to join her husband, but until a couple of months before our release, was always refused on some specious reason or the other. Mrs. Flad and children belonged to the same party, having been left by her husband on his departure, under the protection of the "Gaffat people."

Altogether the number of Europeans with his Majesty during the time of our captivity at Magdala, including Mr. Bardel, was fifteen, exclusive of the two ladies and several half-castes.

Theodore had no sooner returned to Debra Tabor, after sending us to Magdala, than he set to work, with the assistance of the Europeans, casting cannons of various shapes and sizes, and mortars of immense weight and calibre. Gaffat, where the foundry had been erected, was only a few miles from Debra Tabor, and every day Theodore was in the habit of riding down with a small escort and superintending the works. On these occasions, the four who had remained behind (Mr. Staiger and his party) usually came to present their respects, but did not work. Mackerer and McKelvie had been apprenticed to some of the Gaffat people, and did their utmost to please the Emperor, and he, to encourage them, presented them with a silk shirt and 100 dollars each. One morning when the four had come as usual to look on, Theodore, in an angry voice, asked them why they did not work with the others. They perceived by his tone and manner that it was imprudent to refuse; and accordingly bowed in acquiescence and set to work. Theodore, to mark his pleasure, ordered them to be invested with robes of honour, and sent them also 100 dollars each. For some time they worked at the foundry, but were afterwards sent with Mr. Bardel to make roads for the artillery; Theodore, with his usual caution, having two constructed at the same time, one in the direction of Magdala, the other leading towards Godjam, so as to leave every one, his people and the rebels, in doubt as to his movements.

At this time Mr. Brandeis and Mr. Bardel happened to meet at some hot springs not far from Debra Tabor, whither they had gone with his Majesty's permission for the benefit of their health. Though Bardel was not a favourite; being justly distrusted by all, it seems that a kind of intimacy sprung up between the two, and in an hour of confidence Mr. Brandeis revealed to Bardel a plot they had made to run away, proposing to him to join their party. Bardel accepted. A short time afterwards they returned to Debra Tabor, or rather to a short distance from it, where they were making the roads. They at once set to work to complete their arrangements, and at last, everything being ready for the route, they fixed upon the night of the 25th of February for their departure. Towards ten in the evening Bardel looked into the tent where all were assembled, and seeing at a glance that everything was ready, pretended to have forgotten something in his tent, and begged them to wait a few minutes for him. They agreed, and mounting his horse, Bardel started at full gallop to fetch Theodore. That man, so unprincipled that even Abyssinians looked upon him with contempt, had basely betrayed, out of mere love of mischief, those poor men who had trusted in him. Theodore was quite taken aback when Bardel told him that the four he had taken into his service, and Mackerer, were on the point of deserting. "But were you not also one of the party?" Theodore inquired. Bardel said that it was true; but if he had entered into the plot, it was only to be able to prove his attachment to his master by revealing it to him, when he could with his own eyes assure him of the correctness of the assertion. Theodore accompanied him to the tent where the others were anxiously expecting their companion's return.

Fancy their dismay and astonishment when they saw the Emperor quietly walking in followed by their betrayer!

Theodore was calm, asked them why they were so ungrateful, and why they wanted to run away? They replied that they longed to see their country. They were given in charge to the soldiers who had accompanied Theodore, chained hand and foot, each of them to one of their servants; all their followers were stripped naked, tied with ropes, and several of them killed. Their condition ever since was most dreadful: they were confined at first with hundreds of starving and naked Abyssinians, witnessed the execution of thousands, many of whom had been their bed companions, and expected at any instant to be called upon to pay with their lives the penalty of their rash attempt. However, Theodore after a while made a difference between them and his people, he set apart a small tent for them, did not deprive them of all their clothes, and allowed them some servants to prepare their food.

The rebellion had by this time, April, 1867, become so universal, that apart from a few provinces in the neighbourhood of Magdala, that fortress and another one, Zer Amba, near Tschelga, he could only call his own the few acres on which his tents were pitched. His European workmen had cast some guns for him, and afraid that at Gaffat these might be seized by some rebel, he determined upon removing them to his camp. He took advantage of the receipt of a letter from Mr. Flad, to appear displeased at the news he had received, and thereby cover his ingratitude towards those faithful servants by a plausible excuse.

On the 17th of April Theodore went to Gaffat, stopped at the foot of the hillock on which it is built, sent for the Europeans, and told them that he had received a letter from Mr. Flad, containing serious matters, and that, as he could not trust them far from him, they must go to Debra Tabor until Mr. Flad's return, when all would be explained; he added that he had also heard that preparations for the reception of troops were being made at Kedaref, and that "if he was to be killed, they would die first." One of the Europeans, Moritz Hall, remonstrated against the unfair treatment he was subjected to, after long and faithful services: "Kill us at once," he exclaimed, "but do not degrade us in this way; if in the letter you have received, there is anything you can charge against us, then have it read out before your people. Death is better than unjust suspicion." Theodore, in angry tone, ordered him to be silent, and sent them all under escort to Debra Tabor; their wives and families followed; all their property was seized, but afterwards partly returned, and on the tools and instruments being given back to them, they were told to work. The Europeans and guns safe in his camp, Theodore left Debra Tabor on a plundering expedition; but in Begemder he met with such constant resistance from the peasantry, that his soldiers at last objected.

To please them, he led them towards Foggara, a fertile plain to the north-west of Begemder; but he found hardly anything there. All the grain had been buried, and the cattle removed to distant parts of the country. One of our messengers sent to him by Mr. Rassam found him there, and on his return, gave us the most dreadful description of the Emperor's temper: floggings, beatings, and executions were going on all day, and he was so badly off for money, that he had imprisoned several of his own personal attendants, fixing their release at 100 dollars each. During his absence, the Gaffat people had consulted amongst themselves as to the best means of regaining the Emperor's favour, and decided on proposing to cast an immense mortar for him. Theodore was delighted. A foundry was erected, and the "Great Sebastopol," which was destined to be the crushing blow for him, and the means of our salvation, was begun.

CHAPTER XVII

Soon after the Gaffat people had been sent to Debra Tabor, Mr. Flad arrived from England, and met Theodore in Dembea on the 26th of April. Their first meeting was not very friendly. Mr. Flad handed to his Majesty the Queen's letter, with others from General Merewether, Dr. Beke, and from the relations of the former captives. On presenting General Merewether's letter to Theodore, Flad informed him that he had brought as a present to him from that gentleman, an excellent telescope. Theodore asked to see it. The telescope was rather difficult to arrange so as to suit Theodore's sight, and as it took some time before Flad could put it in order, Theodore got impatient and said, "Take it to the tent, we will try it to-morrow; but I know it is not a good telescope: I know it is not sent to me for good."

Theodore then ordered every one to retire, and having told Flad to sit down, asked him, "Have you seen the Queen?" Flad replied in the affirmative, adding that he had been very graciously received, and that he had a verbal message to deliver to him from her Majesty. "What is it?" Theodore immediately asked. Had replied, "The Queen of England has told me to inform your Majesty, that if you do not at once send out of your country all those you have detained so long against their will, you have no right to expect any further friendship from her." Theodore listened attentively, and even had the message repeated to him several times. After a pause, he said to Flad, "I have asked from them a sign of friendship, but it is refused to me. If they wish to come and fight, let them come, and call me a woman if I do not beat them."

The following day Mr. Flad presented him with the several gifts he had brought with him from Government, Dr. Beke, and others; the supplies he had brought for as he put aside, but everything was sent to the royal tent, and 1,000 dollars he had also conveyed for us, Theodore took, saying the roads were dangerous, and that he would send an order for it to Mr. Rassam at Magdala. On the 29th Theodore sent again for the telescope: one of his officers had examined it, and found it excellent, but Theodore pretended not to be able to see anything with it.

"It is not sent for good," he said; "it is the same story as some years ago when Baṣha Falaka (Captain Speedy) sent me a carpet by Kerans; but by the power of God I chained the bearer of that carpet. The man who sends me the telescope only wants to annoy me; he wishes to tell me, 'Though you are a king and I send you an excellent telescope, you will not be able to see through it.'" Flad did his best to disabuse his Majesty of this impression, and convince him of the fact that the telescope was sent to him as a token of friendship; but as Theodore only got more violent, Flad thought it prudent to be silent.

On Monday, the 30th, Theodore sent for Flad again and told him that he was going to send him to rejoin his family at Debra Tabor. Flad took advantage of this occasion to give a full account of the dealings of the rebels with France, and their desire to be acknowledged by us; he assured Theodore that if he did not comply with our Queen's request he would certainly involve himself in a disastrous war, etc. Theodore listened with great coolness and indifference, and when Flad ceased talking, quietly said: "Do not be afraid: the victory comes from God. I trust in the Lord and he will help me; I do not trust in my power. I trust in God who says, If you have faith like a mustard seed, you can remove mountains." He said that even if he had not chained Mr. Rassam it would have been all the same; they would not have sent him the workmen. He knew already, at the time of Bell and Plowden, that the English were not his friends, and he only treated these two well out of personal regard for them. He concluded by saying, "I leave it to the Lord: he will decide it when we fight on the battle-field."

Theodore had vented his rage about the telescope to hide his disappointment; he had said to one of his workmen at the time he wrote to Flad to come up with the artisans, "You do not know me yet; but call me a fool, if by my cunning I do not get them." Instead of artisans, white men to be held as hostages, he received a firm message, holding out no hope of friendship unless he set at liberty all those he had so long unlawfully detained. His answers, so full of meekness, he knew would please his followers; they were superstitious and ignorant, and placed a certain credence in his hopeful words.

Desertions had considerably reduced his army. He well knew the influence of numbers in a country like Abyssinia, and to increase his scanty host, after plundering for the fourth or fifth time Dembea and Taccosa, he issued a proclamation to the peasants in the following terms:—"You have no more homes, grain, or cattle. I have not done it: God did it. Come with me, and I will take you where you will find plenty to eat, cattle in abundance, and punish those who are the cause of God's anger upon you." He did the name for the districts of Begemder he had lately destroyed; and many of these poor starving, homeless creatures, not knowing where to go or how to live, were only too glad to accept his offer.

Theodore's position was not an enviable one. In May, Ras Adilou, together with all the Yedjow men, the only cavalry left to him, departed from the camp in open daylight, taking with them their wives, children, and followers. Theodore was afraid of pursuing the deserters, lest the greater part of his remaining force should seize the opportunity thus offered to them and join the discontented, instead of fighting to capture them. Not long before, a young chief of Gahinte, named Zallallou, at the head of two hundred horse, had fled to his native province, and through his influence all the peasants of that warlike district had aimed and prepared themselves to defend their country against Theodore and his famished host. Zallallou, the very day he left the Imperial camp, fell upon some of our servants *en route* to Debra Tabor, where they were going to purchase supplies; all were plundered of everything they had, stripped, and several detained as prisoners for a few days.

Dahonte and Dalanta not long afterwards, declared themselves for the Gallas, turned out of their provinces the governors Theodore had appointed over them, and seized upon the cattle, mules, and horses belonging to the Magdala garrison, which had been sent there, as was the custom before the rainy season, on account of the scarcity of water on the Amba itself. If Theodore, only a few months before, had but a very insecure portion of his former vast empire that he could call his own, at that date, June, 1867, he was a king without a kingdom, and a general without an army. Magdala and Zer Amba were still garrisoned by his troops; but apart from these forts, he had nothing left: even his camp was only full of mutinous men, and desertions went on at such a rate that he could then only muster from 6,000 to 7,000 men, the majority of whom were peasants, who had followed him to avoid starvation. For miles around Debra Tabor the country was a perfect desert, and Theodore saw with dread the rainy season coming on, for he had no supplies in camp, and a large number of followers, the people of Gondar, and an endless host of useless individuals to support.

In Begemder plundering was out of the: question; the peasants were always on the watch, and on the slightest sign of a move were everywhere on the alert, killing the stragglers and plunderers, and keeping out of the way of the gunmen who stood around the Emperor. Theodore remembered a rich district not as yet plundered, Belessa, at the north-east of Begemder. In order to surprise the inhabitants completely, he proclaimed some days before that he was going on an expedition in quite a different direction, and to make his army appear as formidable as possible, he had given orders that every one who possessed a horse or a mule, or a servant, must send them, under penalty of death, to accompany the expedition. The Belessa people, far from being surprised, had been informed of his intention by their spies, and Theodore, to his disappointment, saw from a distance their villages on fire; the peasants themselves having preferred destroying their homes to leaving them a prey to the invader. Under the conduct of a gallant chief, Lij Abitou, a young man of good family, and a runaway officer, from the Imperial household, the peasants, well armed, took up a position on a small plateau, separated by a narrow ravine from the route Theodore would take. To his surprise, instead of running away at the mere sight of his charger, they not only stood their ground, but several well-mounted chiefs rode out in front and bid defiance to Theodore himself. Astrologers must have told him that the day was not favourable, as after several of his chiefs who had answered the cartel had been laid dead on the field, he still refused to lead his men in person, and before this unexpected resistance gave way and ordered a retreat. Belessa was saved: the hungry, famished robbers that Theodore called soldiers passed a dreadful night; tired, hungry, and cold, they could not sleep, for the peasants might surprise and attack them, in their turn. The cruelties Theodore perpetrated after his return to Debra Tabor were fearful; too horrible to be related. At last, tired of taking his revenge on the innocent, he turned his thoughts to the place he might most easily plunder, and fixed upon the island of Metraha.

That island, situate in the Tana Sea, about twenty miles north of Kourata, is only a few hundred yards from the mainland. It was considered in the light of an asylum, and protected by its sacred character, priests and monks resided there in peace; while merchants and rich landowners sent their goods and stores there for safe custody. Theodore had no scruples about violating the sanctity of the island: the asylum afforded by the churches to all before his time he had long ago violated, and, certain of a large booty, did not hesitate to add another sacrilege to his numerous crimes. On his arrival before Metraha, he at once ordered his people to make rafts. Whilst Theodore was occupied in their construction, a priest came in a boat, and approaching within speaking distance, inquired of the Emperor what it was that he desired. Theodore told him the grain that they had in store. The priest replied that they would send it to him; but Theodore, not satisfied with the grain alone, told the priest not to be afraid, but to send their boats. He took a solemn oath that he would not injure them, nor remove anything but the grain he required. The priest, on his return to the island, informed the people of his conversation with the Emperor, and the majority being in favour of complying with his requests, it was agreed that all the available boats should be taken to the mainland. A few who had no trust in Theodore's word entered their canoes, and paddled away in an opposite direction.

Theodore ordered the Europeans to fire upon them with the small cannons they had brought. They complied; but, to Theodore's great disappointment, failed to hit any of the fugitives. No sooner had Theodore and a select party been admitted on the island than he caused all the remaining inhabitants to be shut up in a few of the larger houses; and after all the grain, silver, gold, and merchandise had been removed, he set the place on fire, and burnt to death priests, merchants, women and children!

For a while, abundance reigned in Theodore's camp. The work of casting the big cannon had been going on for some time: the day of its completion at last arrived, and Emperor and workmen anxiously awaited the result of their labours. The Europeans, to their great dismay, saw that they had failed; but Theodore, not in the least put out, told them not to be afraid, but to try again: perhaps they would succeed another time. Theodore examined carefully everything, connected with the smelting, in order to find out the cause of the failure, and he soon perceived that it was due to the presence of some water around the mould. He at once set to work, and had a large, deep, broad trench constructed from beneath the mould to some distance outside. This drain dried up the place, and on a second attempt being made the success was complete. Theodore was delighted; he made handsome presents to the workmen, and prepared everything requisite to carry away with him his immense piece of ordnance.

During that rainy season (1867) Theodore's difficulties were very great: indeed, the punishment of his evil deeds was falling heavily upon him, and to his proud nature it must have been a daily and constant agony. The rebels were now so little afraid of Theodore that every night they made attacks on his camp, and were always on the watch to seize stragglers, or camp-followers. They had at last become such a terror to the soldiers that, to protect them, and at the same time check, to a certain extent, desertion, Theodore had a large stockade built around the foot of the hill on which his camp was pitched. A war of extermination on both sides now took place; Theodore showing no pity to the peasants whom he succeeded in capturing, and they, on their side, torturing and murdering any one who belonged to the Emperor's camp. A detailed account of the atrocities committed by Theodore during the last month of his stay in Begemder would be too horrible to narrate: suffice it to say that he burnt alive, or sentenced to some cruel death, in that short space of time, more than 3,000 persons! His rage at times was so blind that, unable to satisfy his revenge by punishing those who daily insulted and scorned him, he vented his anger on the few remaining faithful companions who shared his fate: chiefs who had fought by his side for years, friends whom he knew from his childhood, old respectable men who had protected him in former days, all had to suffer more or less for their faithfulness, and fell innocent victims to his mad fits of violence. Many succumbed to a lingering death, or chains and torture, for no reason whatever except that they loved him!

Desertions were still frequent, but the difficulty of escape was greater than before; the peasants often put to death the fugitives; and always stripped and plundered them of everything they had. The gates of the fence were guarded night and day by faithful men, and it required often a good deal of ability and cunning to be able to pass through them. I was told an anecdote which exemplifies the expedients the soldiers resorted to in order to get out of the dreaded camp. One evening, about half an hour before sunset, a woman presented herself at the gate, carrying on her head one of the large flat baskets used for keeping bread; she said, with tears in her eyes; that her brother was lying down some short distance from the fence so dangerously wounded that he could not walk; she had brought him a little bread and water, etc. The guards allowed her to pass. A few minutes afterwards a soldier presented himself at the gate, and asked if they had seen a woman go through, giving the description of the one that had just gone out. The guards said that they had; the soldier appeared to be in a fearful passion, and said that she was his wife, who had made an assignation to run away with her lover; and he threatened to report them to the Emperor. The guards told him that she could not be far off, and that he had better go quickly and overtake her; off he went: as might be expected, neither appeared again.

To the annoyances and difficulties caused by the presence of large bodies of armed peasants, day and night hanging about the outskirts of the camp, were soon added the evils of famine: a small Abyssinian loaf cost a dollar; a salt and a half, a dollar; butter could not by any means be obtained; and hundreds died daily of want and starvation. When the grain plundered at Metraha was consumed, no more could be found; plundering was now quite impossible, and as long as Theodore did not move his camp there was no hope of supplies of any kind being obtained. Almost all the mules, horses, and the few remaining sheep had died from want of food; they could not graze any more in close vicinity to the camp, that pasture being completely eaten up; and as to driving them to some green fields at a distance, that was impossible. The poor animals dropped one after the other, and infected the place by the stench that arose from their dead bodies. The cows had all been killed long before by order of Theodore. One day, when, after one of his first razzias, he had brought back with him to Debra Tabor more than 80,000 cows; at night the peasants came, and from a distance implored him to have pity upon them, and restore them their cattle, without which they were unable to cultivate the soil. Theodore was on the point of acceding to their request, when some of the rascals around him said, "Does not your Majesty know that there is a prophecy in the country, that a king will seize a large amount of cattle, and that the peasants will come and beg him to return them; the king will comply, but soon afterwards die." Theodore replied, "Well, the prophecy will not apply to me." He immediately gave orders for all the cows in camp, those he had lately brought, and all others, to be killed at once; the order was obeyed, and nearly, it is said, 100,000 were killed and left to rot in the plain at a short distance from the camp.

The next day, Theodore, seated outside his hut, perceived a man driving a cow into the fields; he sent for him, and asked him if he had not heard the order. The man replied in the affirmative, but said that he had not killed his cow because his wife having died the day before on giving birth to a child, he had kept that one for the sake of her milk. Theodore told him, "Why did not you know that I would be a father to your child? Kill the man," he said to those around him, "and take care of his child for me."

The waggons being at last ready, Theodore decided upon marching towards Magdala. Pestilence, engendered by famine and the noxious effluvia arising from the heap of unburied dead bodies, now increased the already dismal condition of the Emperor's army; and in a few weeks more he and his whole host must have perished from sickness and want. On the 10th of October, his Majesty set fire to his houses at Debra Tabor, and destroyed the whole place; leaving only, as a record of his stay, a church he had built as an expiation for his sacrilege at Gondar. His march was, indeed, the most wonderful feat he ever accomplished; none but he would have ventured on such an undertaking; and no other man could have succeeded in accomplishing the arduous journey that lay before him: it required all his energy, perseverance, and iron will to carry out his purpose under such immense difficulties.

He had not more than 5,000 men with him, all more or less in bad condition, weakened by famine, discontented, and only awaiting a favourable opportunity to run away. The camp-followers, on the contrary; numbered between forty and fifty thousand helpless and useless beings whom he had to protect and feed. He had, moreover, several hundred prisoners to guard, an immense amount of baggage to carry, fourteen gun-carriages, with cannon or mortars—one of them the famous "Sebastopol," weighing between fifteen and sixteen thousand pounds—and ten waggons, the whole to be dragged by men across a country without roads. Theodore did not let himself be influenced by all these unfavourable circumstances; he seemed, for a time, to have regained much of his former self, and behaved with more consideration towards his followers. His daily marches were very short, not more than a mile and a half to two miles a day. A portion of his camp marched early every morning, carrying the heavy luggage, dragging the waggons, and protecting the followers from the attacks of the rebels, who were always hovering in the distance, watching a favourable opportunity to avenge themselves on the Emperor's people for all the miseries they had suffered at his hand; another portion remained behind to guard what could not be carried; off, and, on the return of the first batch, all started for the spot fixed upon for that day's halt, conveying what had been left behind in the morning. Even then the day's work wast not over; the corn was as yet not quite ripe, and stood in the fields by the side of the road; Theodore would set the example, pluck a few unripe ears of barley, rub them between his hands, and, satisfied with this frugal meal, repair to the nearest brook to quench thirst. From Debra Tabor to Checheo, such was the daily routine of the reduced host of Theodore,—harnessed to waggons, in place of the horses and mules now so scarce in the camp; constantly on the alert, as the country was all up in arms against them; with no supplies available, only the unripe barley plucked by the wayside; no peace by day nor rest at night: in a word, a march unequalled in the annals of history.

The prisoners were very badly off: many—even the Europeans—were in hand and foot chains; to walk a few steps in such a condition is fatiguing in the extreme, but to have to go over a mile or two of broken ground with such fetters equals the cruellest torture. Mrs. Flad and Mrs. Rosenthal every day, as soon as they arrived at the stage, sent back their mules for the Europeans to ride; and some time afterwards, on Mr. Staiger making a gala dress for his Majesty, the hand-chains of all five were taken away. On the native prisoners requesting to be allowed to ride, his Majesty sent them word that, as he knew they had money, he would grant permission to those who would send him a *dollar*. Theodore must have been hard up, indeed, to be satisfied with such a trifle. Several complied with his demand, and, by giving small presents to those chiefs who had mules, they got an occasional lift.

At Aibankab Theodore halted a few days to rest his men; near it two heaps of stones arise, giving to the place the name of Kimr Dengea. [Footnote: "Kimr Dengea," heap of stones.] The story the people of the country narrate with reference to these heaps of stones is that on one occasion a Queen, at the head of her army, went on an expedition against the Gallas; before starting she ordered every one of her soldiers as he passed along to put a stone on a certain spot, and on her return again ordered them to place a stone at a short distance from the former heap. The first is a large mass, the second very much smaller; the Queen knew by that how great her loss had been, and never since then ventured against the Gallas.

At Kimr Dengea Theodore fell in with a caravan of salt-merchants on their route to Godjam. He asked them why they went to the rebels instead of coming to him. The chief of the caravan honestly replied that they had heard from merchants that his Majesty was in the habit of burning people alive, and consequently they were afraid to come near him. Theodore said, "It is true I am a bad man, but if you had trusted and come to me, I would have treated you well; but as you prefer the rebels, I will take care that in future you do not go to them." He then seized the salt and mules, sent all the merchants into an empty house, had it surrounded with dry wood, put guards at the door, and set fire to it.

The peasants of Gahinte, to whom Theodore offered an amnesty, declined to accept it; on three occasions he issued a proclamation offering them a free pardon should they return to him. At last, however, they sent him some priests to see what terms he would make; he received the priests well, and told them that he would not enter Gahinte: he only required a few supplies; but to prove to him their sincerity they must send from each village a person of influence to reside in his camp until he left Begemder. Luckily for them, the peasants declined to comply with his demands; Theodore was too prudent to venture into their valleys, and contented himself by plundering at a short distance from his camp; burning alive, before he left, a few poor wretches who had been simple enough to rely on the faith of his proclamation.

Theodore arrived at the foot of the steep ascent that leads from Begemder to Checheo on the 22nd of November. Up to that spot the road was not bad; but now an almost perpendicular height stood before him, and he was obliged to blast enormous rocks, cut a road through basalt, to enable him to bring his waggons, guns, and mortars on the Zébite plains above.

About that time he must have received the first intelligence of the landing of British troops at Zulla; for one afternoon he said to the Europeans, "Do not be afraid if I send for you at night. You must be on the watch, as I hear some donkeys intend stealing my slaves." The Europeans could not make out his meaning, and retired as usual to their tents. In the middle of the night, all of them, with the exception of an old man called Zander, and McKelvie, who had for a long time been suffering from dysentery, were awoke by soldiers coming into their quarters and ordering them to go at once to the Emperor. They were all ushered into a small tent, and many frivolous charges made against them. They were not allowed to leave that night; even a large bundle of chains was brought in; but on some of the chiefs representing to his Majesty that without their labour it would be exceedingly difficult to make roads and guide the waggons, and that he could always put them in chains when he reached Magdala, Theodore relented. He allowed them to go to their own tents in the daytime, when not on duty; but at night for their own safety, and, as he said, on account of the badness of his people, he made them all sleep in one tent, a few yards from his own: with the exception of a few days, they remained prisoners at night and slaves during the day, until the beginning of April.

From early dawn to late at night Theodore was himself hard at work; with his own hands he removed stones, levelled the ground, or helped to fill up small ravines. No one could leave so long as he was there himself; no one could think of eating, drinking, or of rest, whilst the Emperor showed the example and shared the hardships. When he could capture a few peasants or some of the rebels that crowned all the heights around him, and day and night insulted or laughed at him, he killed them in some cruel way or the other; but towards the soldiers, ever since leaving Debra Tabor, he behaved better, and left off beating or imprisoning them, as had been of late his wont. On one or two occasions only he called them all around him, and, standing on an elevated rock, addressed them in these terms: "I know that you all hate me; you all want to run away. Why do you not kill me? Here I am alone, and you are thousands." He would pause for a few seconds, and add, "Well, if you will not kill me, I will kill you all, one after the other."

On the 15th of December, the road being completed, he brought up his waggons on the plain of Zébite, and encamped there for a few days. The peasants of that district, believing that Theodore would never be able to ascend to their plateau, with all the incumbrances he had with him—though they were themselves ready to fly at the shortest notice—had not removed their cattle and grain; thus Theodore, for the first time for many months, was able to provide food for his small army, and make even some provision for the future. From Zébite to Wadela the road is naturally good, so that, as far as that district, the task before him was easy. He reached that plateau on the 25th of the same month, and encamped at Bet Hor.

But the work now before him would have driven any other man to despair; though not fifty miles from his Amba Magdala, he had, before he could rest there, to make roads down two precipitous descents, cross two rivers, and surmount again two steep perpendicular ascents. He went, however, steadily to work. Little by little he made a road, creditable even to a European engineer, bringing with him his mortars, cannons, &c.; he plundered at the same time, and kept away by his name alone Watshum Gobazé and his uncle Meshisha, who were both watching his movements: not that they intended to attack him, but who were anxious to be able to decamp at the first sign of his marching in the direction of the provinces they "protected." On the 10th of January he began his descent, reached the valley of the Jiddah on the 28th of the same month, ascended the opposite precipice, and encamped on the Dalanta plain on the 20th of February, 1868.

CHAPTER XVIII

We have now followed the Emperor's career from the day of our departure from Debra Tabor to his arrival in our neighbourhood. During that time, apart from the letters he addressed to Mr. Rassam relative to the one from the Queen, and about Mr. Flad and the artisans, we had but little intercourse with him. For a long time messengers passed with the greatest difficulty, and, afraid lest his written communications with the chiefs on the Amba might fall into the hands of the rebels, he had of late sent only verbal messages. Every messenger usually brought us compliments, and when any were sent from the Amba they always came to us by order of the chief before they left, so that Mr. Rassam might return a civil message in answer to the one he had received.

The ordinary staff of messengers were too well known on the road to be able to pass through the districts in rebellion; and for a long time we rejoiced at the idea that all communications were for ever interrupted between the camp and the fort, when one day a young Galla, servant of one of the political prisoners, reached the Amba, bringing a letter from his Majesty. The lad went forwards and backwards many times; but, apart from the presents be received from us, I do not believe he ever even got a salt for so constantly exposing his life; a few more men, who had friends and acquaintances on the road, managed also to pass through. All of them were very useful to us, as they also carried the correspondence between us and Mr. Flad, and, beings well rewarded, could be trusted with the most dangerous letters. We thought it even good fun to make the King's messenger our medium of communication between our friends in his camp and ourselves, often on treasonable matters.

Soon after reaching Bet Hor, Theodore issued a proclamation to the rebel districts of Dahonte and Dalanta, offering full amnesty for the past, and pledging himself, "by the death of Christ," that he would neither plunder nor ill-use them, should they return to their allegiance. For some days both districts refused, as Gobazé had promised to come and defend them; but the people of Dalanta, on seeing that, far from giving them any help, Gobazé was himself getting out of the way of Theodore, thought that, after all, it was perhaps better to accept the latter's offer, and, as they could not help themselves, trust to his pledged word. Dahonte, however, remained in its rebellion, and proposed to resist by force of arms any attempt on the part of Theodore to plunder the province. As the Emperor had spoken in very friendly terms to his workmen and others about Mr. Rassam, that gentleman was advised by the chiefs to write to the King, congratulating him on his safe arrival. This he repeated on several similar occasions; and the messengers he sent with these letters were very cordially treated by his Majesty. Theodore also wrote to Mr. Rassam on one or two occasions; and we had a ludicrous repetition of the courteous and edifying correspondence that had passed formerly between the two in the sunny days of Kourata.

January, 1868, ushered in a period of great mental excitement for us, which lasted until the very end; increasing in intensity as we approached the last days, as we well knew that then our fate would be decided. But there is something in the constant repetition of stimulants, be they moral or physical, which blunts the feelings, hardens the heart, and at last allows the person long submitted to their influence to look upon everything with indifference and impassiveness. We had had so many "shocks" during the last three months—so many times we expected to be tortured or killed— that when the day arrived that we were in reality placed almost beyond hope, the crisis did not affect us much, and once passed, we never thought of the matter again.

Having become "reconciled" with his children of Dalanta, Theodore's task was much easier. Several thousand peasants helped him in his road-making, others carried part of his property to Magdala, and now that the brave garrison of the Amba could cross the Dalanta plateau without fear, he sent for them, leaving only a few old men on the mountain beyond the ordinary number of prisoners' guards. On the 8th of January Bitwaddad Damash, in command, with the "brave" Goji as his lieutenant, and accompanied by seven or eight hundred men, started for Wadela. Many left with beating hearts, trembling at the prospect of meeting the Emperor. He was worshipped at a distance, but dreaded on his approach. His Majesty, however, received them very well; but was not over civil to all. Damash he treated rather coolly; but as he wanted them a little time longer, he did not say much, nor give them any cause to believe that he was greatly displeased with them.

A few days after Theodore had reached Dalanta he sent back the Magdala garrison to the Amba, to accompany thither the prisoners he had brought, with him,—the Europeans included,—and forwarded by them some powder, shot, and the instruments belonging to his workmen. Mrs. Rosenthal was also allowed to accompany the party, and all arrived on the Amba on the afternoon of the 26th of January. The five Europeans were sent to us; and on the interpreter's hut being given to Mr. and Mrs. Rosenthal, the larger one that gentleman had previously occupied was made over to the other five. We were well pleased to be all together. The new comers had much to tell us, and we in return gave them an account of our doings. We were, above all things, rejoiced at the arrival of Mrs. Rosenthal; our morbid idea having been for months, almost up to the end, that some flying column would be detached from the main body of our army to cut off Theodore from the mountain; and our anxiety had been great on account of Mrs. Rosenthal and her child, as Theodore, according to his system of hostages, had kept her near him as a security to prevent the Magdala prisoners from running away.

Messengers now went backwards and forwards daily, sometimes twice in the same day, between the camp and the amba. At first, we saw with anxiety the near approach of Theodore and the renewed facility of his communications with us; but as it was an evil we were powerless to contend against, we consoled ourselves as best we could, and though fearing the worst, hoped for the best. One advantage we gained was the facility of corresponding with Mr. Flad, who always, with great courage, had, ever since his return from England, on all possible occasions, kept us informed of Theodore's doings, and of anything he might have said with reference to the existing difficulties. He wrote to us in the beginning of February to inform us that, from some, conversation he had had with officers of the Imperial household, it was his opinion that his Majesty was aware of the landing of our troops, and had purposely sent to him a chief to find out what the intentions of our Government were concerning himself, and if there was still any hope of the matter being peaceably settled.

There is no doubt that for several mouths past, his Majesty had been advised by his spies that English troops had landed in his country; but under the difficulties he was placed in at the time, he considered it advisable to keep silent on the subject. Since he had reached the vicinity of the Amba, however, he frequently, in his conversation with his people, gave strong hints that he expected before long to have to contend with the soldiers of Europe. On the 8th of February Theodore told Mr. Waldmeier, the head of the workmen—a very intelligent and well-educated man, for whom Theodore had a great regard, though of late he had somewhat roughly used him—that he had received news from the coast informing him that the English had disembarked at Zulla. The following day he sent for Mr. Flad, and calling him aside, told him, "The people from whom you brought me a letter, and who you said would come, have arrived and landed at Zulla. They are coming up by the Salt Plain. Why did they not take a better road? The one by the Salt Plain is very unhealthy."

Flad explained to him that for troops arriving from India, that road was the best, as they would in three or four days reach the highlands of Agam. Theodore said, "We are making roads with great difficulty; for them it will only be play to make roads everywhere. It seems to me that it is the will of God that they should come. If He who is above does not kill me, none will kill me, and if He says, 'You must die,' none can save me: remember the history of Hezekiah and Sennacherib." Theodore appeared very calm and composed during that conversation. Two days afterwards he said to some of his workmen, "I long for the day I shall have the pleasure of seeing a disciplined European army. I am like Simeon; he was old, but before he died he rejoiced his heart by holding the Saviour in his arms. I am old, too; but I hope God will spare me to see them before I die. My soldiers are nothing compared to a disciplined army, where thousands obey the command of one man." Evidently he still entertained some vague hope that the coming event might turn to his advantage, as on another occasion he said to Mr. Waldmeier, "We have a prophecy in our country that a European king will meet an Abyssinian one, and that afterwards a king will reign in Abyssinia greater than any before him. That prophecy is going to be fulfilled at the present time; but I do not know whether I am the king alluded to, or if it is some one else."

We were delighted at the receipt of this intelligence; for a long time we believed that Theodore knew of the landing of our troops, but as he had never made any mention of the fact we still had our doubts on the subject, and were somewhat in dread of his first burst of passion on the intelligence reaching him.

On the 15th of February a letter from the Commander-in-Chief addressed to Theodore was brought to us by the messenger to whom it had been entrusted, as he was afraid of handing it over to his Majesty himself. This placed us in a difficult position; though as regarded the Amharic translation, it was perhaps as well that it had not reached Theodore, as that version, on some important points, gave a totally different meaning from that of the letter itself. I was quite delighted at listening to the Commander-in-Chief's manly and straightforward language. The letter was as firm as it was courteous, and I felt happy and proud, even in my captivity, that at last an English general had torn asunder the veil of false humility which for so long a time had concealed the bold and haughty spirit of England. We felt strengthened by the conviction that the hour was come when right and might would prevail, and the merciless despot who had acted towards us with such unheard-of treachery would meet his fate.

According to the latest news we had received from the Imperial camp, Theodore did not seem inclined to vent upon us his disappointment and anger at seeing all his plans frustrated by the landing of an English army; it was therefore decided to keep for the present the important and valuable document that had so accidentally fallen into our hands, as a powerful weapon to use, should a change take place in the line of conduct Theodore had adopted since he was made conversant of the fact that force was at last resorted to to effect our deliverance: for we had our fears, knowing his changeable and fickle disposition.

Nor did Theodore's peaceful mood last much longer. The Dalanta people, relying on his promises, and anxious to get rid of his presence, gave him every assistance in their power, carrying his baggage to the Amba, or working at the roads under his direction. The honourable way in which he had kept his word with the people of Dalanta induced the neighbouring district to send him deputations begging for pardon, and offering to pay him tribute and send supplies into his camp, if he would proclaim in their favour the same amnesty he had granted to the Dalanta people. Had Theodore been wise, even then he had a good opportunity of regaining part of his lost kingdom; and had he continued to keep to his word, province after province, disgusted with the cowardice of the rebels, would have returned to him. But he was too fond of plundering: the peasants did not, according to his ideas, send sufficient supplies; and as he knew that the district was exceedingly rich in grain and cattle, regardless of his oath, on the 17th of February, he gave orders for his soldiers to plunder the peasants' houses.

Taken quite by surprise, very little resistance was offered. Theodore succeeded beyond his expectations; corn and cattle were now in abundance, and in order to economize his supplies, he allowed; all the Gondar people who were still with him, and many of the women and children of runaway soldiers and chiefs, to leave the camp and go wherever they liked. Since Ohecheo he had formed the strongest and hardiest of the women of his camp into a plundering band; he was always much pleased with their bravery, and one of them having killed a petty chief, and brought to him the sword of her adversary, he was so delighted that he gave her a title of rank and presented her with one of his own pistols. We knew enough of the Emperor's character to fear that, when once he again took to plundering and killing, he would lose much of the amenity and gentleness he had of late displayed, and look upon the arrival of an armed force from England in a very different light; we were not, therefore, much astonished to hear that he had again quarrelled with the Europeans around him. It is also not improbable that a copy of the proclamation the Commander-in-Chief had sent to the different chiefs may have fallen into his hands about this time, as one was found after his death amongst his papers. Whatever may have been the cause of his sudden change, he, without any apparent reason, all at once regarded his workmen with suspicion, and though he ordered them to be in constant attendance upon his person, he would not for many days allow them to work.

Mr. Waldmeier one evening, on returning to his tent to take his evening meal, entered into conversation with a spy of the Emperor's on the subject of the advance of the English army. Waldmeier, amongst other things, told the man that it would be a very unwise act of his Majesty if he did not at once make friends with the English, as he had not a single friend in the country. On the officer reporting that conversation, Theodore in a fearful passion sent for all the Europeans; for a while his rage was such that he could not speak, but kept walking up and down, looking fiercely at them, and holding his spear in a threatening attitudes. At last, stopping before Mr. Waldmeier, he abused him in no measured terms: "Who are you, you dog, but a donkey, a poor man who came from a far country to be my slave, and whom I have paid and fed for years? What does a beggar like you know about my affairs? Are you to dictate to me what I am to do? A King is coming to treat with a King! What do you know about such matters?" Theodore then threw himself on the ground and said, "Take my spear and kill me; but do not revile me." Waldmeier prostrated himself before him and begged for pardon; the Emperor rose, but refused to grant his request, and ordered him to rise and follow him.

On the 18th of February Theodore pitched his camp near the ridge of the Dalanta plateau, and the following day the chiefs of the Amba, with their telescopes, could perceive several working parties engaged in making the road down to the Bechelo. Theodore had made about a thousand prisoners when he had plundered Dalanta, and all of them, under strong escorts, were set to work for him; but when the road was finished half way, he allowed them to return to Dalanta.

For a while the communications between the Amba and the camp were again suspended. The few chiefs and soldiers that had remained at Magdala viewed with great despondency this last breach of faith of their master, as it foreboded anything but gratitude towards them for the many privations they had submitted to in fulfilment of the trust vested in them. With great difficulty we succeeded in getting a messenger to pass through the valley of the Bechelo, on account of the disturbed condition of the country since Dalanta had been plundered. The news he brought was a little more favourable. His Majesty had reconciled himself with Mr. Waldmeier, and now treated all his artisans with consideration and kindness. He did not, however, allow them to work, and they all slept in a tent near his Majesty: a precaution he had for a short time ceased to take. Often he spoke to his soldiers, or to the Europeans, about the coming of our troops; sometimes avowing his intention to fight with them, at other times expressing himself in a more conciliatory tone. He had hardly mentioned our names of late; he spoke about Mr. Stern, but, contrary to his habit, not in anger. He referred several times to a certain letter of Mrs. Flad's, which had given him great offence some years before. That lady alluded in it to the possible invasion of the county by the English and French, giving as her opinion that he would not be afraid. Theodore frequently said that Mrs. Flad was right: "They are coming, and I do not fear."

On the 14th of March his Majesty, with all his waggons, cannons, and mortars, reached the valley of the Bechelo. From a letter we received from Mr. Flad it appears that his Majesty was in a great hurry to reach Magdala. The Europeans were still treated courteously, but, day and night, were strictly watched. He evidently received good information of what was going on in the British camp. To Mr. Waldmeier, who was more than any other in his confidence, he said, "With love and friendship they will overcome me; but if they come with other intentions I know they will not spare me, and I will make a great blood-bath, and afterwards die."

On the 16th he despatched a messenger to the Amba to rejoice his people with the good news of his approach, and sent us a courteous message. Mr. Rassam at once wrote to him, complimenting him on his success. Mr. Rassam is certainly deserving of praise for endeavouring, by every means in his power, to impress upon his Majesty the fervent friendship he felt for him, and the sincere admiration and deep devotion which time had only strengthened, and that even captivity and chains could not destroy. Mr. Rassam's official position gave him great advantages over the other captives; he was able to make "friends" of all the royal messengers, of all the personal attendants, of his Majesty, and of every one on the Amba or in the camp, who could say a good word for him. Ignorant of the source of Mr. Rassam's liberality, the chief courtiers, and even his Majesty himself, came to the conclusion that Mr. Prideaux and myself were very inferior beings—harmless individuals, whom it would be perfectly absurd to place on a footing of equality with the open-handed, sweet-talking gentleman, who alone, and out of mere regard, again congratulated his Majesty.

Theodore was so pleased with Mr. Rassam's letter that early on the 18th he sent Mr. Flad, his secretary and several officers, with a friendly letter to that gentleman, and instructed the chief of the Amba to remove at once *his friend's* fetters. Theodore, in his letter to Mr. Rassam, forgetting that he himself had on several occasions made mention of his fetters, said that he had no quarrel with him, and that when he had sent him to Magdala he had only told his people to watch him, but out of precaution they put him in chains. He sent him also 2,000 dollars for the money and things Flad had brought with him, and said that, on account of the rebellious condition of the country, he had not been able to forward them, and hoped he would, at the same time, accept a present of a hundred sheep and fifty cows. No one else was included in the order; and I confess that we were foolish enough to feel this disappointment bitterly. Probably twenty months of captivity weakens the mind as well as the body, as at other times we should not have given even a thought to the matter. Even as it was we soon forgot all about it, wisely remembering that freedom and liberty would be ours when the British flag should float over our former gaol. It appears that our displeasure had been remarked, and a spy started at once for the camp to inform his Majesty that we were angry at our chains not being opened.

Mr. Flad returned that evening to the Imperial camp, already pitched on the northern banks of the Bechelo; and the following morning the Emperor sent for him and asked him if he had seen us all, and if we were looking well. He inquired especially about Mr. Prideaux and myself; Flad told his Majesty that we were in good health, but sorry that he had made a difference between us and Mr. Rassam. At this the Emperor, smiling all the while, said:—"Yes, I have heard of it: when they were put in chains by my people Mr. Rassam did not say a word, but both of them looked angrily at the chains. I have no anger against them, nor have they done me any wrong; as soon as I shall meet Mr. Rassam I will take off their chains also."

Mr. Flad explained to his Majesty that we had felt disappointed, as some one, on Mr. Rassam's chains being ordered to be opened, had come to the conclusion that the Consul, Dr. Blanc, and Mr. Prideaux would be included in the same order, and had run on ahead to bring us the *miserach* (good news); that Mr. Rassam was also very sorry his two companions were separated from him, and had asked him the reason why it was so, but as he did not know his Majesty's motives he could not answer him, &c. Theodore, still smiling, said to Mr. Flad, "If there is only friendship, everything will be right."

On the evening of the 25th of March, his Majesty pitched his camp on the small plateau of Islamgee; he had brought his cannons and even the monster mortar as far as the foot of the ascent, and was hard at work making the road required for them to be dragged up.

Early on the morning of the 26th, the priests of the Amba, in full canonicals, carrying crosses and gaily-tinselled umbrellas, went to Islamgee to congratulate the Emperor on his safe arrival. Theodore received them with great courtesy, and shortly afterwards dismissed them, saying, "Go back, my fathers, be of good cheer; if I have money I will share it with you. My clothes will be yours, and with my corn I will feed you." They were on the point of starting when an old bigoted priest, who had always shown himself badly disposed towards us, turned round and addressed his Majesty in the following terms:—"Oh, my King, do not abandon your religion!" Theodore, quite surprised, inquired of him what he meant. The priest, rather excited, exclaimed, in a loud voice, "You do not fast, you observe no more the feasts of the saints! I fear that you will soon follow entirely the religion of the Franks." Theodore turned towards some of the Europeans that stood near him and said, "Did I ever inquire of you about your religion? Did I ever show any desire to follow your creed?" They all replied, "Certainly not." Theodore then addressed the priests, who were listening with dismay to this conversation, and told them, "Judge this man." The priests did not consult long, and with one accord gave as their decision, that "the man who insults his king is worthy of death." On that, the soldiers fell upon the old priest, tore off his clothes, and would have, killed him on the spot had not Theodore mitigated the punishment. He ordered him to be put in chains, sent to the Amba, and for seven days not to be allowed either bread or water.

Another priest, who had also on a former occasion grossly insulted his Majesty, was sent up to the prison at the same time. That priest had said to some of the Emperor's spies that their master wore three matabs: [Footnote: *Matab*: a string made of blue silk, and worn round the neck as the sign of Christianity in Abyssinia.] one, because he was a Mussulman, having burnt the churches; the second because he was a Frank, never observing the fast days; the third, to make the people believe he was a Christian.

The following morning we were awoke by the merry *elelta*—the shrill cry of joy uttered by the Abyssinian *beau sexe* on great and happy events. On this occasion a peculiar mixture of joyous and plaintive strains slightly modified its usual character, and it was a sharp but also tremulous sound that greeted the arrival of the Emperor Theodore on the Amba. Carpets were at once spread on the open space in front of his house, the throne was brought out and decked with gorgeous silks, and the state umbrella unfolded to protect the reclining Emperor from the hot rays of the sun. We expected, on seeing all these preparations made and the large number of courtiers and officers assembled in front, that before long we would be called for, and that something similar to the trial and reconciliation of Zagé was going to be acted over again. We were, however, mistaken: it was on account of some private affairs that the Emperor, abandoning for a day his work, had called a court of justice.

For a long time various charges had been whispered against two of the chiefs of the Amba, Ras Bisawar and Bitwaddad Damash. His Majesty now desired to investigate them; he listened quietly to the accusers, and having heard the defence, he asked the opinion of the chiefs around him. They advised him to forgive them on account of their former good services, but that they should not be trusted any more. Had not a chief, they said, deserted a few nights before—a feat he could not have accomplished had not several of the garrison helped him in his escape?—and moreover, should an enemy present himself before the Amba during one of the Emperor's absences, they would most probably quarrel amongst themselves instead of defending the place. The Emperor accepted their decision and said that he would send a new garrison, that the former one should proceed that very day to his camp, and that as their store of grain would only be a burden to them, they should leave it behind; he would give orders to the writers to make out a correct account of all they had, and, *to oblige them*, he would keep the grain himself and pay them the value in money. He afterwards sent for the two priests he had imprisoned the day before, released them from their fetters, and told them that he forgave them, but that they must leave his country at once. On going away, he sent word by Samuel to Mr. Rassam that he had intended to come and see him but that he felt too tired; he added, "Your people are near; they are coming to deliver you."

The soldiers of the garrison were greatly annoyed at having to leave, and were much pleased early the next morning to learn that Theodore had rescinded his order. He had, he said, pardoned them on account of their long and faithful services. The Ras was put on "half-pay," and a new commandant, Bitwaddad Hassanié, sent to take over the charge, while the garrison was reinforced by some 400 musketeers.

It is probable that Theodore wanted simply to know what amount of corn the garrison possessed, as he might perhaps require it himself before long, and possibly also the clemency shown by him was due to his being pleased at the soldiers having complied with his orders and purchased grain, as he had directed them, with the money he had a short time before given them.

CHAPTER XIX

On the 28th of March, all of us, with the exception of Mr. Rassam, were called out and made to stand in a line to be *counted* by the new Ras; then at about ten at night, as we were undressing, Samuel came to inform us that he had received orders to put us all, with the exception of Mr. Rassam, in one hut for that night, but that as none of our huts was large enough, he had obtained leave that we should be distributed into two. Cameron, Mr. Rosenthal, and Mr. Kerans were made to join us company, and four villanous-looking rascals, with lighted candles burning all night, were posted inside the door to prevent our going out. Samuel and two chiefs slept in Mr. Rassam's room, and I strongly suspect that Samuel was on that occasion more in the position of a prisoner than a guardian.

We slept but little, expecting that the morning would bring some change for the worse. To our day guards some ten or fifteen of the greatest scoundrels of the camp had been recently added, and we felt rather anxious when we learnt early the next morning that Theodore had sent word he would come up in the course of the day to muster the garrison.

At about three in the afternoon some of our servants came rushing into our hut to tell us that Theodore had arrived on the Amba, and that he appeared to be a *little* drunk. Shortly afterwards Mr. Flad came with a message to Mr. Rassam from the Emperor, to the effect that if his Majesty had time he would send for him after his return from the church. A red-flannel tent, the sign of royalty, was, in the meanwhile, pitched in the plain, and all around carpets were spread. When Theodore issued from the church he was in a great passion, seized a priest by the beard, and said to him, "You say that I want to change my religion; before any one could force me to do so I would cut my throat." He then thrust his spear with violence into the ground, "fakered," cursed the Bishop,—in a word, acted in all respects as if drunk or mad. He called Mr. Meyer, who was standing at a short distance from him, and told him to go to Mr. Rassam with the message, "Your people are coming. I put you in chains for that purpose. I have not obtained what I wanted. Come to me, and in the same dress you used to wear before."

We all felt very nervous about the interview, as Theodore seemed in a bad disposition; however, all went on well. As soon as Mr. Rassam approached the tent, Theodore advanced a few steps to meet him, shook hands with him, and asked him to sit down. He then said, "I cannot say that I could not bring my throne today, as you are aware that it is at Magdala; but out of respect for my friend the Queen, whom you represent here, I desire to sit on the same carpet as yourself." After a while, he said to Mr. Rassam, "Those two persons who came with you are neither my friends nor my enemies, but if you consent to become their security, I will have their chains opened." On that Mr. Rassam rose, and said, "Not only will I become their security, but should they do anything displeasing to your Majesty, do not say it is Blanc or Prideaux, but that Rassam did it." Theodore then asked Mr. Rassam to send two persons to have our chains taken off, and as his Majesty insisted upon it, Mr. Rassam mentioned Mr. Flad and Samuel.

The servants had heard the good news and rushed in before Flad came to us with the welcome intelligence. On the arrival of Flad and Samuel, we were taken to Mr. Rassam's house, where Mr. Flad delivered to us from his Majesty the following message:—"You are neither my friends nor my enemies. I do not know who you are. I chained you because I chained Mr. Rassam: now I open your chains because he promised to be your security. If you run away it will be a shame for you and for me."

On that we were told to sit down; an iron wedge was first hammered in where the ring was joined, and when the intervening space was considered sufficient, three or four loops of strong leather rope were passed inside the irons, and we were told to put one leg on a large stone brought in for the purpose. On each side a long pole was then fixed in the leather loops, and five or six men pulled on them with all their strength, using the stone as a "point d'appui" for the lever. As the leather thongs acted on the iron ring, little by little it gave way and stretched out, until at last it was wide enough to pass over the foot: the operation was then performed on the other leg. It took at least half an hour to take mine off, and even more to open Prideaux's. Though we were delighted at the prospect of having again the free use of our limbs, we did not enjoy the rude operation at all; and although (as we were in favour) the soldiers did their best not to hurt us, still the pain was at times quite unbearable, as the "point d'appui" now and then slipped from the stone to the chain itself, and pressing on the shin it seemed to us as if the leg would be crushed to pieces.

At first we could hardly walk. Our legs seemed to us as light as feathers; we could not guide them, and we staggered very much like drunken men: if we met with a small stone in our way, we involuntarily lifted up the foot to a ridiculous height. For days the limb was painful, and the slightest exertion was followed by great fatigue.

Theodore having expressed his desire that we should present ourselves before him in uniform, we dressed ourselves immediately the chains were taken off. As I was the first to get rid of my twenty-one months' friends, I was ready when Prideaux came in; but no sooner had he begun taking off his prison garb to dress himself, than messenger after messenger rushed in, sent from Theodore to hurry us on. Well knowing the fickle disposition of their master, all the chiefs present, Samuel, the guards, every one kept continually shouting out to Prideaux, "Make haste, make haste!" Flurried, and unaccustomed since so many months to the civilized way of putting on his clothes, and unable to guide his feet properly, in his hurry he tore his uniform trousers almost in two. But no one _would hear of waiting any longer: off we must go. Luckily a few pins were at hand, and what with his cap as a screen, the accident, if not repaired, was hidden. On reaching the Imperial tent, his Majesty, after greeting us cordially, said, "I chained you because your people believed that I was not a strong king; now that your masters are coming I release you to show them that I am not afraid. Fear not; Christ is my witness, and God knows, that I have nothing in my heart against you three. You came to this country knowing what the Consul had done. Do not fear, nothing will happen to you. Sit down."

Once seated he ordered some tej to be given to us, and conversed with Mr. Rassam; amongst other things he said, "I am like a woman in the family way, and know not if it will be an abortion, a girl or a boy; I hope it will be a boy. Some men die when they are young, some at middle age, some when they are old; some are prematurely cut off, but what my end will be, God only knows." He then introduced his son to Mr. Rassam. He inquired if we had carpets, and if our houses were comfortable; and on Mr. Rassam telling him that by his favour we had everything we required, and that his Majesty would be pleased if he saw the nice home he had, Theodore looking up to heaven said, "My friend, believe me, my heart loves you; ask me for whatever you like, even for my own flesh, and I will give it to you."

His Majesty, during the whole of the interview, was most courteous and appeared much pleased with Mr. Rassam's answers, and laughed heartily more than once. When he dismissed us, he sent his son and the Europeans to accompany us to our huts.

I heard, both from Mr. Rassam and from the Europeans that were present all along, that before as well as during the time we were present, Theodore had shown himself most friendly and kind. The Europeans told me that whilst our chains were being opened he talked on many subjects with Mr. Rassam. Amongst other things, he said to him, "Mr. Stern has wounded me in the arm, but if anything bad is to happen, before that I will wound him also." He also said, "I will fight; you may see my dead body, and say there is a bad man, who has injured me and mine; and perhaps you will not bury me."

After we left he mustered his troops and spoke to them about us. "Whatever happens, I will not kill these three—they are messengers; but amongst those that are coming, and here also, I have enemies; those I will kill if they want to injure me." As he was passing the gate on his way back to his camp, he called the Ras and told him, "Mr. Rassam and his companions are not prisoners, they may play and run; watch them with the eye only."

That night we had no guards inside our room; they slept outside as before. We, however, did not venture to avail ourselves of the order and walk about the Amba, but remained quietly in our inclosure.

On reaching his camp, Theodore assembled his people and said to them:—"You hear of white men coming to fight me; it is no rumour, but quite true." A soldier shouted out, "Never mind, my king, we will fight them." Theodore looked at the man, and said, "You fool! you do not know what you say. These people have long cannons, elephants, guns, and muskets without number. We cannot fight against them. You believe that our muskets are good: if they were so they would not sell them to us. I might kill Mr. Rassam, as he brings these soldiers against me. I did him no harm: it is true I put him in chains; but it is your fault, you people of Magdala, you should have advised me better. I might kill him, but he is only one; and then those who are coming would take away my children, my women, my treasures, and kill me and you."

The following morning, the 30th, a message was sent to the five who had lately joined us, asking them to work again for him, as he wanted more stone shots. On accepting his offer, their foot chains were taken off, hand chains put by pairs, and they were conducted to the camp. A tent was pitched for them, and on their arrival they received a present of tej, meat and bread, from his Majesty.

None of us were over sanguine at the recent good treatment we had received at the hands of Theodore; we knew how suddenly he changed, and that often,—as formerly in our case,—he pretended great friendship, when he intended all the while to ill-use, or even kill his dupes. We were, however, in good spirits and kept up our courage, knowing that the end was near: we left the result in God's hands, and hoped for the best.

On the 1st of April we learnt that the evening before, Theodore, being very drunk, had "fakered" a great deal. At about ten in the forenoon a large number of soldiers came rushing in from the camp below (we always disliked very much those abrupt movements of the soldiers), but instead of coming towards our fence, as at first we feared, they went in the direction of the magazines, and shortly afterwards we saw them again passing along on their way back, carrying the cannons Theodore had on the mountain, powder, cannon-balls, &c. We supposed that Theodore had either decided on defending Selassié, or had sent for his guns, as he intended, such was the general opinion, to have a great "faker."

Early on the morning of the 2nd, some of the chiefs were sent by the Emperor to inform us that his Majesty required us immediately to proceed to Islamgee. From our former experience of Theodore's fickle disposition we knew not what would be our fate, whether a polite reception, imprisonment or something worse; but as there was no help for it, we dressed, and, accompanied by the chiefs, left our huts, (perhaps never to see them again,) and walked down to the camp below the mountain. It was the first time, with the exception of the short distance we had gone on the day our chains had been opened, that we had left our inclosure. We had but a very indifferent idea of the Amba, and were astonished to find it much larger than we expected, the road between the gates longer and steeper, and the paths along the side of the Amba more abrupt and more lengthy than we had supposed from our recollections of twenty-one months before.

We found Theodore seated on a heap of stones about twenty yards below Islamgee, on the side of the road just completed, and through which the cannons, mortars, and waggons were going to be dragged. From the spot he had chosen he could see all the road down to the foot of Islamgee, where all his people were busily engaged fixing long leather ropes to the waggons, and, under the supervision of the Europeans, making everything ready, for the ascent. The Emperor was dressed very simply: the only difference in his attire from the chief in attendance standing some ten yards on his side, was in the silk border of his shama: he held a spear in his hand, and two long pistols were fixed in his belt. He greeted us cordially and made us sit down *behind him*: a proof of confidence, he would certainly not have accorded to his dearest Abyssinian friend, as we had only to give him a sudden push, and he would have rolled down the precipice below.

The road he had made on the side of Islamgee was broad but very steep on the average at a gradient of one in three; half way an almost straight angle intersected it, and we feared that there might be some difficulty in turning the heavy waggons without upsetting them. He did not speak much at first, being intent on examining the waggons below; but as soon as the big mortar came in sight he pointed it out to us, and asked Mr. Rassam his opinion about it. We all admired the huge piece, and Mr. Rassam, having complimented his Majesty on his great work, added, that before long he hoped that our people would have the same pleasure of admiring it as we did. Samuel, who translated on that occasion, turned quite pale, but as the

Emperor understood a little Arabic he was obliged to render the sentence, though he evidently did not like it. Theodore laughed, and sent Samuel to tell Mr. Waldmeier what Mr. Rassam had just said. A few minutes afterwards his Majesty got up; we rose also, and Mr. Rassam told him, through Samuel, that to gladden his heart still more he begged him to be gracious enough to release from their fetters our companions still in chains on the Amba. This time Samuel not only turned pale, but shook his head, declining to open such a subject; but on Mr. Rassam repeating his request, this time in a higher tone of voice, Theodore looked round, and Samuel, having no option left, complied. His Majesty looked sullen and a little annoyed, but after a short pause gave orders to some of his attendants and to Samuel to proceed at once to the Amba and have the chains of the five remaining captives opened at once.

The Emperor then walked down to the spot where the road made a sharp angle, and directed the laborious task of having such heavy masses dragged up the precipitous incline. He sent us to the other side of the road, where we might witness the whole scene well, and appointed several of his high officers to attend upon us. None but Theodore, I believe, could have directed that difficult operation; the leather ropes, from long use, were always breaking, and we were very much afraid that some accident might happen, and that, at the very last stage, the ponderous mortar "Sebastopol" would tumble over the precipice. We fancied the rage his Majesty would be in; and our close proximity to him made us earnestly pray that nothing of the kind would occur. The sight was well worth witnessing: Theodore standing on a projecting rock, leaning on his spear, sent his aide-de-camp at every moment with instructions to those who directed the five or six hundred men harnessed to the ropes. At times when the noise was too great, or when he wanted to give some general instructions, he had but to lift up his hand and not a sound would arise from the thousands engaged in the work, and the clear voice of Theodore would alone be heard in the deep silence that his simple gesture had produced.

At last the big mortar was safely landed on Islamgee. We climbed up as fast as we could, and complimented his Majesty on the achievement of his great undertaking; he sent us word to examine the mortar. We all three jumped on the gun-carriage, greatly admired it, and loudly expressed our astonishment and delight to the bystanders. His Majesty was evidently well pleased with the praises we had bestowed upon his great favourite, and made us sit down near him on the verge of the Islamgee plateau whilst the remaining cannons and waggons were being drawn up. The wonderful work of dragging up the 16,000 pounds weight of "Sebastopol" once over—though some of the cannons were also of a considerable size,—the rest of the operation was only child's play, and his Majesty, though present, never interfered.

We must have remained with him for at least several hours in quiet and friendly talk. As the sun was getting hot, his Majesty insisted on our putting on our caps, and, on Mr. Rassam a short time afterwards asking his permission to open an umbrella, he not only granted it, but, seeing that I had none, kindly sent one of his pages for his own, opened it, and gave it to me. He told us of all the difficulties he had undergone, and how the peasants refused every assistance. He said, "I was obliged to make roads during the day and drag my waggons, and to plunder at night, as my people had nothing to eat." All the country, he said, had been against him, and when they could seize any of his followers they immediately put them to death; in return, when he made any of them prisoners, to avenge his friends, he burnt them alive: this he told us in the quietest way possible, just as if he had done the right thing. He then asked about our troops, the elephants, the rifles, &c. Mr. Rassam told him everything we knew; that about 12,000 troops had landed, but that not more than 5,000 or 6,000 would advance on Magdala—adding, "It will only be friendship." Theodore said, "God only knows; before, when the French came into my country, at the time of that robber 'Agau Negussi,' I made a quick march to seize them, but they had run away. Do you believe that I would not have gone to meet your people, and asked them what they came into my country for? but how can I? You have seen to-day my army, and"—pointing to the Amba above—"there is all my country. But I will wait for them here, and then let God's will be done."

He next spoke about the Crimean war, of the late contest between Austria and Prussia, of the needle-gun, and asked us if the Prussians had made the Emperor of Austria a prisoner, or seized his country. Mr. Rassam told him that the needle-guns, by their rapid fire, had gained the victory for the Prussians; that on peace being made the Emperor of Austria was obliged to pay a large sum of money; that a part of his territory had been annexed by the conqueror, and all his allies had lost their kingdoms. His Majesty listened with great composure, only when he was told that only 5,000 men were coming, the proud curl of his lip expressed how much he felt his fallen condition when so few men were considered sufficient to conquer him. He afterwards spoke to us about his old grievances against Cameron, Stern, and Rosenthal. About us he said, "You have never done me any wrong. I know that you are great men in your country, and I feel very sorry to have ill-treated you without cause."

After the last waggon had been drawn up, he rose and told us to follow; we walked a few yards behind him, and when Samuel, who had gone to give orders for a tent to be pitched for us, returned, he asked us, through him, several questions about shells, the charge required for his big mortar, &c., to all of which Mr. Rassam replied, that being a civilian he knew nothing about it. He then told him to ask me, but Mr. Rassam replied that I was only acquainted with medicines. On that he ceased his inquiries and conducted ne to the tent prepared for us; then bidding us good afternoon, retired to his apartment. An Abyssinian breakfast, tej, and a few European dishes and cakes that Mrs. Waldmeier had prepared; according to his instructions, were then sent for us to partake of. A short time afterwards he sent for Mr. Waldmeier and Samuel.

It seems that Theodore had already been drinking, as he talked to them in a very excited manner, inquiring why he had not received any intimation of the landing of our troops and if it was not customary for a king to inform another that he was invading his country &c. Mr. Waldmeier and Samuel, when they returned, appeared rather alarmed, as it was no unfrequent case with Theodore to be very friendly in the morning, and, when in his cups, to change his demeanour and ill-treat those he had petted a little while before. Samuel and Waldmeier were a second time sent for. Theodore then abused Samuel a great deal, told him that he had many charges to bring against him, but that he left it for another day; he then ordered him to take us back to the fort, gave instructions for three mules to be brought, and for the commandant of the mountain, together with the former one, to escort us. To Mr. Waldmeier he said, "Tell Mr. Rassam that a small fire, the size of a pea, if not put out in time, may cause a great conflagration: it is left to Mr. Rassam to extinguish it before it spreads." We were glad to return safe and sound to our old prison, and rejoiced on seeing our companions freed from their fetters and looking happy and hopeful.

On the following morning Mr. Rassam sent word to the Emperor, requesting his permission to be allowed to inform the Commander-in-Chief of the British army of his Majesty's good-will towards the Europeans in his power; but Theodore answered that he did not desire him to write, as he had opened the chains of the captives not out of fear, but simply on account of his personal friendship for Mr. Rassam.

As Theodore had on several occasions expressed his astonishment at not receiving any communication from the Commander-in-Chief, we thought it advisable to request Sir Robert Napier, through our friends, to be kind enough to send a short courteous letter to the Emperor, informing him of the object of the expedition; as the letter he had addressed to him before landing had been detained by Mr. Rassam, and the ultimatum sent by Lord Stanley previous to the intervention of an armed force, having also fallen into Mr. Rassam's hands, instead of reaching the Emperor, had been destroyed by that gentleman.

The five (Mr. Staiger and his party) were making stone balls for his Majesty's cannons, but as none of the Europeans in his service would stand security for them, every evening the hand chains were hammered on after their day's work was over. On the evening of the 3rd Theodore sent to Mr. Rassam, asking him to become their guarantee; but he refused, as he could not, he said, hold himself responsible for them so long as they were working for his Majesty and resided at a distance from him. However, Mr. Flad and one of the other Europeans consenting to become security, the torture of having the chains daily fastened on was discontinued, and the captives were simply guarded at night in their tent.

Provisions were running short, and for some days a foraging expedition was much talked about, Dahonte being considered as the place selected. But Theodore, unwilling to expose his small force to a repulse, did not venture so far, but on the morning of the 4th of April plundered his own people, the few small villages situate at the foot of the Amba; and he unsuccessfully attempted to sack the village of Watat, where his *own cattle* were kept. Theodore met with much more resistance than he expected from the Galla peasants; many of the soldiers were killed, and the booty brought back was very small.

The soldiers on the mountain were more despondent than ever: little aware of the great change that before long was to take place, they viewed with great concern and anxiety this last raid, as, were the Emperor to go away, they would be left to starve on their rock. From Mr. Munzinger we frequently received short notes, which reached us sewn in the worn-out trousers of some peasant or messenger; thus we knew that our deliverers were now near, and we longed for the day, not far distant, when our fate would be decided: for we suffered more from constant anxiety and doubt— as to what every minute might bring, than from the certainty of death: even the few hopeful thoughts we now and then indulged in were nothing compared to regained liberty.

CHAPTER XX

On the evening of the 7th of April we heard indirectly that the next morning all the prisoners, ourselves included, would be called before his Majesty, who was at the time encamped at the foot of Selassié, and that in all probability we should not return to the Amba. At day-dawn a messenger came from Theodore ordering us to go down, and take with, us our tents and anything else we might require. As was our wont on such occasions, we put on our uniforms, and proceeded to the Emperor's camp accompanied by the former captives. On approaching Selassié we perceived his Majesty, surrounded by many of his chiefs and soldiers, standing near his guns in conversation with some of his European workmen. He saluted us courteously, and told, us to advance and stand near him. Cameron was staggering from the effects of the sun, and could with difficulty keep himself from falling to the ground. On perceiving his condition his Majesty asked us what was the matter with him. We answered that Cameron was unwell, and begged permission for him to sit down, a request that was immediately granted. Theodore then greeted the other prisoners, asked them how they were, and on perceiving the Rev. Mr. Stern he said, smiling all the while, "O Kokab (Star), why have you plaited your hair?" [Footnote: Only soldiers plait the hair; peasants and priests shave the head about once a month.] Before he could answer Samuel told the Emperor, "Your Majesty, it is not plaited; it falls naturally on his shoulders."

Theodore then retired a little way from the crowd, and told us three and Cameron to follow him. Seating himself on a large stone, and telling us also to sit down, he said, "I have sent for you, as I desire to look after your safety. When your people come and fire upon me I will put you in a safe place; and should you even there be in danger I will remove you to somewhere else." He asked us if our tents had arrived, and on being informed that they had not, he ordered one of his own, of red flannel, to be pitched in the meanwhile. He remained with us about half an hour conversing on different topics; he narrated the anecdote of Damocles, asked us about our laws, quoted Scripture—in a word, jumped from one subject to the other, discoursing on topics quite foreign to his thoughts. He did his best to appear calm and amiable, but we soon detected that he was labouring under great excitement. When, in January, 1866, he received us at Zagé, we were struck by the simplicity of his dress, in every respect the same as that of his common soldiers; of late, however, he had adopted a more gaudy attire, but nothing compared to the harlequin coat he wore that day.

After he had dismissed us, he ascended the hill under which our tent was pitched, and for two hours, at about fifty yards from us, surrounded by his army, he "fakered" (bragged) to his heart's content. He discoursed first on his former deeds, or what he intended to do when he should encounter the white men, speaking all the while in contemptuous terms of his advancing foe. Addressing the soldiers whom he was sending as an advanced post to Arogié, he told them, on the approach of the white men, to wait until they had fired, and before the enemy had time to reload, to fall upon them with their spears; and showing the gaudy dress he had put on for the occasion, he added: "Your valour will meet with its reward, and you will enrich yourselves with spoils, compared to which the rich dress I am wearing is but a mere trifle." When he had concluded his harangue he dismissed his troops, and sent for Mr. Rassam. He told him not to notice what had taken place, as it meant nothing; but that he was obliged to speak publicly in that manner to encourage his soldiers. He then mounted his mule and ascended to the top of Selassié to examine the road from Dalanta to the Bechelo, and ascertain the movements of the English army.

The next day, the 8th, we only saw his Majesty at a distance, seated on a stone in front of his tents, and talking quietly to those around him. In the afternoon he ascended to the top of Selassié, and on his return sent us word that he had seen nothing; but that our people could not be far off, as a woman had come to inform him that, the evening before, horses and mules had been taken down to the Bechelo to be watered.

As we came down from the Amba the day before, we had met on the road all the prisoners crawling along, many of them in hand and foot chains, having in that condition been obliged to walk down the irregular and steep descent. Their appearance was enough to inspire pity in the most callous heart; many had no other covering than a small piece of rag round the loins, and were living skeletons, covered with some loathsome skin disease. Chiefs, soldiers or beggars, all wore an anxious expression: they had but too much reason to fear that they had not been dragged out of the prison where they had spent years of misery for any good purpose. However, on that morning Theodore gave orders for about seventy-five to be released, all either former servants of his, or chiefs whom he had imprisoned, without cause, during his fits of madness, so frequent of late.

Soon after his return from Selassié, his merciful mood being over, Theodore sent orders to have seven prisoners executed; amongst them the wife and child of Comfou (the storekeeper who had run away in

September)—poor innocent beings on whom the despot vented his rage for the desertion of the husband: they were shot by the "brave Amharas," and their bodies hurled over the nearest precipice. Theodore sent me word to go and visit Bardel, who was lying dangerously ill in a tent close by. Having seen him and prescribed, I afterwards visited some of the Europeans and their families; I found them all exceedingly anxious and none could arrive at any conclusion as to the probable course Theodore would adopt.

Early on the morning of the 9th some of the European workmen informed us that Theodore was making roads to drag part of his artillery to Fahla, where it overlooks the Bechelo; they also told us that before parting he had given orders for the release of about one hundred prisoners, most of them women or poor people. Towards 2 P.M. the Emperor returned, and sent us word by Samuel that he had seen a quantity of baggage coming down from Dalanta to the Bechelo—four elephants, but very few men. He had also remarked, he said, some small white animals, with black heads, but he could not make out what they were. Did we know? We made a rough guess, and answered that they were probably Berbera sheep. He sent a last message, saying, "I am tired from looking out so long; I am going to rest awhile. Why are your people so slow?"

A severe storm then broke out; and it had hardly subsided when we saw soldiers rushing from all directions towards the side of the precipice—a couple of hundred yards from our tent. We soon heard that his Majesty, in a fearful passion, had left his tent, and had gone to Mr. Rassam's servants' houses, where the Magdala prisoners had been shut up since they had been taken down to Islamgee.

As I have said, that morning Theodore had released a large number of his prisoners. Those who remained, believing that they might avail themselves of the Emperor's good disposition, clamoured for bread and water, as for two days they had been deprived of both, all their servants having decamped and kept away since they had been removed from Magdala. At the cries of "abiet, abiet," [Footnote: "Abiet," master, lord. The usual expression used by beggars when asking alms.] Theodore, who was reposing after indulging in deep potations, asked his attendant, "What is it?" He was told that the prisoners begged for water and bread. Theodore, seizing his sword, and telling the man to follow him, exclaimed, "I will teach them to ask for food when my faithful soldiers are starving." Arrived at the place where the prisoners were confined, blind with rage and drink, he ordered the guards to bring them out. The two first he hacked to pieces with his own sword; the third was a young child; though it arrested his hand, it did not save the poor creature's life, and he was hurled alive over the precipice by Theodore's order. He seems to have been somewhat calmer after the two first murders, and something like order prevailed during the remainder of the executions. As every prisoner was brought out he inquired his name, his country, and *his crime*. The greater part were found guilty, hurled over the precipice, and shot below by musketeers sent there to despatch any one who still showed signs of animation, as many had escaped with life from the awful fall. Some 307 were put to death, and 91 reserved for another day. These last, strange to say, were all chiefs of note; many of whom had fought against the Emperor, and all, he knew, were his deadly enemies.

What our feelings were all this time can easily be surmised: we could see the deep line of soldiers standing behind the Emperor, and counted up to two hundred discharges of fire-arms, when we left off the agonizing calculation of how many victims were being slaughtered. A friendly chief came to us, and implored us to remain very quiet in our tents, as it would be very dangerous if Theodore remembered us in his present mood. At dusk he returned, followed by an admiring crowd. He, however, took no notice of us; and, after a while, seeing all quiet, we felt pretty confident that we were safe for *that day* at least.

There is no doubt that when Theodore sent for us and all the prisoners, he had made up his mind to kill every one. His apparent clemency was merely used as a blind to mask his intent and inspire hopes of freedom in the hearts of those whose death he had already determined upon.

Early on the morning of the 10th his Majesty sent us word to get ready to return to Magdala. Shortly afterwards one of his servants brought us the following message:—"Who is that woman who sends her soldiers to fight against a king? Send no more messengers to your people: if a single servant of yours is missing, the covenant of friendship between you and myself is broken." A few minutes afterwards a boy whom I had some days previously sent to General Merewether, with a request that a letter should be sent to Theodore, who had on several occasions manifested great astonishment at not receiving any communication from the army, returned with a letter from his Excellency the Commander-in-Chief for the Emperor. The letter was perfect; just what we had wished for—firm, courteous; it contained no threats, no promises, except that Theodore would be honourably treated if he delivered the prisoners uninjured into his hands. We at once sent Samuel to inform the Emperor that a letter from Sir R. Napier had arrived for him. His Majesty declined to receive it. "It is of no use," he said; "I know what I have to do." However, shortly afterwards he sent for Samuel privately, and asked him its contents, and as Samuel had translated it, he informed him of the principal points. His Majesty listened attentively, but made no remarks. A mule from the Imperial stables was sent for Mr. Rassam's use to ride; Lieutenant Prideaux, Captain Cameron, and myself were told that we might ride our own mules; but this favour was denied to the other captives. On our return to Magdala we were hailed by our servants, and the few friends we had on the mountain, as men who had returned from the grave. We sent for our tents, bedding, &c., and awaited with anxiety the next move of the fickle despot.

About noon the whole of the garrison of the Amba were told to arm and proceed to the King's camp; a few old men only and the ordinary prisoners' guard remaining on the mountain. Between 3 and 4 P.M. a violent thunderstorm burst over the Amba. We thought now and then that we could distinguish amidst the peals of thunder distant guns, and some close at hand. At other times we were almost certain that the sound we had just heard was a volley; but we only laughed at the idea, and wondered how the echoes of the almost constant thunder could to our excited imagination bear such close resemblance to the welcome music of an attack by the army of rescue. Shortly after 4 P.M. the storm subsided, and then no mistake was possible; the deep, dull sound of guns, and the sharp reports of small arms, now reached us plainly and distinctly. But what was it? No one would or could say. Twice during the next hour the joyous *elelta* resounded from Islamgee to the Amba above, where it was responded to by the soldiers' families. Then all doubts vanished: evidently the King was only "fakering;" no fight could have taken place, as no *elelta* would be heard if Theodore had ventured to encounter the British troops.

We were fast asleep, quite unaware of the glorious battle that had taken place a few miles from our prison, when we were aroused by a servant, who told us to dress quickly, and come over to Mr. Rassam's house, as messengers had just arrived from his Majesty. We found on entering Mr. Rassam's room Messrs. Waldmeier and Flad, and several of the Emperor's chiefs, who had come up to deliver the Imperial message. Then for the first time we heard of the battle of Fahla; heard, indeed, that we were now safe; that the humbled despot had acknowledged the greatness of the power he had for years despised. The Imperial message was as follows:—"I thought that the people that are now coming were women; I now find that they are men. I have been conquered by the advance guard alone. All my musketeers are dead. Reconcile me with your people."

Mr. Rassam sent him back word that he had come to his country to make peace, and now, as well as formerly, he only wished to see that happy result obtained; he proposed, he said, sending Lieutenant Prideaux for himself, and that his Majesty should send Mr. Flad, or any other European whom he trusted, together with one of his noblemen, to the British camp to make terms; but that unless he was willing to deliver over to the Commander-in-Chief all the prisoners, the proposed steps would be quite useless. The two

Europeans and the other messenger remained some time with us to rest and refresh themselves: they told us that his Majesty had mistaken a battery of artillery for Baggage, and seeing only a few men at Arogié, he had given in to the importunities of his chiefs, and allowed them to have their own way. On a cannon being fired, the Abyssinians, excited by the prospect of a large booty, rushed down the hill. His Majesty commanded the artillery, which was served by Abyssinian workmen, under the direction of a Copt, the former servant of the Bishop, and of Lij Engeddah Wark, the son of a converted Bengal Jew. At the first discharge the largest piece of ordnance, "Theodoros," burst, the Abyssinians by mistake having rammed in two cannon balls. Towards dusk he had sent to recall his troops, but messenger after messenger was despatched to no purpose: at last the broken-down remnants of his army were seen slowly climbing the steep ascent, and he heard for the first time the dismal tale of their disaster. Fitaurari [Footnote: *Fitaurari*, the commander of the advanced guard.] Gabrié, his long-attached friend, the bravest of the brave, lay dead on the battle-field; he inquired for others, but the answer was Dead, dead, dead!! Cast down, conquered at last, Theodore, without saying a word, walked back to his tent with no other thought but an appeal to the friendship of his captives and to the generosity of his foe.

Returning to the Emperor's tent Messrs. Flad and Waldmeier informed him of their arrival by one of the eunuchs who had accompanied them for that purpose. It appears that in the meanwhile Theodore had been drinking hard; he came out of his tent very much excited, and asked the Europeans, "What do you want?" They told him that as he had commanded them, they had spoken on his behalf to Mr. Rassam, and that that gentleman had proposed sending Mr. Prideaux, &c. &c. The Emperor interrupted them, and in an angry tone exclaimed, "Mind your own business: go to your tents!" The two Europeans stood still, in the hope that his Majesty might change his mind; but seeing that they did not depart, he got into a rage, and in a high tone of voice ordered them to retire at once.

At about 4 A.M. a messenger was sent by his Majesty to call Messrs. Flad and Waldmeier before him. As soon as they arrived he asked, "Do you hear this wailing? There is not a soldier who has not lost a friend or a brother. What will it be when the whole English army comes? What shall I do? counsel me." Mr. Waldmeier told him: "Your Majesty, peace is the best." "And you, Flad, what do you say?" "Your Majesty," replied Mr. Flad, "ought to accept Mr. Rassam's proposal." Theodore remained a few minutes silent, his head between his hands, apparently in deep thought, and then said, "Well, go back to Magdala, and tell Mr. Rassam that I trust in his friendship to reconcile me with his people. I will do what he thinks best." Mr. Flad brought us this message, Mr. Waldmeier remaining with the Emperor.

On Lieutenant Prideaux and Mr. Flad reaching Islamgee they were conducted to the Emperor, whom they found sitting outside on a stone and dressed in his ordinary manner. He received them very graciously, and immediately ordered one of his best mules to be saddled for Prideaux's use. Noticing that he was rather exhausted from the rapid walk, he gave him a horn of tej to refresh himself with on the road. He then dismissed them with the following message:—"I had thought before this that I was a strong man, but I have now discovered that they are stronger; now reconcile me." They then left, and accompanied by Dejatch Alamé, the Emperor's son-in-law, proceeded to the British camp at Arogié, where they arrived after a two hours' ride, and were warmly cheered and greeted by all. After a short stay in the camp, they returned to his Majesty bearing a letter from Sir Robert Napier, couched in firm but conciliatory terms, and assuring Theodore that, provided he submitted to the Queen of England and brought all the prisoners and other Europeans to the British camp, honourable treatment would be accorded to himself and his family.

Sir Robert Napier received Dejatch Alamé with great courtesy (a fact that was immediately reported to Theodore by a special messenger), invited him into his tent, and spoke plainly to him. He told him that not only all the Europeans must at once be sent to the camp, but the Emperor himself must come in also and submit to the Queen of England. He told him that if he complied he would be honourably treated, but that if any one of the Europeans in his hands were injured, he could expect no pity; and that had he (Sir Robert Napier) to remain for five years in the country, he would not leave until the last murderer was punished, had he even to buy him from his mother. He then showed Alamé some of the "toys" he had brought with him, and explained to him their effects.

On the return of Prideaux and his companions to Theodore's camp, they found him sitting on the brow of Selassié, overlooking the British camp, and in anything but a pleasant humour. They had been joined on their arrival by Mr. Waldmeier, and together they presented themselves before him, and delivered the letter into his hands. It was twice translated, and at the conclusion of the second reading he asked, in a deliberate manner, "What does honourable treatment mean? Does it mean that the English will help me to subdue my enemies, or does, it mean honourable treatment as a prisoner?" Prideaux replied, that on the first point the Commander-in-Chief had said nothing; that all his wishes were contained in his letter; and that the English army had simply come into the country to rescue their fellow-countrymen, and that object effected they would then return. This answer did not please him at all. Evidently his worst passions were aroused; but, controlling himself, he motioned them to stand a little distance from him, while he dictated a letter to his secretary,—a letter begun before the arrival of Prideaux, an incoherent epistle, not sealed, stating, amongst other things, that he had hitherto surrendered to no man, and was not prepared to do so now. He inclosed with his letter the one he had just received from Sir Robert Napier, handed it over to Prideaux, and bade them be off at once; not allowing Prideaux even to wait for a glass of water, telling him that there was no time to lose.

Another couple of hours' ride brought Prideaux and Flad again to the British camp. Sir Robert Napier, however reluctant he must have felt, after allowing them time to rest, despatched them back to Theodore. It was, indeed, the proper way to deal with him: firmness alone could save our lives; as we had but too ample proofs that the kind of adoration for so long bestowed upon him resulted in nothing but a nonsensical correspondence, and no real advantage had ever been gained. No answer could possibly be given to the mad production Theodore had sent; a verbal message to the same purport as the first communication from the Commander-in-Chief was all that was required.

We were still in the power of Theodore; had not, as yet, tasted liberty; whatever, before long, would be our fate, we were passive, and ready to submit with as much good grace as possible to the sentence we every minute expected. Mr. Flad had left his wife and children on Islamgee, and could not well decline to go back; but for Prideaux the case was quite different: he returned, like a brave, gallant man, ready to sacrifice his own life in endeavouring to save ours, and going willingly to almost certain death in obedience to his duty. None of the brave soldiers who gallantly wear the Victoria Cross ever did a nobler deed. Fortunately, however, as they were nearing Selassié, they met Mr. Meyer, one of the European workmen, who communicated to them the welcome intelligence that we were all liberated and on our way to the camp. They gladly turned round the heads of their tired mules, and, together with Mr. Meyer, brought back the good news to our anxious countrymen.

But we must return to ourselves, still shut up in Magdala. We remained all day in great suspense, not knowing at any moment what course Theodore would adopt. I dressed several of the wounded and saw many of the soldiers who had taken part in the fight of the previous day. All were much cast down, and declared that they would not fight again. "Of what use is it," they said, "fighting against your people? When we fight with our countrymen each side has its turn; with you it is always your turn. See how many dead and wounded we have! We did not see any of your men fall: and then you never run away." The rockets terrified them greatly, and if their description of the shells is correct they must indeed be terrible weapons.

Shortly after receiving an answer from Sir Robert Napier, and despatching Prideaux and Flad for the second time, Theodore called his principal chiefs and some of his European workmen before him and held a kind of council; but he soon became so excited, so mad, that it was with difficulty he was restrained from committing suicide. The chiefs reproved him for his weakness, and proposed that we should all be killed, or kept in a hut in the camp and burnt alive on the approach of our soldiers. His Majesty took no notice of these suggestions, dismissed his chiefs, and told Messrs. Meyer and Saalmüller, two of his European workmen, to get ready to accompany us to the English camp. At the same time he sent two of his high officers, Bitwaddad Hassanié and Ras Bissawur, to us with the following message:—"Go at once to your people: you will send for your property to-morrow."

We did not like that message at all. The two chiefs were sullen and downcast, and Samuel was so excited that he would give us no explanation of this sudden decision. We called our servants to pack up a few things, and many of them bade us good-by with tears in their eyes. The best disposed of the guards looked sad and sorrowful: no doubt the general impression was the same as ours, that we were sent for, not to go to the English camp, but to certain death. There was no use in remonstrating or in complaining, so we dressed; glad that at all events the end of our captivity had arrived, whatever it might be; we bade good-by to our servants, and under a strong escort left the Amba. Whilst we had been dressing, Samuel had consulted with the two chiefs; they told him that Theodore was quite mad, and that anything which might delay our meeting should not be neglected, as time to allow him to cool down a little was of the utmost importance. They decided on sending a soldier in advance with a supposed message from us, to ask from his Majesty the favour of a last interview, as we could not depart without first bidding him good-by.

Arrived at the foot of the Amba, we found that the Emperor had sent no mules, as was his custom, and we had to have ours saddled, or borrow some from the European workmen. The place seemed almost deserted, and on our way to the Imperial tent we met only a few soldiers; but as we advanced we perceived that the heights of Selassié and Fahla were crowded with the remnants of the Imperial host.

At about a hundred yards from the King's tent we met the messenger whom Samuel and the chiefs had sent to request a last interview, coming back towards us. He said that the King was not in his tent, but between Fahla and Selassié, and that he would only see his beloved friend Rassam. Orders were then given by the chiefs who escorted us to conduct Mr. Rassam by one road, and the remainder of the captives by another. We had to follow a small pathway on the side of Selassié, and Mr. Rassam was conducted by a road some fifty yards above. We advanced in that manner for a couple of hundred yards, when we were ordered to stop. The soldiers told us that the Emperor was coming towards Mr. Rassam, and that we must wait until their interview was over.

After a while we were told to advance, as Mr. Rassam had left the King and was moving on.

I was walking in front of our party, and great was my surprise, after a few steps, on arriving at a sudden turn in the road, to find myself face to face with Theodore. I at once perceived that he was in a fearful passion. Behind him stood about twenty men in a line, all armed with muskets. The spot on which he was standing is a small platform, so narrow that I would have almost to touch him on my way onwards. Below the platform the precipice was abrupt and deep; above, the rocks rose like a huge wall: evidently he could not have chosen a better place if he had any evil intentions against us.

He could not have seen me at first, as his face was half turned; he whispered something to the soldier nearest to him, and stretched out his hand to take the man's musket. I was quite prepared for the worst, and, at the moment, had no doubt in my mind that our last hour had come.

Theodore, his hand still on his musket, turned round; he then perceived me, looked at me for a second or two, dropped his hand, and in a low sad voice asked me how I was, and bade me good-by.

The chief on the following day told me that, at the time, Theodore was undecided as to whether he would kill us all or not; only allowing Mr. Rassam to go on account of his personal friendship for him, and that we owed our lives to the mere accident that his eye first fell upon me, against whom he had no animosity; but that the result would have been quite different had his anger been roused by the sight of those he hated.

A few minutes later we rejoined Mr. Rassam, and moved on as fast as our mules could amble. Mr. Rassam told me that Theodore had said to him, "It is getting dark; it is perhaps better if you remained here until to-morrow." Mr. Rassam said, "Just as your Majesty likes." Theodore then said, "Never mind; go." He shook hands with Mr. Rassam, both crying at the idea of parting, and Mr. Rassam promising to return early the next morning.

We had nearly reached the outposts of the Imperial camp when some soldiers shouted for us to stop. Had Theodore again changed his mind? So near liberty, were we again doomed to captivity or death? Such thoughts immediately crossed our minds; but our suspense was short, as we perceived running towards us one of the Emperor's servants, carrying Prideaux's sword, as well as my own, which his Majesty had seized at Debra Tabor some twenty-one months before. We sent back our thanks to his Majesty by the servant, and resumed our march.

Little did we know at the time the narrow escape we had just had. It appears that, after our departure, Theodore sat down on a stone, and, putting his head between his hands, began to cry. Ras Engeddah said to him, "Are you a woman, to cry? Let us bring back these white men, kill them, and run away; or fight and die." Theodore rebuked him in these words:—"You donkey! have I not killed enough these two last days? Do you want me to kill these white men, and cover Abyssinia with blood?"

Though now fairly out of the Imperial camp, and in sight almost of our pickets, we could hardly credit that we were not the victims of some delusion. Involuntarily, we would look back, fearful that, regretting his clemency, Theodore might follow and overtake us before we reached our camp. But God, who had almost by a miracle delivered us that day, still protected us; and shortly afterwards, with grateful and joyful hearts, we entered the British lines; and heard the gladdening sound of English voices, the hearty cheers of our countrymen, and shook hands with the dear friends who had laboured so zealously for our release.

CONCLUSION

On the morning of the 12th, the day following our deliverance, Theodore sent a letter of apology, expressing his regret for having written the impertinent missive of the day before. He at the same time requested the Commander-in-Chief to accept a present of 1,000 cows; this, according to Abyssinian custom, implying a peace-offering, which once accepted, removed all apprehension of hostilities.

The five captives who had joined us in January, 1868 (Mr. Staiger and his party), Mrs. Flad and her children, several of the Europeans, and the families of all of them, were still in Theodore's power. The Europeans who had accompanied us the evening before, and who had spent the night at the camp, were early that morning sent back to Theodore; and Samuel, who was one of the party, was instructed to demand that the whole of the Europeans and their families should be allowed to depart at once. A dhoolee and bearers were also sent at the same time for Mrs. Flad, whose state of health did not allow her to ride. Before starting, Samuel was told by Mr. Rassam that the Commander-in-Chief had accepted the cows: an unfortunate mistake, as it misled and deceived Theodore, but so far opportune, that it probably saved the lives of the Europeans still in his power.

When the Europeans who had returned to Selassi to bring down their families, and Samuel, approached the Emperor, his first question was, "Have the cows been accepted?" Samuel, bowing respectfully before him, said: "The English Ras says to you, 'I have accepted your present: may God give it back to you.'" On that Theodore drew a long breath, as if relieved of a deep anxiety, and told the Europeans, "Take your families and go." To Mr. Waldmeier he said, "You also want to leave me; well, go: now that I have friendship with the English, if I want ten Waldmeiers I have only to ask for them." In the afternoon the European workmen and their families, Mr. Staiger and his party, Mrs. Flad and children, Samuel, and our servants, all came into the British camp. They had been allowed to take away their property, and on their departure Theodore, in good spirits, bade them good-by.

On Saturday, the 11th, Sir Robert Napier had clearly pointed out to Dejatch Alamé, the course he had adopted, and that not only the captives, but Theodore also, must come into the British camp before twenty-four hours, otherwise hostilities would begin anew; but at the urgent request of Dejatch Alamé, who knew how difficult it would be for Theodore to comply with that part of the order which referred to himself, he promised to extend to forty-eight hours the term he had fixed upon for his ultimatum to be acceded to.

On the morning of the 18th, the Emperor having not as yet made his submission, it became necessary to compel him to obey, and steps were being taken to complete the work so ably begun, when several of the greatest chiefs of Theodore's army made their appearance, stating that they came in their own name and in that of the soldiers of the garrison, to lay down their arms and surrender the fortress; they added that, Theodore, accompanied by about fifty followers, had made his escape during the night.

It appears that the evening before, Theodore, on hearing that the cows had not been accepted, but were still outside the English pickets, believed that he had been deceived, and that, if he fell into the hands of the English, he would either be doomed to chains or to a cruel death. All night he walked about Selassié anxious and cast down, and towards early morn called upon his people to follow him. But instead of obeying they retired to another part of the plain. Theodore shot the two nearest to him; but this daring act did not quell the mutinous disposition of the soldiery: on the contrary, they only retreated further back.

With the few men who followed him, he passed through the Kafir Ber, but had not gone far before he saw the Gallas advancing from all sides in order to surround him and his party. He then said to his few faithful followers, "Leave me: I will die alone." They refused; on that he said to them, "You are right; but let us return to the mountain: it is better to die by the hands of Christians."

The surrender of the army, the storming of Magdala, the self-inflicted death of Theodore, are too well-known facts for me to enlarge upon them I entered the place shortly after it had been occupied by our troops. One of the first objects that attracted my attention was the dead body of Theodore. There was a smile on his lip—that happy smile he so seldom wore of late: it gave an air of calm grandeur to the features of one whose career had been so remarkable, whose cruelties are almost unparalleled in history; but who at the last hour seemed to have recalled the days of his youth, fought like a brave man, and killed himself rather than surrender.

I remained that night in Magdala. It seemed passing strange to spend a night as a free man in the same hut where I had been so long confined a prisoner. English soldiers now guarded our former gaolers, the queen was our guest, the dead body of Theodore lay in one of our huts: in the short span of forty-eight hours our position had so completely changed that it was difficult to realize it: at times I was apprehensive of being the victim of a delusion. I was too excited to sleep.

General Wilby, his aide-de-camp Captain Cappel, and his brigade-major Major Hicks, shared my hut; hungry and tired they enjoyed quite as much as I did, the simple Abyssinian dish of teps, the peppery sauce, and some tej, which we ourselves went to fetch from the cellars in the royal buildings. The next day we returned to Arogié, and during my stay there I received the kind hospitality of General Merewether. On the 16th, some of the released captives and myself started for Dalanta, where we waited a few days until all had joined; and on the 21st, after Sir Robert Napier had presented us to our deliverers, we proceeded on our way to the coast, and reached Zulla on the 28th of May.

Looking back now, a free man in a free country, the past appears to me like a horrible dream, a kind of missing link in my life; and when I remember that our deliverance was followed so shortly afterwards by the self-destruction of the passionate despot who held us in his power, I can find no truer solution to this difficult problem, than the words inscribed by the warm-hearted countrymen of Kerans, on the banner that floated at Ahascragh to welcome his return, "God is good, who set you free."

ERRATUM

For "Samuel, the Georgis balderaba" *Read* "Samuel Georgis, the balderaba"